Suicide Protest in South Asia

The radical act of suicide protest is undertaken by social movement participants in order to demand a particular previously articulated political outcome. This book examines the history and strategic impact of suicide protest, which has been increasingly used as a protest tactic since World War II, adding to a growing area of research on the ability of certain actions to impact policy in favor of movement goals.

   The book offers a combination of historical and contemporary case analysis from South Asia, where different iterations of this tactic have been used extensively throughout the latter half of the twentieth century, including the use of fasting to the death, self-immolation and deliberate drowning. Focusing on the success or failure of a particular action relevant to the movement's broader mobilization strategy, the author examines the internal impact this has on the movement and the mechanisms by which suicide as a form of protest evolves.

   Providing a unique contribution to the field of comparative politics, political violence and social movement studies this book will be of interest to scholars working on political science, sociology and South Asian studies.

Simanti Lahiri is Assistant Professor of Political Science at the University of Alabama, USA.

Routledge Advances in South Asian Studies
Edited by Subrata K. Mitra
South Asia Institute, University of Heidelberg, Germany

South Asia, with its burgeoning, ethnically diverse population, soaring economies and nuclear weapons, is an increasingly important region in the global context. The series, which builds on this complex, dynamic and volatile area, features innovative and original research on the region as a whole or on the countries within it. Its scope extends to scholarly works drawing on the history, politics, development studies, sociology and economics of individual countries within the region, as well as those that take an interdisciplinary and comparative approach to the area as a whole or to a comparison of two or more countries from this region. In terms of theory and method, rather than basing itself on any one orthodoxy, the series draws broadly on the insights germane to area studies, as well as the tool kit of the social sciences in general, emphasizing comparison, analysis of the structure and processes, and the application of qualitative and quantitative methods. The series welcomes submissions from established authors in the field as well as from young authors who have recently completed their doctoral dissertations.

1. **Perception, Politics and Security in South Asia**
   The Compound Crisis of 1990
   P. R. Chari, Pervaiz Iqbal Cheema and Stephen Philip Cohen

2. **Coalition Politics and Hindu Nationalism**
   Edited by Katharine Adeney and Lawrence Saez

3. **The Puzzle of India's Governance**
   Culture, context and comparative theory
   Subrata K. Mitra

4. **India's Nuclear Bomb and National Security**
   Karsten Frey

5. **Starvation and India's Democracy**
   Dan Banik

6. **Parliamentary Control and Government Accountability in South Asia**
   A comparative analysis of Bangladesh, India and Sri Lanka
   Taiabur Rahman

7. **Political Mobilisation and Democracy in India**
   States of emergency
   Vernon Hewitt

8. **Military Control in Pakistan**
   The parallel state
   Mazhar Aziz

9. **Sikh Nationalism and Identity in a Global Age**
   Giorgio Shani

10. **The Tibetan Government-in-Exile**
    Politics at large
    Stephanie Roemer

11. **Trade Policy, Inequality and Performance in Indian Manufacturing**
    Kunal Sen

12. **Democracy and Party Systems in Developing Countries**
    A comparative study
    Clemens Spiess

13. **War and Nationalism in South Asia**
    The Indian state and the Nagas
    Marcus Franke

14. **The Politics of Social Exclusion in India**
    Democracy at the crossroads
    Edited by Harihar Bhattacharyya, Partha Sarka and Angshuman Kar

15. **Party System Change in South India**
    Political entrepreneurs, patterns and processes
    Andrew Wyatt

16. **Dispossession and Resistance in India**
    The river and the rage
    Alf Gunvald Nilsen

17. **The Construction of History and Nationalism in India**
    Textbooks, controversies and politics
    Sylvie Guichard

18. **Political Survival in Pakistan**
    Beyond ideology
    Anas Malik

19. **New Cultural Identitarian Political Movements in Developing Societies**
    The Bharatiya Janata Party
    Sebastian Schwecke

20. **Sufism and Saint Veneration in Contemporary Bangladesh**
    The Maijbhandaris of Chittagong
    Hans Harder

21. **New Dimensions of Politics in India**
    The United Progressive Alliance in power
    Lawrence Saez and Gurhapal Singh

22. **Vision and Strategy in Indian Politics**
    Jawaharlal Nehru's policy choices and the designing of political institutions
    Jivanta Schoettli

23. **Decentralization, Local Governance, and Social Wellbeing in India**
    Do local governments matter?
    Rani D. Mullen

24. **The Politics of Refugees in South Asia**
Identity, resistance, manipulation
Navine Murshid

25. **The Political Philosophies of Antonio Gramsci and Ambedkar**
Subalterns and dalits
Edited by Cosimo Zene

26. **Suicide Protest in South Asia**
Consumed by commitment
Simanti Lahiri

Suicide Protest in South Asia
Consumed by commitment

Simanti Lahiri

LONDON AND NEW YORK

First published 2014 by Routledge

2 Park Square, Milton Park, Abingdon, Oxfordshire OX14 4RN
711 Third Avenue, New York, NY 10017

Routledge is an imprint of the Taylor & Francis Group, an informa business

First issued in paperback 2017

Copyright © 2014 Simanti Lahiri

The right of Simanti Lahiri to be identified as author of this work has been
asserted by her in accordance with sections 77 and 78 of the Copyright,
Designs and Patents Act 1988.

All rights reserved. No part of this book may be reprinted or reproduced or utilised in any
form or by any electronic, mechanical, or other means, now known or hereafter invented,
including photocopying and recording, or in any information storage or retrieval system,
without permission in writing from the publishers.

Notice:
Product or corporate names may be trademarks or registered trademarks, and are used only
for identification and explanation without intent to infringe.

British Library Cataloguing in Publication Data
A catalogue record for this book is available from the British Library

Library of Congress Cataloguing in Publication data
Lahiri, Simanti.
    Suicide protest in South Asia: consumed by commitment / Simanti Lahiri.
        pages cm. – (Routledge advances in South Asian studies)
    Includes bibliographical references and index.
    1. Protest movements–South Asia. 2. Suicide–Political aspects–South Asia. 3. Social
    movements–South Asia. 4. South Asia–Social conditions. 5. South Asia–Politics and
    government. I. Title.
    HN670.3.M6L35 2014
    303.48′4–dc23
    2013034758

ISBN: 978-0-415-82099-8 (hbk)
ISBN: 978-0-8153-7359-9 (pbk)

Typeset in Times New Roman
by Out of House Publishing

For my family
Baba, Ma, Didi, Alberto, Octavio and Noor

Contents

	List of illustrations	x
	Acknowledgments	xi
1	Introduction	1
2	Gandhi and the development of suicide protest in India	20
3	Successful suicide: Potti Sriramulu and the question of Andhra	40
4	Short-term success: the Narmada Bachao Andolan	61
5	Failure of the tactic: the Anti-Reservation Movement	85
6	The tactical approach and suicide bombing in Sri Lanka	100
7	Suicide protest from a global perspective	120
8	Conclusion	143
	Bibliography	153
	Index	163

Illustrations

Figure

1.1	Suicide protest outcomes: the tactical approach	11

Tables

1.1	Cases and tactics	16
7.1	A comparison of the IRA and Tibetan protestors	134
8.1	A comparison of suicide protest inputs and outcomes	146

Acknowledgments

In 1996, when I was a senior at Barnard College, a number of students went on a political fast on Columbia's campus. I had just returned from a year abroad at the School of Oriental and African Studies (SOAS) where I took a year-long seminar on Gandhi. I was intrigued by the application of his tactic, fasting, in the middle of this college campus – and the reactions to it. Was fasting a useful tactic at the time? Did it make sense in the context of such an institution? I never really found satisfying answers to those questions at that time. But I took them with me when I returned to SOAS the following year for a Masters degree.

It was at SOAS that I began to seriously investigate what I then called self-sacrificing politics vis-à-vis Gandhi's use of the fast. By the time I received my degree, I knew that I wanted to see how the practice of self-sacrifice may have transformed, or not, in the context of contemporary Indian politics. Thus, I have either been actively or passively preparing to write this book for the past 16 years. Focusing on a topic like suicide protest has been both fascinating and maddening. Trying to really discern the motivations and impacts of something like suicide protest has taken me in directions I never thought I would go. Throughout this whole process it was clear to me that suicide protest is both an important and oddly relatable phenomenon, and I am not the only one to think this way. When I first began this project as a PhD student at the University of Wisconsin-Madison, it was a struggle to find other scholars who were interested in issues of suicide protest. Now there are a number of people who work on this topic, making this an emerging field of study.

The journey, from those first days watching the fast on my walk to class, to the completion of this book, has been very long but not unrewarding. Over the course of these years I have met and been influenced by a number of extraordinary individuals who have helped me bring this book to fruition. It would be impossible to acknowledge all of the people who have supported this project, and me, in both large and small ways. However, there are some without whom this book would not exist.

First, I was very lucky to not only find my path as an academic, but also to find my scholarly focus early. That certainty can be attributed to my education at Barnard College, and Dennis Dalton, who steered me to my interest

xii *Acknowledgments*

in Gandhi and social movements. Very often he and I would be walking from class in front of the fast together and I cannot thank him enough for the intellectual foundation that I have (hopefully) built on. I must also thank my professors at SOAS, especially Sudipta Kaviraj, David Arnold and David Taylor, who helped to develop my interest in Gandhi and South Asia; Chapter 2 was substantially influenced by my time at SOAS.

I was very fortunate to be a graduate student in the political science department of the University of Wisconsin-Madison. A number of people there made direct and important contributions to this project. Aseema Sinha has not only been a supportive advisor and friend, but also provided keen insight into this topic. Mark Beissinger set me on the pathway to the comprehensive study of social movements and political contention. Both of these individuals have provided crucial critiques of my approach to this topic. This book is immeasurably better because of them. I would like to thank Aili Tripp for her help, both intellectually and emotionally. I also owe thanks to the political science department as a whole for providing a truly supportive academic community where I could develop my research agenda; and the Center for South Asian Studies, which supported me financially and intellectually.

I would like to thank the Helen Kellogg Institute of International Studies at the University of Notre Dame for giving me the time after grad school to reconceptualize my dissertation into this book project. I was able to present my project during my time there and my discussions with the fellows and the faculty helped me to substantially make this book better.

I would like to thank friends and colleagues at the University of Alabama who have read versions of the book and been very supportive of my work, such as Jennifer Caputo, Andrew Raffo Dewar, Greg and Beth Vonhamme, Rekha Nath, Nikhil Bilwakesh, Jennifer Shoaff, Barbara Chotiner, Emilia Powell, Ted Miller, Utz McKnight and Wendy Richman. I would especially like to thank Nancy Rubin – this book would not exist without her support and help.

I must also thank Professor Subrata K. Mitra, editor of the *Advances in South Asian Studies* series at Routledge, as well as Dorothea Schaefter, Jillian Morrison and Rebecca Lawrence for their help throughout the editorial process. Finally, thank you to Peter Kenyon, Alison Evans and the production team for the careful editing of this book.

Over the years a number of students and friends have helped me with stages of this book. Melba Jesudasen in Madison helped with translations of Tamil material. Chanley Rainey and Ishita Chowdhury helped with organization and other important components of this book. I would also like to thank friends who helped me while I was doing fieldwork: Sunalini Kumar, Mr. and Mrs. Dipendra Maitra, Baljit Singh, Judy Grayson and Parveen Nair. I also need to thank Teen Murti Library in New Delhi and the Andhra Pradesh Archives in Hyderabad.

I have been most lucky to have a number of people that I can call my friends and family who have all helped me in ways, tangible and intangible, too numerous to account for here. I hope that they all know how important they have been to me during this process – I know that my acknowledgements are wholly unequal to the level of support, understanding, critical engagement, laughter and sanity that they have provided over the years. I must thank Travis Nelson, Bahareh Lampert, Joe Lampert, Ayse Zarakol, Erin Grunze, Paul Scholmer, Dan Kapust, Mike Franz, Alex Caviedes, Tim Bagshaw, Omar Khan, Shamus Khan, Kristin Springer, Eric Lipton, Amy Wexler, Jinna Shin, Bridget Burns, Freyda Spira, Esther Berg, Ben Tyler and Aranya Ghatak.

Finally, I dedicate this book to my family, Amar K. Lahiri, Tapati Lahiri, Jhumpa Lahiri, Alberto Vourvoulias, Octavio Vourvoulias and Noor Vourvolious. This was a very hard section for me to write, as I really cannot put into words how much this book and I owe to them. Not only have they put up with my travels, my periodic inattentiveness and stress, they also have never faltered in their love, support and kindness towards me. My father has a saying that "the last two feet of the palm tree are the hardest to climb," and writing this book it sometimes felt like I was on a never-ending stretch for those last two feet. If not for my family, I would never have been able to finish the climb.

They poked into the straw with sticks and found him in it. "Are you still Fasting?" asked the overseer, "when on earth do you mean to stop?" "Forgive me, everybody," whispered the hunger artist; only the overseer, who had his ears to the bars, understood him. "Of course," said the overseer, and tapped his forehead with a finger to let the attendants know the state the man was in, "we forgive you." "I always wanted you to admire my fasting," said the hunger artist. "We do admire it," said the overseer, affably. "But you shouldn't admire it," said the hunger artist. "Well then we don't admire it," said the overseer, "but why shouldn't we admire it?" "Because I have to fast, I can't help it," said the hunger artist. "What a fellow you are," said the overseer, "and why can't you help it?" "Because," said the hunger artist, lifting his head a little and speaking with his lips pursed, as if for a kiss, right into the overseer's ear, so that no syllable might be lost, "because I couldn't find the food that I liked."

Franz Kafka
The Hunger Artist
(Franz Kafka, 1971, *The Complete Stories.*
New York: Schocken Books Inc.)

1 Introduction

In 1990 Rajiv Goswami set himself on fire during an anti-government protest in New Delhi. That act of self-immolation seemed to encompass months of frustration on the part of high caste students who were fighting the adoption of government policy that they felt would limit their future economic options.[1] Witnesses described the event as the burning of a living effigy. Goswami survived, but that act sparked a wave of student suicides in solidarity and protest.[2] The drama of these acts cannot be denied, but tracking their effectiveness in creating political change is much more problematic. The agitations of 1990 did help change the government, but they could not change the policy that so many people had protested against and died for. In contrast, when Potti Sriramulu, a Telegu activist, fasted to death in 1952, his act of suicide protest not only resulted in the creation of the Andhra state but also provided the impetus needed to reorganize many Indian states along linguistic lines in subsequent years. The brief comparison of these two cases of suicide protest in India illustrates the relevant empirical puzzles at the heart of this book. How, why, and more importantly *when*, does suicide protest contribute to movement success or movement failure? To answer these questions, I compare cases of suicide protest in India to determine when the tactic succeeds and when it fails. In the process, I develop what I call the tactical approach to understanding movement success and failure. This approach systematically examines the effectiveness of a particular type of protest tactic – suicide protest – and identifies certain mechanisms that help or hinder adoption of political outcomes in favor of the movement. I cite a combination of internal movement dynamics, the performance of the tactic, and the political structure as important conditioning factors for movement success.

Suicide protest is a relatively recent addition to the canon of usual protest tactics.[3] As such, it is under-examined within academic scholarship, though this has been changing in the last ten years (Biggs 2005; Hyojoung 2002). This book is primarily concerned with how these tactics may create policy changes in favor of the movement and in the process I also explore the history, contours and practice of suicide protest.

2 Introduction

As is the case for many, the puzzling motivations behind suicide protest initially captured my attention to these phenomena.[4] These acts are so extreme and self-annihilating that they seem to directly contradict our understanding of self-interest and self-preservation. However, the systematic and organized ways in which these tactics are often deployed indicates that it is not simply an idiopathic practice; so why do groups use suicide to express themselves politically? The first response to this question is often "because it works." On the face of it, this is a simple and logical response; groups use suicide protest because it can get them what they want from the state, or from their opponent. However, the simplicity of that logic is misleading. If suicide protest is practiced because it can create change, then what makes it so effective? Is there something special about suicide protest in particular, or do all tactics have the same ability to succeed? Does suicide protest always "work?" If not, then when is it more likely to create political change? These questions allow us not only to examine the tactic of suicide but also to explore how tactics, social movements, and the state interact and relate to one another.

There is a rich literature on social movements in a number of academic disciplines. While this work explores many facets of social movement behavior, the lion's share tends to focus on the area of movement mobilization and motivation. Of primary concern has been how and why social movements will organize and then choose to act in furtherance of their particular goals. The preoccupation with the moment of mobilization stems in part from the desire of contemporary scholars to discard previous considerations of social movements as "abnormal," and instead place movement phenomena firmly within the realm of regular political and social behavior (Gamson 1968).

Concentrating on movement mobilization has left other areas of social movement research underdeveloped. In particular, the impact that movements can have on states, political policy, social life and individuals, has been under-examined within scholarly literature. This book adds to this growing area of research through a focus on the ability of a certain *category* of tactic to impact policy in favor of movement goals. In other words, this project examines the effectiveness of suicide protest in creating policy shifts in favor of the movement.

Scope of the suicide protest in India

The frequency of suicide protest in India and the world seems to be on the rise, especially if we included instances that were not connected to active social movements, such as the thousands of farmer suicides since 1991,[5] or the recent series of self-immolations in support of the creation of Telengana. The ramifications of high levels of suicide protest have also not been adequately studied. I think however, that it is safe to say that high levels of suicide protest can demonstrate issues of state capacity, governance and democratic institutionalization. Since Independence, the Indian state has had a very uneasy relationship with suicide protest. The Indian Emergency was sparked (though not caused) by a series of fasts to the death conducted by a number of opposition leaders. While anecdotal evidence suggests that suicide protest is both frequent and significant, that has not been reflected in systematic study. Based on an event analysis database that I have been collecting I can provide a certain amount of description of the scope of suicide protest within India. This dataset is based on a close reading of the *Times of India*, Bombay edition, between the years 1975 to 1983.[6]

Preliminary analysis of this dataset indicates some counterintuitive aspects of the practice of suicide protest in India during the time period. Between 1975 and 1983 I counted 224 actual and 30 threats of suicide protest. Among the events only 11 actors actually died. Fasting, of all the types of suicide protest, was predominant, and was used 121 times. Other types of suicide protest included drowning and self-immolation. During this period more men engaged in suicide protest, though there were some women who also utlitized the tactic. Because I use the Bombay edition of the *Times of India* there is a selection bias in favor of events from the western part of the country. Despite this, the reporting indicates that suicide protest was used mostly in urban environments (though it was not limited to cities) throughout the country. Interestingly, during this period the majority of suicide protest events can be traced to economic, not cultural, social or political motivations. I suspect that the salience of economic motivations can be traced to a number of structural issues relevant at the time, and that as approaches to political mobilization change in India the stated motivations for suicide protest may also change.

This data allows us to draw some tentative conclusions regarding the scope of suicide protest within India. Between 1975 and 1983 suicide protest is clearly a commonly used tactic, which indicates both a familiarity and ease of its use. While it does seem puzzling that so many of these events did not end in actual death, I believe that this fact reveals two aspects of how suicide protest was used at the time. First, fasting was the most popular form of suicide protest in India during this period. Unlike other forms of suicide protest, fasting allows a certain amount of time for actors to change their mind, or negotiate with the state. I discuss some reasons why fasting is so popular in India in Chapter 2. Second, suicide protest, while popular, also begs a certain level of commitment. The data can't tell us what individual protestors, or groups, were thinking as they began to use this tactic, but during this period death remained an uncommon result of suicide protest; this changes in a decade. Extrapolating from this data, we can see that suicide protest is a common choice within India; this book focuses on a particular aspect of these phenomena that I believe needs further examination. One reason why forms of protest can attain popularity is because they are perceived as being effective in creating political change; what make suicide protest an effective tactic?

4 *Introduction*

Bringing tactics back in

Measuring the effects of a particular protest tactic has rarely been done within social movement literature. If we accept Tarrow's definition of social movements as "sustained challenges" (1998), then one assumes that most movements not only engage in a range of behaviors to get what their members want, but that those desires can and do change. Moreover, movements do not work in a vacuum, but rather occur within a matrix of supportive and competing movements; other organizations, campaigns and political institutions that determine the success or failure of the movement as a whole. This complexity often obscures the importance of a single act. Previous work done on the power of tactics tries to get around this issue by focusing on the context surrounding the protests and not the protests themselves. According to these theories the success or failure of strikes or demonstrations depends on their political context, not on the tactics themselves. If taken to its logical conclusion then, tactics become interchangeable. Focusing on the political context to the exclusion of examining tactics and their deployment strips them of any power.

Groups use protest to communicate with their opponents, the public and other movements. They make claims against the state through protest actions. There is also strong evidence that tactics are not interchangeable, but that the choice to use particular ones often stems from the cultural, social and political (Tilly 2003) milieu. Put more simply, tactics will not convey much meaning if they are not in some way rooted in society, though that rootedness may come from many different places. While it might again sound like I am proposing that context is all that matters, even in choice of tactic, that is not the case. Instead, I am pointing out that tactics themselves are meaning-makers as well as tools for the movements and should be studied with both of these aspects in mind. If we accept that tactics are important, then we must also examine the ability of particular acts to propagate political change. To do this I present disparate cases of suicide protest that highlight both the way that movements deploy tactics, and their context. The effectiveness of suicide protest is not determined by any one factor but by a concert of movement and state behavior that can either accentuate or muffle the inherent power of these dramatic acts.

Successful suicide protest?

When confronted with acts of suicide protest, we tend to recoil from them or relegate them to unique instances that won't be repeated. Our instinctive reaction aside, suicide protest has been on the rise around the world since the latter half of the twentieth century. One explanation for this is that suicide protest may be more effective than we want to believe. This book provides insight both into the particular tactic of suicide protest, as well as the manner and methods through which all protest tactics can lead states to either comply, deny or ignore demands from social movements. Theories on social movements look closely at the motivations for why and when groups form, and then act in particular ways.[7] Though the question of movement success and failure has been explored by a number of authors, few theories link the use of particular tactics to outcomes.[8] To understand the salience of tactics for movements I closely examine one particular type of political expression: suicide protest.

Watching someone set herself on fire, or reading about the event afterwards, is disturbing; we almost instinctively shy away from it. Despite the powerful visible impact that suicide protest has, we don't know enough about when or why this tactic succeeds or fails in creating political outcomes for the movement.[9] In this study I explain the reasons why suicide protests result in successful contestation against the state for some groups, but not for others. I posit that suicide protest is more likely to result in policy shifts when there is a combination of four different factors.

First, I determine whether the movement utilizes other protests tactics, such as strikes or demonstrations, in addition to suicide protest. The presence of other protest tactics indicates a high level of *tactical depth*. Second, I measure the *intensity* of the suicide act; in other words does death occur or not? Third, I examine the ability of the movement to construct a favorable *emotional narration* of the event, including emotional fields. Finally, I examine the capacity of the political system to accommodate oppositional forces, indicating a high level of *political competition* both in and outside of the government. The extent to which each of these four elements is realized determines the probability of a movement's success.

I examine three cases of suicide protest within India. These cases are: the fast to the death by Potti Sriramulu for the linguistic state of Andhra in 1952 India; the use of fasting and drowning by the Narmada Bachao Andolan (NBA) in 1991 and 1993 India; and the self-immolation of high caste students in Northern India in 1990. Among these three cases, only one, the movement for Andhra, did the use of suicide result in long-term policy change in favor of the movement. The Anti-Narmada Dam movement attained short-term goals through suicide, but did not create long-term change. The students protesting against reservation policies failed to create policy change in their favor. The variation among and between these cases suggests that the manner in which suicide protest is used will have an impact on the tactic's ability to generate political transformations. Next, I broaden my analysis to examine its applicability to the tactic of suicide bombing, which is related to suicide protest but qualitatively different. By extending the argument to include this type of tactic, I hope to make clear that my theory can apply to other types of extreme tactics. I investigate suicide bombings conducted by the Liberation Tigers of Tamil Eelam (LTTE) in Sri Lanka throughout the 1990s and the early twenty-first century. Similar to the NBA, the LTTE gained short-term success with suicide bombing but failed to create long-term favorable outcomes. I also compare four secondary cases of contemporary suicide protest around the

6 *Introduction*

world. These cases provide insight into the limits of my theory of protest success and failure. They are: the fasts conducted by the IRA in 1980 and 1981; the self-immolation death of Mohammed Bouazizi in Tunisia; the series of self-immolations by Tibetans protesting China's presence in Tibet; and the self-immolation of war protestor Malachi Ritscher in Chicago in 2006.

The violent non-violence of suicide protest

I define suicide protest as actions carried out by social movement participants that are intended to knowingly result in their own deaths. These actions are undertaken to demand a particular previously articulated political outcome.[10] I believe that the collective and organized aspect of suicide protest is crucial when trying to understand policy change. There have been cases in India, and other places, of individuals who have committed suicide for political, economic or social reasons; they may even enact their suicide in public places. However, those actions, which I call "political suicides," are not only empirically difficult to analyze, but also theoretically less significant to the overall concern of this book: movement success and failure. That said, there have been some startling cases of individual suicide protest that have helped to spur (or not spur) political change. I examine two such cases in Chapter 7. Generally speaking this book sidesteps questions of individual motivations and impacts in favor of examining group dynamics.

As such, definition explicitly distinguishes between intention and results. Not all suicide protests result in the death of the protestor; protestors must have a real commitment to the possibility of death. This distinction allows us to include suicide protests that are pre-empted by external forces, such as the state. Also, this definition excludes simple verbal threats of suicide. An illustrative example would be the protests surrounding the staging of the Miss World pageant in Bangalore, India, in November 1996. Numerous groups opposed the pageant, ranging from women's organizations to conservative religious groups. At the time, one women's organization, the Mahila Jagran Samiti, published an open letter to the government in which some of their members threatened to self-immolate themselves if their demand to move the pageant was not met. The group claimed that the pageant did not reflect Indian culture and was vulgar. As the event drew closer, this organization threatened a mass self-immolation protest on the day of the closing ceremony, although the protestors were ultimately dissuaded from carrying out this threat by the state. While this was a serious situation that certainly has a bearing on the topic of political suicide, it would not be included in our definition of suicidal protest; it is too difficult to unearth the actual degree of intention from a simple verbal threat. Were these women actually prepared to die for their causes? With no action to back up their statements it is hard to tell. In contrast to the Miss World Pageant protests, in 1932 Gandhi declared a fast to the death in protest against the creation of separate electorates for Untouchables in India. The fast ended after a few days as B.R. Ambedkar,

Introduction   7

a leader of the Untouchable community, was forced to concede to Gandhi's wishes (Ambedkar 1946). Despite the fact that Gandhi did not die as a result of his 1932 fast, this event *would* be included under the definition of suicide protest used in this book; Gandhi began his fast knowing that it would end in death unless there was external intervention.

Thus, my understanding of suicide protest rests in part on the perceived intentionality of the participating actor, by which I mean the group. By doing so I complicate another aspect of how we may understand this phenomenon. Should suicide protest be considered an act of violence, or of non-violence? Gandhi believed the intention of the faster was the most important factor when considering whether the fast was a true act of non-violent *satyagraha*, or a violent act of emotional blackmail.[11] Most current practitioners of suicide protest would describe the tactic as non-violent, based both on their intentions and the fact that such acts do not harm other people. In fact, that perception of suicide protest most likely imbues it with a degree of symbolic power. While there is a case to be made for the non-violence of suicide protest, that reading can also lead to troubling consequences, canonizing certain movements and protestors above others, or even misunderstandings regarding the nature of movements.[12]

As I have defined it, suicide protest can also fall into the larger rubric of political violence. William Gamson defines political violence as "deliberate physical injury to property or persons" (Gamson 1975, p. 74). This does not explicate the *direction* of harm. Violence not only means harm that one individual will commit against another, but also can include the harm that a person can do to herself. In other words, suicide protest is a form of self-directed violence that intends death, but which is often framed as non-violence. The duality of suicide protest is key to its ability to create political change. It is a tactic that can be both feared and revered. The ambiguity of suicide protest makes it a good tactic to study, as these acts illustrate potential strengths and weaknesses of radical tactics in protest action and adds to our understanding of both violent and non-violent protest.

Suicide protest versus suicide bombing

While suicide protest straddles the conceptual line between violence and non-violence, the same could not be said of suicide bombing, which is firmly embedded within the rubric of political violence. I argue that suicide bombing is a related but qualitatively different type of tactic from suicide protest. As such, applying my analytical argument to suicide bombing reveals interesting aspects of the tactical approach to movement success and failure, while also testing its applicability on other types of extreme protest tactic.

Despite some similarities the tactic of suicide bombing is not a type of suicide protest. For example, unlike suicide protest, it is impossible to discuss suicide bombing with the language of non-violent resistance, placing the tactic outside of the category as a whole. Despite this, there are some significant

8   *Introduction*

commonalities between the two. Both tactics are meant to end in the death of the protestor. Moreover, groups that use suicide bombing often emphasize the self-sacrificing nature of the tactic, not its ability to cause high levels of violence. The conceptual separation between the two tactics illustrates the fundamental characteristics of both. Suicide protest, by my definition, must lie in a contested space between violence and non-violence, making it a radical choice. Suicide bombing is purely violent, though the tactic can often highlight the sacrificing nature of political violence more effectively than other types of violent action.

The similarity between these two tactics creates an opportunity to test the applicability of my theory on this similar, but unrelated, tactic. I include suicide bombing in my analysis for two reasons. First, suicide bombing illustrates the ways that my argument applies to other violent tactics. If we can understand how tactics work then we can also understand why groups use them. This is especially important for a tactic like suicide bombing, which continues to be used in various contexts. My second purpose in including suicide bombing is that I believe isolating certain stratagems as "terrorism" doesn't actually help to deepen our understanding of them. These acts reside on a continuum of protest actions and therefore should be studied together.

Do tactics matter? Alternative explanations for movement success and failure

Before I engage deeply in my argument, I think it is important to examine the issue of movement success and failure and the ambiguity of both of these categories. Notions of movement success or failure are contested within social movement literature (Gamson 1975; Giugni 2004; Tarrow 1998; MacAdam 1999). Scholars have cited different combinations of policy shifts, process shifts, co-option, perception change and personal transformations, as some of the elements that could constitute successful contestation of the state by movements. Generally these scholars examine the movement as a whole, or the pattern of the protest cycle that the movement is embedded in, to determine success or failure. I draw from this work to determine the importance that particular tactics can have on social movement outcomes.

I use a basic understanding of success and failure in order to track the implications of a singular tactic. By definition, social movements contend for some political effect from the state. Regardless of size, all movements have a particular agenda. In the process of trying to realize that agenda movements also identify contingent political goals. Movements that have a long history will more likely have both short- and long-term goals as part of their agenda. Very often campaigns may concentrate on short-term, or intermediate, goals as opposed to the long-term, or ultimate goals for which the movement was created.[13] Making a distinction between long- and short-term goals is important for several reasons. First, it problematizes our notions of success and failure with regard to social movements. Are movements only

Introduction 9

successful if they have "won the war?" Shouldn't winning the battle count for something? If battles do count, how should that affect our understanding of success or failure? Additionally, disaggregating outcomes allows us to examine the relative effects of one tactic over the other. How do movements decide which tactic should be used for which goal? Is there a pattern to this choice? This work makes a clear distinction between intermediate and ultimate goals to make a more nuanced analysis of the tactic of suicide. I argue that while suicide protest seems to be more effective in attaining short-term goals, there are situations where the tactic may result in realizing ultimate political goals as well.

I am primarily concerned with discovering when and how suicide protest results in policy shifts in favor of the movement. In order to understand the success or failure of suicide protest we must first shift our focus from explaining protest to explaining how protest affects other aspects of political life: in this case policy change. Few people have seriously looked at whether or not protest "works." Gamson (1975), Piven and Cloward (1979) and Giugni (2004) each present alternative theories regarding the success and failure of movements. Scholars have cited different combinations of policy shifts, process shifts, and co-option as some of the elements that could constitute successful contestation of the state by movements.. In contrast to scholars that have examined the success or failure of movements, I focus on the impact of a particular type of tactic on the success of the movement as a whole. It is unclear why so few scholars have been concerned with the effect of distinct tactics on movement outcomes. By addressing this question we can not only understand the nuances of internal movement dynamics, we can also investigate how social movement claims can be accommodated or denied by states.

There have been a number of different theories regarding the success or failure of movements. I group these disparate theories into two broad categories. First, theories that focus on internal movement dynamics to explain the possibility of success and failure; and second, those that cite external or structural elements as most important in creating political outcomes.

Falling into the first category, Gamson (1975) provides a methodical analysis of the impacts of social movements. He cites violence and disruption as a key to successful contestation of the state. Gamson looks closely at the internal structures of the movement to determine its chances of success or failure. The more organized movements are, the more likely they will be successful. In contrast to Gamson's argument, scholars such as Piven and Cloward (1979) and Burstein (1999) cite external factors as the key to movement impacts. As states provide more institutional support to movements, so movements will increasingly be unable to stand in opposition to the state. According to Piven and Cloward movements can be co-opted by the state, hindering their ability to create real change in their favor. Burstein presents a theory of democratic representation, which cites legislative and public perceptions as important factors in determining movement impacts. He blurs the line between movement organizations and other types of interest group. His argument provides

10 *Introduction*

needed contextual analysis for the salience of movements, but suggests that the movements themselves are less important than the context they act in.

Based within the political process approach, Giugni (2004) attempts to bridge these contrasting theories of movement success. He points to the fact that external alliances and the internal organization of movements are often dependant upon one another. I agree with Giugni that these two theories are not mutually exclusive. To this theory he adds the role of public opinion in trying to understand the success or failure of movements. Giugni's understanding of a movement's effects speaks to the particular role that suicide protest can play in its overall success. Like Giugni, I believe that both internal movement dynamics, and the political context of a state, aid in determining their political efficacy. I apply his theory to examine the effect that a particular tactic – suicide protest – can have on policy change.

Other factors could also play a role in determining the level of movement success. International pressures, moral approbation, and the type of demands made may greatly effect the ability of suicide protest to create change. While these factors may be important, I believe that my argument provides a more nuanced and comprehensive understanding for why *tactics* matter, not just the movement as a whole. Moreover, the tactical approach considers both internal and external factors in its analytical framework. This allows a holistic examination of the ways movements try to communicate, and the political context at the time.

The argument

Having differentiated between the different types of political outcomes that suicide protest can create, the question still remains: under what conditions will suicide protest engender intermediate or ultimate goals, or both? I argue that the presence of four different factors will increase the probability that suicidal protest can result in either type of political outcome: first, the presence or absence of other tactics used by the movement, indicating a high level of *tactical depth*; second, the *intensity* of the protest; third, the ability of the movement to *narrate* the events; and finally, the level of viable *political competition* within the state. Three of these elements depend on movement actions: tactical depth, intensity and emotional appeals. The fourth element, the level of political competition, examines the political context at the time of protest. Figure 1.1 is a visual representation of how these elements work together in order to increase the likelihood of policy outcomes in favor of the movement. I then proceed to explain each factor more fully, starting with tactical depth.

Tactical depth

I measure the tactical depth of a social movement by looking at whether or not groups use other, particularly non-violent, protest tactics. In other words,

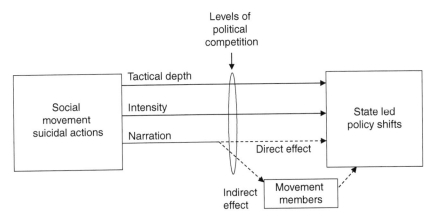

Figure 1.1 Suicide protest outcomes: the tactical approach

can the movement contest the state on multiple levels? From the wide range of tactics possible, I identify purely non-violent, or traditional,[14] forms of protest as particularly important to movement success. Having a number of tactics in their repertoire would indicate the presence of short-term campaigns that support the overall goal of the group; the presence of alternative protests and campaigns indicates a high level of tactical depth within the movement as a whole.

The need for tactical depth illustrates a weakness inherent within the practice of suicide protest and other radical events – these tactics are unlikely to create long-term change when used on their own. Though suicide protest does have the ability to shock the public, it is also an extreme act that often garners a negative reputation among states and the media. Movements that utilize suicide protest tread a fine line between the labels of "committed" and "crazy." In order to mitigate negative reactions and create positive outcomes, movements must use other types of protest to show that they are adaptive and willing to negotiate with their opponents. The presence of non-violent protest tactics is more likely to lead to a positive long-term outcome in favor of the movement. Non-violent tactics indicate that the movement has leaders who are willing to negotiate with the state. Suicide protest seems like an all-or-nothing option; there is usually little or no room for negotiation.[15] Yet more often than not, movements must negotiate with the state and other political actors. Movements that only utilize suicide protest, or become identified with the use of suicide protest, will not be in a good bargaining position vis-à-vis the state once the protest has ended. Gamson (1975) makes a claim that violence can help create political change precisely because it is so disruptive; however, this does not explain why so many violent movements fail. Andrews (2001) and others argue that movements that apply protest and regular tactics will be more effective than purely violent movements. I

12 Introduction

combine these two approaches in the tactical approach to suicide protest. The inherent violence of these acts can be very disruptive, but that violence cannot be harnessed unless the movement can also demonstrate its non-violent aspects. In order to achieve a long-term goal, movements must be able to prove that they are not only extreme, but also can deal with the state in good faith. The presence or absence of tactical depth highlights a particular weakness of violent political mobilization; violence has the ability to be effective, but it is less likely to do so when it is the only method utilized.

Intensity

Tactical depth measures a movement's resources and relative power. The next two factors – the intensity of the tactic and the emotional narrative surrounding suicide protest – look more closely at the protest act itself. Drawing from Tilly's use of the term "intensity" (1978), I define intensity as the presence of death in a suicide event. It seems odd to consider the use of death as an indicator for the strength of a political protest. Yet, though death is exactly what these movements desire, it is not an inevitable end to suicide protest. Death increases the intensity of a protest act. I also expand the notion of intensity to look across protest acts. In other words, will groups be able to suicide protest more than once? I believe that there can be diminishing returns when one group uses suicide protest too much. We will see this play out in the Anti-Reservation movement; the power of the tactics rest on their dramatic nature. As the number of deaths increase, the efficacy of the tactic decreases. This phenomenon is also evident in the case of the LTTE's use of suicide bombing.

Despite the previous arguments, high levels of intensity are important to the success of the tactic because the possible or actual death of the protestor is the lever that can be used against the state. Protests with high intensity garner media and public attention. Also, high-intensity protests can signal the level of commitment within a movement.

Emotional narratives

The third factor that increases the probability of movement success is the extent to which they succeed in creating emotional appeals both within and towards the state. This does not measure whether or not movements are actually able to create emotional responses, or affective ties, but the ways in which they attempt to do so, either consciously or unconsciously.[16] If groups that use suicide protest attempt to harness or engender emotional ties through direct and indirect appeals, then it is more likely that acts of suicide will spur a political outcome. I identify two audiences for suicide protest; first, active and potential members of the movement and second, the primary opponent – in most cases the state. In order to examine this aspect of suicide protest, I conduct dramaturgical analyses of suicide protest events and any celebrations

Introduction 13

or rituals that are centered on those events (Blumer 1969; Esherick and Wasserstrom 1990; Hare and Blumberg 1988). I analyze the way in which movements describe the event to the public, media and the state, as well as the staging of the event itself. Acts of protest do not speak for themselves; social movements that want such acts to say particular things create their meanings. What do movements want suicidal protest to say? Is it an act of martyrdom or anger? Does it invoke feelings of support or hatred? Do they emphasize the suicidal aspects of the protest or do they underplay it? I argue that movements attempt to engender or construct emotional ties with both the public and the state. I contend that movements will particularly access pride, sympathy, shame and fear in their desire to create emotional bonds with the community and the state.

I closely examine both the duration and memory of suicidal events to determine the extent to which certain audiences can identify themselves with the act and the actor. Pride and sympathy depend on a sense of intimacy with the object of these emotions (Ahmed 2004). The ability of movements to re-enact suicide events helps to generate these emotional responses. The manner with which movements discuss, remember and celebrate acts of suicide will help to create or stifle emotional ties. I also contend that movements will actively seek to create negative emotional responses among and within their opponents: in most cases the state. I identify shame as the primary emotion directed towards the state, and examine the rhetoric surrounding suicide events, as well as their staging, to see if movements intend to create and re-create these negative emotions in their opponents.

The emotional narrative is one area where there is a significant difference between suicide protest and suicide bombing. As with other types of terrorist action, the group will try to create a sense of fear, not shame, within the state.

It is important to discern the emotional resonance of a suicide protest because the success of this tactic is, in part, dependent on how the public and state view the event. Petersen (2002) cites the negative emotional responses to ethnic violence as one reason why the tactic may fail. Suicide is a type of violence, but one that has the ability to create positive emotional responses. By playing on notions of martyrdom and pride, movements can gain public and political support. Of course, the stigma that accompanies normal political violence can attach itself also to suicide protest. Groups must carefully navigate the possible negative aspects of this particular tactic.

Level of political competition

The final component that adds to the relative success of suicide protest is the level of effective political competition within the state, including other political parties, supporting social movements, and international actors. I measure the level of political competition based both on the number, and strength, of opposing forces in the state. The number of opposing forces is

14 Introduction

a simple measure. The simple existence of other political parties does not convey how effective those forces may be. Therefore I will also examine the viability of other political parties, and movements, and their relative strength vis-à-vis the state.

The level of political competition is determined by two specific structural contexts. First, what exactly is the political situation at the time of the protests? Are there viable competitive parties? Is political power dispersed in any way? Second, I also take into account the actual or perceived ability of these movements to take advantage of that political context and competition. To that end, this variable is both concrete and interpretative. Higher levels of competition will increase the probability of movement success; as competition decreases so does the possibility of successful long-term policy shifts. Higher levels of competition also indicate a more open state structure. This factor is embedded within the political process approach to social movements, though I only cite one specific point of that broad theory. Proponents of the political opportunity theories are mainly concerned with how and when movements mobilize. They pinpoint political and institutional shifts that indicate to movements the times and spaces in which to mobilize. The political context has bearing on the creation of movements and mobilization (McAdam 1996; Tarrow 1996, 1998). As the political process approach has grown, so too has the number of structures that can influence mobilization. McAdam (1996, p. 27) defines four dimensions of political opportunity:

1 the relative openness or closure of the institutionalized political system;
2 the stability or instability of that broad set of elite arrangements that typically undergird a polity;
3 the presence or absence of elite allies;
4 the state's capacity and propensity for repression.

It is necessary to gage the levels of political competition as they can have clear effects on the ability of movements to create political change. However, there may be a tendency to place the level of political competition as a dependent variable; in other words, movements are trying to create competitive political contexts. I am not using this variable like that here. Instead, I use this factor to understand the possible spatial, temporal and institutional openings in place in the state, and the ability of the movement to take advantage of these openings.

Each of these four dimensions encapsulates a number of structural shifts. In trying to determine how political structures impinge on the possibilities of success and failure of the movement, I isolate the first dimension – openness – and use the presence or absence of viable competition as the indicator of that openness.[17] I argue that as the level of viable political competition increases, so does the possibility of successful suicide protest. When states must contend with a number of different political forces they will be more willing to negotiate or jockey for support both from these other political groups and the

Introduction 15

public. Suicide protest is more likely to have a positive effect when conducted in a more competitive and open state.

Unlike suicide protest, there is a larger body of work that investigates the effectiveness of suicide bombing. Pape (2005) argues that while suicide terrorism is less likely to create long-term political change, it is effective in engendering short-term success. Additionally, not only is suicide bombing more likely to take place in democracies, it is more likely to create short-term political change in these contexts as well. While I agree with Pape that the level of democracy can help make suicide protest effective, I do not believe that regime type is the only determining factor for the success or failure of this tactic. I argue that the presence or absence of oppositional political actors will affect the likelihood of tactical success in addition to regime type.

Research design, case analysis and chapter outline

Suicide protest exists within a liminal space; it is simultaneously moral and immoral, violent and non-violent, and can spur negative and positive emotional responses. The contested nature of suicide protest gives the tactic visceral power, but that power does not always translate into political success. I believe that these four factors (tactical depth, intensity, narration and competition) when taken together, present a dynamic picture of the different forces that increasingly improve the chances of a positive political outcome. Ultimately I present a relational story between social movements, external actors and states, all of which are embedded within a social and cultural context. No *single* condition is either necessary or sufficient for the creation of political change. Instead they all interact with one another to create different outcomes.

I examine the success or failure of suicide protest through a comparative analysis of three relevant cases in South Asia. This work fits into a larger tradition of comparative political inquiry that uses in-depth analysis of fewer cases in order to generate particular theoretical implications. While suicide protest is increasingly used, it is still relatively rare, and therefore difficult to adequately study through large-scale quantitative methodologies. The comparative case study approach allows me to trace out complex matters, such as movement dynamics and the multiple interactions between states and movements, without losing relevant details to abstraction.

Case analysis

I compare three different movements located in South Asia that all use varying forms of suicide in conjunction with other tactics: The movement for Andhra in 1952, the Anti-reservation movement in 1990, and the Narmada Bachao Andolan. I selected cases based on variation of suicide protest types as well as variation across the four factors I previously outlined (see Table 1.1).

16 Introduction

Table 1.1 Cases and tactics

Movement name	Movement type	Suicide tactic type
Movement for Andhra (1952)	Sub-national	Fast to the death
The Narmada Bachao Andolan (1986–2000)	Environmental	Fast to the death; drowning
The Anti-Reservation Movement (1990)	Student movement	Self-immolation
Liberation Tigers of Tamil Eelam (1981–2009)	Ethno-nationalist separatist movement	Suicide bombing

I broaden the scope of my analysis to examine a case of suicide bombing, focusing on the Liberation Tigers of Tamil Eelam's use of the tactic from 1987 until the group's demise in 2009. Through this comparison we can understand the relative value of each type of suicide tactic. Is one form of suicide more successful than another? What implications does this framework have for suicide terrorism?

This comparative case analysis is based on in-depth field research conducted in India and Sri Lanka in 2005, 2006 and 2010. For each case I examined government documents, archival material and newspaper accounts of suicide protests. I also conducted semiformal interviews with relevant actors.

This book is organized into eight chapters. Chapter 2 examines the historical and cultural development of suicide protest in South Asia, focusing on two specific types of suicide protest: self-immolation and fasting. The chapter investigates ways that cultural practice transformed into political protest. Suicide protest is not the obvious choice when planning a protest event, yet it has become increasingly commonplace in South Asia. What accounts for this increase? When suicide protest is used why does it take certain forms and not others? In this chapter I examine two particular themes. First, what is the relationship between cultural practice and protest type? Do they implicate one another, and if so how? I posit that the form of protest is implicated by relevant social rituals and then examine those rituals in the light of this conclusion. Second, I investigate Gandhi and the Nationalist Movement's influence on modern political practice in India. The Nationalist Movement lasted for about 50 years, but continues to exert influence on modern Indian politics; most especially in the way that it chooses to challenge the state. Gandhi was one of the first activists to utilize ritual within politics, but not the last. Chapter 2 also briefly examines the scope of suicide protest within India, using event data I have collected, providing a glimpse into the pattern and frequency of suicide protest.

In the next three chapters I consider my overall argument through a comparison of three critical cases of suicide protest in South Asia. I argue that the success or failure of suicide protest depends on the presence or absence of four factors: (1) the tactical depth of the movement; (2) the intensity of the event; (3) the ability of the movement to construct emotional narratives about the event; and (4) the level of political competition in the political context. In these chapters I present an historical analysis of the movements and then investigate their use of suicide. These cases illustrate three possible outcomes for suicide protest: long-term success, short-term success and failure.

Chapter 3 presents the first empirical case analysis: Potti Sriramulu's fasting to death in 1952. He conducted this fast so that the Government of India would create a linguistic state for Telegu speakers. This suicide protest event resulted in long-term change for the movement; within days of his death Nehru declared the establishment of the state of Andhra. In this chapter I explore the events of the fast in light of my overall argument. Sriramulu's fast resulted in long-term policy change in favor of the movement.

Chapter 4 investigates the case of the Narmada Bachao Andolan (NBA), an environmental movement that mobilized in opposition to the Sardar Sarovar Dam project in Western India. I focus on the movement's most active period, the mid-1980s to 2000. The NBA utilized suicide protest to gain short-term success in their favor. This chapter highlights the importance of intensity and political competition.

Chapter 5 considers the Anti-Reservation Movement in 1990. This conservative student movement failed to achieve any political ends, despite the use of self-immolation. This chapter traces the history of the problem and analyzes why the students were unable to shift policy in their favor. This movement highlights the importance of narrative, and also problematizes the issue of intensity and it's role in movement success.

The next two chapters are a departure from the core analysis of the book. In Chapter 6 I address a related, but different, type of suicide protest: suicide bombing. Suicide bombing is a much more widely known method of protest, and utilized throughout the world. Though it is qualitatively different from the types of suicide protest I consider earlier in the book, its relevance indicates that analysis of its efficacy is warranted. I investigate the Liberation Tigers of Tamil Eelam's (LTTE) use of suicide bombing throughout their existence. Based on this analysis it is clear that the four critical factors I outlined earlier are applicable to cases of suicide bombing as well as to other forms of suicide protest. The LTTE deployed suicide bombing as a tactic more than 200 times, and were able to create short-term success.

Chapter 7 examines four secondary cases of suicide protest in other areas of the world. By doing this I am able to examine the boundaries of my argument as well as more contemporary instances of suicide protest. The book is concerned with suicide protest in South Asia, and when it is embedded within a movement. However, acts of suicide protest occur in other regional and organizational contexts; can the model also be applied to suicide protest in Europe or the Middle East? What impact can single acts have on a movement? I examine four global cases of suicide protest:

1   the fasts in the Maze prison in Northern Ireland;
2   the self-immolation of Tibetan monks in India and China;

18 *Introduction*

3 the self-immolation of Mohamed Bouazizi in Tunisia in December 2010;
4 the self-immolation of Malachi Ritscher in Chicago in 2006.

These cases present empirical and theoretical challenges to my model. I determine that the four identified factors do have implications for these cases.

In the final chapter I present my conclusions regarding the efficacy of suicide protest as a social movement tactic. I compare the cases, and explore some of the implications of my argument. For instance, to what extent does violent action depend on the presence of non-violence to generate success? Is suicide protest more, or less, effective in democratic contexts? These discussions shed new light on the issue of suicide protest and its relationship to mobilization and politics.

Notes

1 High caste students were fighting the implementation of the Mandal Commission, which would increase the number of spaces reserved for *dalits* (Untouchables) in public sector jobs.
2 Though numbers vary, reports seem to agree that approximately 200 students attempted self-immolation. However, not all of these attempts resulted in the death of the actor. I consider the actions of this group fully in Chapter 5.
3 Though acts of fasting and self-immolation have cultural relevance within Hindu, Muslim and Christian religions, the use of these actions as a political act can only be traced back to the early twentieth century. Suffragettes in North America and Europe, as well as Northern Irish prisoners, were the first to use hunger strikes: a form of fasting. Self-immolation is thought to have originated in the 1960s.
4 I discuss the motivations for using both suicide protest and suicide bombing in an article entitled "Choosing to Die: Suicide Bombing and Suicide Protest in South Asia" in *Terrorism and Political Violence* (forthcoming).
5 The number of farmer suicides is disputed. Based on his analysis of Ministry of Crime Statistics, Nagaraj (2008) claims that 166,304 farmers committed suicide between 1996 and 2005. While the causes and impacts of farmer suicides are related to the types of suicide protest under discussion in this book, the farmers themselves are not actively engaged in political mobilization.
6 I use this dataset in a number unpublished articles. These articles make tentative claims regarding the relationship between suicide protest and democratic institutionalization.
7 See Tarrow (1998), McAdam (1996), and political opportunity structure theory of social movement analysis.
8 Though some scholars of social movements have discussed the failure or success of movements (Giugni 2004; Piven and Cloward 1979) for the most part these authors examine the movement in sum, and are not primarily concerned with the effect that a specific protest can have on movement and state politics. For more on this type of analysis I draw from work done on political violence (Brass 1997; Horowitz 2001; Petersen 2002), as well as terrorist activity (Bloom 2005; Pape 2005). These types of work are more likely to look at a particular tactic, in this case violence, and track the effects that violence can have. Though these works are not usually embedded within a larger analysis of contentious politics, I combine these two understandings of tactics and political mobilization in this work.

Introduction 19

9 Success is defined as the ability of a tactic to create policy or state shifts in favor of the movement. I provide an in-depth examination of movement success later in the chapter.

10 This definition draws extensively from Durkhiem's theory of *altruistic suicide* outlined in his seminal work, *Suicide* (1979). Altruistic suicide occurs when individuals are subordinated to a strong social community, and usually out of a sense of obligation. I also draw from Biggs and his discussion of self-immolation, which he states should include more than death by fire. Biggs defines self-immolation as an "extreme form of protest" (2005, p. 173) that is public.

11 I discuss Gandhi's philosophy of fasting extensively in Chapter 2.

12 See Ackerman and Kruegler (1994) for a systematic discussion on some of the unintended consequences of what they call "strategic nonviolent conflict." The authors examine the conditions under which non-violent action may "work," suggesting that the decision to choose non-violence as a tactic can have impacts on the outcome of conflicts.

13 The discussion differentiating between political outcomes disregards one other type of outcome – the shift in the political discourse surrounding the movement. This can be intended or unintended, as well as positive or negative. An example of this would be an environmental movement that does not successfully attain its ultimate goal, but the existence of the movement instils an awareness of the environment in both the public and the state that did not exist previously. Though shifts in political discourse often result from protest, I do not incorporate this notion within my analysis of the success and failure of a movement.

14 By this I mean strikes, demonstrations, marches and other protest types that do not cause bodily harm. I also include the ability of the movement to use non-disruptive tactics, such as court and legislative appeals.

15 This does not always hold true for the tactic of fasting, which will be discussed further in Chapter 3 and Chapter 4.

16 There is a methodological issue when trying to ascertain emotions and emotional responses. First, memories of emotions are unlikely to be consistent or accurate. Feelings and memories about past emotional states are colored by intervening events. Unless one is present during acts of suicide protest it is difficult to gage the public's actual emotional reaction. I examine emotional narratives directed to the state. But can the state feel emotions at all? Should we simply aggregate the emotions of all of those who make up the state? If so, then this runs into the same problems of recollection and retelling that I describe with regard to public emotions. Even if people in government do feel emotional responses to suicide protest, how does this translate into governmental action? While all of these questions are interesting I have not found direct evidence to support any claims on this matter. Instead I only discuss how movements harness and create emotional ties and responses with these two audiences, not their success in doing so.

17 See Giugni (2004) for an alternative use of these four dimensions of political opportunity structure.

2 Gandhi and the development of suicide protest in India

In this chapter I track the development of two crucial types of suicide protest, fasting to the death and self-immolation, from ritual practice to political protest tactics within the particular political history of India. While there can be as many types of suicide protest as there are ways to commit suicide, these two events seem to be more frequently used both in and outside South Asia. It is this frequency that makes it necessary to contextualize the use of these two tactics, not only to explain how they entered the lexicon of protest tactics within Indian political history, but also to understand why they remain powerful in contemporary politics. A major claim of this book is that suicide protest can be meaningful; in order to understand that meaning we must examine the historical and cultural significance of these particular types of suicide protest. Why is fasting more resonant than something like ingesting poison, another type of suicide protest practiced in India? Can the power of political self-immolation be attributed to the importance of burning within Hindu tradition? I examine these questions by tracing both the use of these practices as ritual and their adoption as protest tactics.

I contend that a complex dance of cultural practice, personality, political innovation and critical political junctures helped establish fasting to the death and self-immolation as acceptable forms of political expression in India. In particular, I argue that the Indian Nationalist Movement and Gandhi's adoption of innovative protest tactics, including fasting to the death, helped to inculcate the notion of physical self-sacrifice as a desired and effective type of political protest contra the state – in effect, making suicide protest, or self-sacrifice, a regular form of political expression. In order to examine the theoretical scope of this argument I briefly discuss the importance of political communication and language in society in this chapter, linking that notion to the adoption of particular protest tactics, focusing on the role of cultural ritual within political practice. I then explore the transformation of cultural ritual in India into suicide protest. Finally, I concentrate the majority of this chapter on an examination of what I believe to be a critical era of political innovation in India: the Nationalist Movement. In particular, I explore Gandhi's adoption of the fast to the death in politics, tracking the evolution of his practice through descriptions of two of his fasts. Through this analysis, as well as his theories of fasting and sacrifice in politics, I draw some conclusions regarding the shifting nature of political discourse and suicide protest within contemporary India.

Suicide protest in political idiom

Acts of suicide protest, especially fasting to the death and self-immolation, have become common and maybe even habitual aspects of political expression in India. This commonality suggests that suicide protest is now, in some ways, an acceptable type of practice within Indian politics. In other words, suicide protest has become a part of the political idiom of India. I use the term political idiom to denote the current paradigm of political communication within a state. Broadly speaking, political idiom covers multiple types of communication, including verbal, visual, metaphorical, figurative and symbolic forms of speech and praxis. But political idiom is also narrow, as it creates a linguistic and expressionistic shorthand within politics. Thus, political idiom should be considered a type of *episteme* of political communication and practice.[1] As new forms of political expression enter the idiom they change and constrain what will be acceptable in the future. The political idiom of a state reconstitutes itself, even as it changes. Thus, my conceptualization of political idiom is a system of discourse that explicates "acceptable" and "normal" forms of political practice and language.[2] There are a number of different political idioms, depending on the political structure or institutions at play. In particular, I examine the construction and propagation of a mobilizational political idiom, which shapes the ways that challengers can and will articulate their claims.

In practice, political idiom is the combination of actual and symbolic actions and interactions that construct and constrain the political space. Focusing on the importance of symbolic speech and political theater, I draw from scholars who examine the production and effects of symbolic discourse (Edelman 1967; Edelman 1988; Blumer 1969; Turner 1974, 1982). These scholars investigate the ways that political actors use symbolic discourse to both reinforce and break down the "normal" in politics. Edelman (1967) describes two types of symbols that are deployed by the state. "Referential symbols" are used to create a common discourse, which often pertains to the state itself. For example, the creation of flags and anthems allows states to construct a collective language about itself. In contrast, "condensation symbols" are invoked to convey the meaning behind particular acts. "Practically every political act that is controversial or regarded as really important is bound to serve in part as a condensation symbol. It evokes a quiescent or aroused mass response because it symbolizes threat or reassurance" (Edelman 1967, p. 7). In order to direct the meaning and understandings behind these symbols states will often construct "political spectacles," which are intended to create action or non-action on the part of the public (Edelman 1988). Edelman directly connects the interpretation of symbols and spectacles to political actions. In addition,

22   *Gandhi and suicide protest in India*

Edelman's division between different types of symbols illuminates the complex purposiveness of symbolic discourse. These symbols help the public to understand the political world, but in particular ways. Edelman focuses on the ways that the state chooses to construct and deploy these spectacles, but they aren't the only game in town – movements and other contending groups also attempt to construct and deploy these types of symbolic discourses. Herbert Blumer (1969) references the relational aspects of discourse, emphasizing the importance of social interaction as the location of meaning-making. This theory illustrates the role that contending groups and other actors can play as they attempt to create meaningful political discourse and idiom. Both Edelman and Blumer provide important insights into the elements that help to shape political idiom. They highlight the relational and complex nature of symbolic communication. However, my work draws more extensively from Turner's identification of the social drama as a critical space for social and political communication.

Turner (1982, p.10) believes that the social drama fundamentally plays out contention in society:

> a public breach ... in the normal working of society, ranging from some grave transgression of the code of manners to an act of violence ... Such a breach may result from feeling, a crime of passion perhaps, or from cool calculation – a political act designed to challenge the extant power structure.

The social drama has a life of its own which is laden with hidden meanings, antagonists, heroes and villains, and does not simply relay an interesting story. Instead, social and political dramas can be used to point out weaknesses, spark redressive actions, or even call leaders to account (ibid., p.11). Turner (1974, p. 38) describes four phases of public action in a social drama. First, there is a "breach" of normal social relations. This breach must be public, and even if a single person undertakes it, that person is representing a group. Second, after the breach occurs there will be a period of crisis; at this time if the crisis cannot be contained within a small part of the community "there is a tendency for the breach to widen and extend until it becomes coextensive with some dominant cleavage in the widest set of relevant social relations to which the conflicting or antagonistic parties belong" (ibid, p. 38). Third, there is the redressive action that occurs when acts to contain and redress the crisis will be brought to bear; these acts can vary from legal action to giving advice (ibid., p. 39). Finally, there is either a period of reintegration of the antagonist into society, or a legitimating of the divide between the ruling structure and whatever social relation is estranged (ibid., pp. 41–2).

Turner's approach can easily accommodate social movement action. Protest events often engage in this type of drama, thereby taking part in the iterative process of meaning-making in political life. Social movements will either construct or heal breaches in society in order to shift the parameters of what is "acceptable" in politics. Protest represents the "breach" in the social fabric, which can possibly become a part of the common political parlance. Through the performance of political "breaches" protest has the ability to shape both the meaning and form of political expression. These breaches also help to shift the nature of political idiom in a state, as they are accepted or rejected by relevant actors.

Edelman, Blumer and Turner explicate the ways that language and social drama become a part of everyday lexicons. Focusing on the political, we see how protest helps to construct the political idiom of the time. Since this type of political communication can be crucial to the articulation and consideration of interests within a polity, social movements try to contour political language in order to make their own claims more relevant; by doing this movements actively constitute and reconstitute what has meaning within political and social space. This project questions when and how the particular form of political expression, suicide protest, can be transformed into political gains for the movement. Some argue that the power of suicide protest lies within its uniqueness and the fact that it can be considered a break with "normal." The extraordinary aspects of suicide protest are important yet, if suicide protest is only an alien artifact, a curiosity, then it would be unlikely that it could actually engender real political change; it would simply be marveled at, and then forgotten. The tactical approach highlights the manner with which movements deploy and then narrate their use of suicide protest. In doing so, movements try to situate suicide protest as acts that are simultaneously rooted within society, but also are dramatic and traumatic shocks to the public. The duality of suicide protest is a key component of its ability to create political change. The astounding aspects of suicide protest seem self evident; acts such as self-immolation or fasting to the death set the stakes of political communication very high, and no matter how often they may be used within a particular political context there remains an element of surprise when they are utilized. And yet, these acts are not completely alien in nature.

The previous discussion frames how social movements are meaning-makers as well as practical political organizations; they make claims to change how politics and the world around them is perceived in some way. One way they do this is by accessing and transforming socially and culturally relevant actions in furtherance of their own political goals. The predominant argument to explain the genesis of protest actions cites a combination of regime type and cultural practice (Tilly 2008; Tarrow 2011; Scott 1992) as crucial factors in that process, though there is debate regarding how these two elements interact to create particular protest actions. What is clear is that protest must be rooted within the particular context; it does not simply appear fully formed like Athena from Zeus's head. Tilly's work on contentious performances (2008) directly engages with how different forms of protest transform into accepted repertoires that can be repeated across time and space. He claims that contention is a product of "historically grounded performances" which limited the way that protestors can articulate claims

24   *Gandhi and suicide protest in India*

(Tilly 2008, p. 4). He further claims that once protest repertoires are in place, they change very incrementally, but they *can* change. Periods of rapid change to the opportunity structure may lead to innovation by challengers (ibid., p. 44).[3] Tilly's notion that protest tactics evolve slowly is persuasive. However, I focus on his idea that protest innovation will occur during periods of rapidly changing opportunity. The Indian Nationalist Movement in the twentieth century was a perfect example of such a time period. As such, I believe that it was a critical juncture of political, social, cultural and economic change that lead to intense and rapid shifts in the way that people articulated their claims towards the state and each other. These shifts were facilitated by active movement entrepreneurs who were searching for ways to create a new language of mobilization against the entrenched British state. In keeping with other aspects of the Nationalist Movement,[4] activists like Gandhi turned to indigenous cultural rituals and traditions as they searched for new ways to challenge the state.

Ritualistic social behavior is symbolically and culturally laden, and a perfect well from which social movement actors can establish new types of protest action.[5] This is due, in part, to the function that cultural ritual usually plays in society. "Traditionally prescribed cultural performance that serve as a model *of* and *for* what people believe" (Esherick and Wasserstrom 1990, p. 844). So, the performance of cultural rituals within a political setting, or for political reasons, is not, in and of itself, enough to ensure political responses or resonance.[6] The performance and transformation of these rituals can serve as the type of public breach described by Turner, which helps society create new understandings of social and political life. In particular, I believe that the contemporary use of fasting and self-immolation can be linked to Gandhi and a particular aspect of his mobilizational politics during the time of the Nationalist Movement. I argue that within the Indian context the Nationalist Movement represents a critical historical period of political experimentation during which the idea of physically subsuming the body for a political cause gained popular support. I focus on Gandhi – and his philosophy of *satyagraha* and his practice of fasting to death – as crucial elements that contributed to the contemporary acceptance of suicide as a protest tactic within India. Before engaging with Gandhi's fasting I first, very briefly, examine cultural antecedents of both self-immolation and fasting within the Indian context. In particular I examine the ritual practices of *sati* and votive fasting. Based on my analysis, it is clear that votive fasting directly influenced Gandhi's adoption of political fasting.

Sati and fasting in India

The separate practices of fasting and self-immolation are both culturally and ritually significant within South Asia. Both acts have considerable purchase within Hinduism and other religious traditions in the South Asian context. In particular I examine the use of votive fasts by women within Hindu families as well as the practice of *sati* and Hindu death rituals. The practice of these particular rituals informs the general acceptance and attitude about the act of denying oneself food, or the setting oneself or others on fire, and may explain how they were so easily adapted for use as types of political expression.

Fire holds a powerful place within religious and cultural iconography for most of the religions within South Asia, especially Hinduism. As such, burning the body, either in funerary rites or as a type of suicide, is not unusual in India. One of the most iconographic and problematic forms of self-immolation[7] is *sati*, the practice of widow burning, though this paper is more concerned with how self-immolation is used within recent social movement protests. In order to understand how self-immolation has evolved into a social movement practice we must explore the origins of the custom itself. *Sati*[8] "describes the ritual according to which a Hindu wife follows her husband to his death by ascending his pyre with him or ascending one of her own shortly afterward" (Hawley 1994, p. 1). The practice can be traced back to early Hindu texts; it was first banned under British rule. Since Independence in 1947 there have been no special legal provisions made for *sati*, but it has been subsumed under laws against murder and assisted suicide (Oldenburg 1994), thereby conferring no distinction on the religious connotations of the practice. I will not go into an historiographical analysis of *sati* at this time; it is not necessary for our purposes. Instead, I focus my analysis on a more recent example of *sati* in India, the Roop Kanwar case of 1987. The reactions to this case explicate contemporary attitudes surrounding this practice. Responses to Roop Kanwar's death can be divided into two categories: traditionalist or legalistic. Traditionalists framed the Kanwar *sati* as an act of pure and unblemished self-sacrifice. This stems from a belief that since *sati* is rooted within the cultural and religious tradition of India, it should not be thrown away (Nandy 1994). In contrast, legalists, including a number of feminist groups, had a very different reaction to Kanwar's death. These groups saw Roop Kanwar's *sati* simply as an act of murder. In the aftermath a multitude of possible explanations were created by women's movements in order to explain the impossible; no sane young woman would willingly burn herself alive, she must have been coerced through some unknown means. The particulars of the feminist response are not as important as the fact that a self-immolation of a widow was seen to be an impossible act; that no woman, acting out of her own agency, would ever willingly self-immolate herself for her husband (Oldenburg 1994).

These two reactions to Kanwar's *sati* illustrate the often uneasy relationship between cultural practice and modern liberal democratic norms in India. But they also tell us something about how practices like sati and self-immolation are interpreted in modern India. The contemporary practice of self-immolation will often draw from religious tradition, and yet the same acts can seem contrary to modern conceptions of India and political expression. Reactions to self-immolation will depend on the ability of movements to narrate the tactic.

26   *Gandhi and suicide protest in India*

In contrast to self-immolation, ritual fasting is significant in many different cultures,[9] especially in religious practice. Fasting was often used as a means to prove one's level of devotion to god. It has also been used as a pathway to achieve a closer relationship to god in both Western and Eastern traditions. In his book, *The Holy Anorexia*, Rudolph Bell argues that "the suppression of physical urges and basic feelings – fatigue, sexual desire, hunger, pain, frees the body to achieve heroic feats and the soul to communicate with God" (Bell 1985, p. 13). Many practice fasting in India, but I focus on one particular type of fast: the votive fast conducted by Hindu women. Within the orthopraxy of Hinduism, women are often called to fulfil a caretaker role within their families and communities. One prevalent method used by women is to habitually fast in order to maintain the well-being and health of their families. In some households women will conduct complete or partial fasts on a weekly basis. These fasts are interesting. Not only are they meant to be a personal expression of religious devotion, they are also a means by which to attain something: the well-being of the family. In this way these votive fasts are inherently altruistic and self-sacrificing. The Judeo-Christian idea that the denial of bodily urges may lead to some type of religious ecstasy impacted upon Gandhi as he began to formulate his own theories of fasting (Parekh 1989a). However, what influenced Gandhi most was rooted in his own observations of the women around him, especially his mother (Gandhi 1982).

In addition to the votive fast, I must also mention the practice of *dharna*[10] which was used as a type of shaming of injustice. Still used today, *dharna* involves fasting at the doorstep of somebody one has a grievance with, such as a debtor; the notion being that the person in power (in this case the debtor) will be shamed if she allows the protestor to die. Thus, there are already antecedents for relational and practical fasting within India.

Fasting in the Nationalist Movement: Gandhi

According to Tilly, protest repertoires change incrementally, over long periods of time. But protest tactics can also be created in times of dramatic political upheaval. I argue that the time of the Indian Nationalist Movement was one of those periods. The methods used by the Indian National Congress (INC), the Muslim League (ML) and other groups helped to outline the way that activists would challenge the Indian state for years to come. In particular, I examine Gandhi's theory of *satyagraha* and his introduction of the political fast within the movement. Gandhi's legacy has been well examined by scholars since his death in 1948 (Dalton 1993; Brown 1989; Parekh 1989a; Parekh 1989b; Rudolph and Rudolph 1983; Erikson 1969). In this section I propose that Gandhi's use of fasting not only introduced this particular tactic to India as a viable and effective form of political challenge, but also that Gandhi's fasts, writings, speeches and lifestyle also introduced the idea that the body could and should be utilized as a locus for political mobilization, especially the sacrifice of the body.[11]

Gandhi's philosophy of fasting within political mobilization is rooted within his comprehensive approach to political and spiritual mobilization, known as *satyagraha*, which he first used in South Africa. According to Gandhi, *satyagraha* was more than simply a tactic; it was also a guiding moral code for living. "Gandhi's theory of *satyagraha* is at once both epistemological and political, a theory of both knowledge and action" in everyday life (Parekh 1989b, p. 143). For Gandhi, the epistemic nature of *satyagraha* meant that political mobilization and liberation were meaningless unless simultaneously enacted out of a desire to achieve the goals of personal and spiritual liberation – a standpoint that suggests Gandhi thought of *satyagraha* as a moral code which could be utilized for (but was not limited to) the pursuit of political protest. This reading of *satyagraha,* as a type of moral action was meant to penetrate all aspects of life, public and personal. You could not be a true *satyagrahi* while believing in the use of force for personal matters. Another reading of *satyagraha* suggests that it should be considered as a type of "transformational realism" (Matena 2012), which highlights the strategic nature of Gandhi's political practice. I believe that either interpretation (and more likely both) makes sense when trying to explain Gandhi's decision to make use of fasting to the death. For Gandhi there was no division between the personal and the political; all aspects of life impact and influence one another. The practical result of Gandhi's theory can best be seen in his philosophy and practice of *swaraj*, and fasting.

The ways that political or social life constitute personal beliefs and vice versa can be clearly seen in Gandhi's own conceptualization of the term *swaraj*, or self-rule: the ultimate goal of *satyagraha.* Unlike others in the Nationalist Movement, Gandhi adhered to a vision of *swaraj* that was simultaneously broader and stricter than simple independence or freedom. Gandhi (*CWMG*, vol. 83, p. 180) states:

> [T]he root meaning of *swaraj* is self-rule. *Swaraj* may, therefore, be rendered as a disciplined rule from within … 'independence' has no such limitation. Independence may mean license to do as you like. *Swaraj* is a sacred word, a vedic word meaning self-rule and self-restraint, and not freedom from all restraint, which 'independence' often means.

For Gandhi, true liberation was predicated on a thick and comprehensive theory of freedom, of which freedom from British rule played only a small part. His conceptualization of both *satyagraha* and *swaraj* demand that the means are just as important as the desired end; for Gandhi there would be no point in obtaining political freedom if it was achieved by violence. Armed or violent struggle may end in a thin understanding of "freedom" but would in no way liberate the soul from fear. Short-term goals were important only if they could be attained in the "right way" (Horsburg 1968, p. 43). As Gandhi states (1997, p. 81): "[T]he means may be likened to a seed, the end to a tree; and there is the same inviolable connection between the means and the end

28   *Gandhi and suicide protest in India*

as there is between the seed and the tree." This strict understanding of the means–ends question can be seen throughout his career as a strategist for the Indian Nationalist Movement; time and again Gandhi subsumed the importance of political or mobilizational success to the means by which that success could be achieved.

Gandhi's conceptions of *satyagraha, swaraj,* and his means–ends paradigm, directly influenced his adoption of the fast to death as a protest tactic during the time of the Nationalist Movement, and the particular circumstances when this tactic could be an acceptable form of political expression. Influenced by his mother and others (Gandhi 1982), Gandhi began to fast for religious purposes early in his time as an activist. He often fasted to purify himself and felt that fasting was a necessary expression of religious devotion and liberation. As he states (CWMG vol. 19, 1968, p.487): "[A] genuine fast cleanses the body, mind and soul. It crucifies the flesh and to that extent sets the soul free." In the previous case Gandhi is speaking of the effect of personal fasting, which for him becomes a means to self-liberation and freedom. Based on these statements it should be no surprise that Gandhi would utilize such a transformative (for him) act within the context of mobilizational politics. The adoption of fasting by nationalist politics was not as drastic or strange as one might think. If religious fasting was conducted to maintain the health and well-being of the family, then the political fast was meant to achieve the same, but in this case for the benefit of the health and well-being of the nascent Indian state and the Nationalist Movement. Fasting for personal reasons frees the individual; fasting for political reasons would help to free the state.

However, the transformation of the fast from a sacred personal act to a secular public act was not done without thought or consequence. Consistent with Gandhi's approach to all political action, the fast to death could and should only be undertaken in certain ways and for certain reasons. His care in introducing the fast was in part to distinguish his fasts to death from the more common, and for Gandhi problematic, hunger strike, a term that he abhorred. Hunger strikes were not unheard of in the early part of the twentieth century in and outside India, but under Gandhi's strict rules for non-violent actions, the actions of the suffragettes and of Irish prisoners would not pass muster. In particular, Gandhi was opposed to using the tactic in prison to ask for better conditions as the underlying reason for such fasts was, in his opinion, selfish. As discussed in Chapter One, I argue that suicide protest is in part powerful due to its liminal aspects: its ability to be both non-violent and violent. This is doubly true when taking into account Gandhi's own theories of what constituted violence, which includes both emotional and physical suffering. Based on Gandhi's comprehensive notions of violence, fasting could easily, depending on the way it was deployed, descend into a form of coercive political violence. To stop this from happening the intent of the activist becomes just as important as the means he uses to make his point.

Though he never published a guide to the Gandhian fast, based on a close reading of Gandhi's writings I believe there are three important factors that contribute towards ensuring its non-violence. First, Gandhi felt that the fast should be used relatively rarely: "[A] *satyagrahi* should fast only as a last resort when all other avenues of redress have been explored and have failed" (CWMG, vol. 83, p. 401). Second, the intent of the faster, his motivations and goals, come under scrutiny: "Fasting with a spiritual purpose behind it is praiseworthy only under well defined conditions. It must not be for a selfish end...it must not be in the nature of violence" (Gandhi 1965, p. 28). Finally, he goes on to emphasize that there must be love present between the faster and his opponent, which is central to his moral justification of the fast (Gandhi 1965). A fast unto death absent of love would and should be considered a type of violence, as it would create a situation of emotional blackmail or coercion against the opponent. This would be unacceptable to Gandhi's theory of his own project of spiritual truth through *satyagraha*. To better understand the evolution of Gandhi's fasting, as well as general attitudes towards fasting at the time, I examine two instances of its use during the time of the Nationalist Movement: the Yervada fast in 1932 and the Calcutta fast in 1947.

Gandhi first used fasting for a political purpose in 1932.[12] The early 1930s was a fruitful time for Gandhi and the development of his brand of political activism; he was clearly instrumental in planning the Indian National Congress (INC) approach to the movement for Independence, resulting in his importance to both the general Indian population and the British Raj (Brown 1989) Among his achievements at this time Gandhi completed the Salt March to Dandi in 1931,[13] a success which led to the creation of the Gandhi–Irwin Pact, and his attendance of the Second Round Table Conference in London. Central to Gandhi's perceived leadership of the movement was his development of *satyagraha* as the cornerstone of the movement's strategy against the British Raj. It was at this moment that Gandhi decided to transform fasting from what had until now been used as a spiritual action, into a cornerstone of his political tactics.

Prior to 1932 Gandhi had fasted publicly, but not politically.[14] However, a particular policy outcome of the Second Round Table Conference convinced Gandhi to commit to a "Fast unto Death."[15] The 1931 Conference represented an attempt by the British to establish certain Indian political institutions; as such, a number of community and political leaders attended in order to design a nascent electoral system. Prior to this Conference the British had already divided the Indian electorate between Hindus and Muslims with a "communal award." During the Conference the communal award was extended to include "Depressed Classes."[16] Functionally this award would separate traditionally marginalized communities, including Untouchables, from the larger Hindu voting block. Propelled by B.R. Ambedkar, the communal award for Untouchables was considered to be a necessary step to gain political power in either the Raj or an Independent India. Ambedkar and his supporters justified the award by stressing the need to distinguish the Depressed Classes

30 *Gandhi and suicide protest in India*

from the larger Hindu community in order to guarantee access to protected freedoms and rights (Ambedkar 1946). In his view a single Hindu electorate would be a modern mechanism for continuing the traditional dominance of caste Hindus.

Gandhi vehemently opposed Ambedkar's political solution to caste discrimination. Gandhi believed that untouchables were intrinsically a part of the larger Hindu community; any separation would destroy the religion as a whole. While he acknowledged the historical and endemic discrimination and repression of untouchables within Hinduism, he was committed to finding an internal solution to the problem.[17] According to Gandhi, Harijan empowerment could only happen from within the religion, not from outside it. The communal award was extended in August 1932; to Gandhi, this signaled the creation of divisions that would make *swaraj* an impossible goal (CWMG, vol. 50, p. 466). At this time Gandhi himself was incarcerated in Yervada Prison in Poona. By September he had escalated his agitation to the point of declaring a fast to the death. In the following excerpt Gandhi (CWMG vol. 51, p. 62) announces his decision to the press on September 16, 1932:

> The fast which I am approaching was resolved upon in the name of God for his work, and I believe in all humility, at his call ... The impending fast is for against [sic] those who have faith in me, whether Indians for foreigners, and for those who have it not. Therefore, it is not against the English official world, but it is against those Englishmen and women who, in spite of the contrary teaching of the official world, believe in me and the justice of the cause I represent. Nor is it against those of my countrymen who have no faith in me, whether they be Hindus or others; but it is against those countless Indians (no matter what persuasion they belong) who believe that I represent a just cause. Above all it is intended to sting the Hindu conscious into the right religious action.

Gandhi's statement illustrates his own justifications of his decision to fast. For Gandhi it wasn't an act of pure political strategy, but was an example of religious and ethical sacrifice. By choosing the fast, Gandhi relocated this political (and therefore moral) conflict onto his own body. Throughout the fast, which lasted six days, Gandhi adamantly restated his perspective of the fast: "My message to the British and American people is that they must not mistake this for a political move. It is a deep spiritual effort, a result of 50 years constant application to an ideal. It is a penance" (CWMG, vol. 51, p. 132). Despite Gandhi's framing of the fast as a purely moral act, it was also clear that this was a political move. Gandhi wanted to create a tangible change in policy, which occurred when Ambedkar agreed to give up the communal award.[18]

Reactions to Gandhi's decision to fast were mixed, but in analyzing the responses of Congress leaders, the Raj and Dr Ambedkar, I have determined some similar attitudes on the practice of fasting at the time. First, all of these

Gandhi and suicide protest in India   31

actors were surprised that Gandhi made the decision to fast at all. Nehru (1973, p. 407), who was not consulted about the fast before the fact, states:

> What a capacity Bapu [Gandhi] has for giving shocks to his people! A week ago – on the 14th – I read about his decision to "fast unto death" in disapproval of the separate electorates given by Ramsay Macdonald's award to the Depressed Classes. Suddenly all manner of ideas rushed into my head – all kinds of possibilities and contingencies rose up before – and upset my equilibrium completely.

Nehru's reaction is telling; clearly the fast was not a well thought out and planned strategy by the Congress to dispute the award. Indeed, it seems that Gandhi's decision to fast was more personal than political at the beginning. Nehru's surprise tells us something about fasting at the time. It was not a common tactic and had not necessarily been discussed by movement leadership, indicating that fasting was not at this point a part of the political idiom of the Indian nationalist politics at that time.

Second, in addition to surprise regarding the choice to fast, many were also perplexed by what had driven Gandhi to do it. In other words, the stakes of the fast did not seem to fit the stakes of the Communal Award. Nehru describes himself as being "annoyed with [Gandhi] for choosing a side issue for his final sacrifice – just a question of an electorate. What would be the result on our freedom struggle?" (ibid.) The notion that the Communal Award was not a worthy reason for risking Gandhi's life was echoed in reactions from British elites. In an August 1932 letter from Lord Willingdon, then Viceroy of India, to Sir Samuel Hoare, the Secretary of State of India, he states: "[I]t seems extraordinarily stupid of the little man to definitely go out on this issue" (Willingdon, unpublished letter, 1932). Reactions such as these clearly indicate the lack of importance that many within the Indian and British political system had assigned to the question of the Depressed Classes and their treatment; but they also reveal something about attitudes towards fasting as well. The tactic was viewed as something unique, something that should only be deployed for the most serious reasons. For Nehru, that meant fasting should be reserved for the freedom struggle as a whole. For the British, it is unlikely that anything could approach a level of importance such that fasting to the death would be a logical course of action.

Third, in exploring the political and strategic reactions to the fast, the overwhelming concern of all parties seems to be the unpredictability of fasting and the possible ramifications of Gandhi's death. Congress, realizing that Gandhi could actually die, was worried about how his death would affect the movement as a whole (Brown 1977). The British, having dealt with the death of a number of Irish hunger strikers in the early part of the twentieth century, were also wary. As Lord Willingdon (1932) describes: "[W]e shall have to consider quite seriously what to do with the little man when he takes to this unfortunate exercise, for I don't suppose we can allow him to die of a

32 *Gandhi and suicide protest in India*

hunger strike in prison at this." Willingdon's letter indicates that the British not only realized that Gandhi was serious, but also, to a certain extent, recognized the power that fasting could have on the population as a whole. In the end, responding to the strategic considerations of the fast, the British took themselves out of the picture completely by acceding to his wishes as soon as the decision to fast had been made. They did this by revoking their previous support for the communal award as long as representatives from the Depressed Classes also agreed, effectively placing the entire burden of the fast on Ambedkar's shoulders.

Since Ambedkar and his community were forced into the role of being Gandhi's main antagonist, I want to spend a bit more time exploring his complex reactions to the fast and Gandhi as a political leader. Though Ambedkar was an undisputed leader of his community, there remained a high level of support for Gandhi and his tactics within the Depressed Classes. Gandhi had embarked on a campaign of *"harijan* uplift" to help shift attitudes on untouchability.[19] In contrast to Gandhi, Ambedkar had a more traditional approach, predicated on empowering the community from within. The communal award would be a positive step in that direction both by ensuring that the community would be politically represented, but also by divorcing the community from the larger group of Hindus who had very different political concerns. The conflict over the award, and Gandhi's stance, did not soften Ambedkar's opposition to Gandhi. Ambedkar felt that the fast was nothing short of political coercion that "would not win the Depressed Classes to the Hindu fold if they were determined to go out" (Ambedkar 1946, p. 327). Despite his resistance to Gandhi and the fast, Ambedkar was also cognizant of the political reality of the time; Ambedkar in particular, and the untouchables in general, could not be seen to be the cause of Gandhi's death. Ambedkar agreed to get rid of a separate electorate in return for reserved seats for Depressed Classes within the Hindu electorate, thereby conceding to Gandhi's wish that untouchables remain under the aegis of the Hindu community. Ambedkar was fairly unrelenting in his disappointment in both Gandhi and Congress in the aftermath of the fast. He subsequently not only questioned Gandhi's motives, but even his commitment to the fast itself, indicating that Gandhi "wanted very much to live" (Ambedkar 1946, p. 88).

Finally, Gandhi himself was able to evaluate the Yervada fast later in his life. His own response demonstrates the strict nature of Gandhian fasting. By many evaluations Gandhi "won" the fast – the Depressed Classes remained part of the Hindu voting block. This victory prompted Gandhi's continued use of the tactic, in conjunction with his own spiritual fasts, throughout the rest of his life. But by his own admission this first use of the political fast may have crossed his own restrictive definitions of nonviolence and violence: "I do admit that my fast of September did unfortunately coerce some people into action which they would not have endorsed without my fast" (Gandhi 1965, p. 41). Despite his own reservations, the Yervada fast is the moment when fasting enters the nationalist dialogue in a

Gandhi and suicide protest in India 33

meaningful way. Moreover, Gandhi's apparent success guaranteed that the tactic would be used again.

Exploring the various reactions to the fast provides a glimpse into the general feelings about fasting at the time among political elites. Clearly all concerned parties took Gandhi's actions fairly seriously. Both the Congress and the British were worried about the possible reactions to Gandhi's death, and Ambedkar actually changed his political stance to prevent this from happening. Despite this, all of the actors seemed both shocked and annoyed that Gandhi would take such a drastic step to stop the creation of a separate electorate, indicating that fasting was both uncommon and problematic at the time. At this point fasting to the death in particular, and suicide protest in general, was clearly not a part of the political idiom. However, as the movement continued, Gandhi's use of the tactic increased. An examination of one of his last fasts illustrates how his own fasting practices changed over time, as well as how the reception to and expectations of fasting had changed within the political elite.

Compared to his politically powerful position in 1932, by 1947 Gandhi's influence and reputation among the general population had grown, but his voice was increasingly marginalized in the politics of transition (Brown 1989). Much of this was due to Gandhi's own disenchantment with the notion of states, which did not make sense as the Raj began to withdraw. Gandhi's mobilizational politics, which had been so powerful within the context of the Nationalist Movement, were much less important in a nascent state. Moreover, Gandhi's notion of the "thick" form of *swaraj* that I previously discussed no longer seemed to be on the agenda. Finally, Gandhi's opposition to Partition served to further marginalize him from the center of power within Congress, now held by other elites such as Nehru and Vallabhbhai Patel. Of course, Gandhi was positioned as the moral conscience of the new nation, and he did still garner a fair degree of popular support, though this no longer translated into the kind of political power he had wielded two decades before. It was within this context of diminished political, but heightened moral power that Gandhi embarks on one of his most admired and powerful fasts.

The events surrounding the Calcutta fast of 1947[20] are rooted in the "Great Calcutta Killings" of 1946, a violent instance of communal killings perpetrated by both Hindus and Muslims in the city. The massacre resulted in at least 4,000 deaths, and represented a new form of urban violence in India (Dalton 1993). The 1946 riots exacerbated existing communal tensions in religiously diverse Calcutta and unfortunately became a template for future Partition violence in the rest of the country. With this history in mind, violence again broke out in the city in May 1947 in response to news that Bengal would be partitioned again.[21] The subsequent violence was quick and programmatic: "The Calcutta riot rapidly transformed the political scene in Bengal, indeed over the whole of India" (Das 1993, p. 61). This time the violence was a threat not just to the people of Calcutta but also to

34 *Gandhi and suicide protest in India*

the entire project of Partition and the transfer of power. It was to this context that Gandhi was dispatched to Calcutta on August 9, 1947. He was met with increasing collective violence (Dalton 1993). Gandhi's response to this heightened and violent atmosphere was to invite the Muslim Governor of Bengal, H.S. Suhrawardy, to live with him, hoping that a demonstration of inter-faith cooperation among the political elite would trickle down to the general public. Helped greatly by the granting of Indian Independence on August 16, at first Gandhi's plan seemed to work. However, by the end of August, riots resumed in the city, now spurred by the mass migrations taking place on the border between West Bengal and East Pakistan.[22] By September of that year rioting had taken a huge toll on the city, and Gandhi declared one of his last fasts to the death. Despite initial opposition to it by Bengali elites and Congress, the fast was amazingly effective. Gandhi's own goal was to fast until a sense of complete peace ruled the city; this only took four days. There are many reasons why the violence abated, but the fast was clearly a factor.

Reactions to Gandhi's fast within the city demonstrate a shift in local attitudes towards the tactic of fasting itself. As late as May 1947 the main English language newspaper of Calcutta, *The Statesman*, published an editorial excoriating Gandhi and his threat of fasting in support of the joint appeal:

> It is however, with regret that Mr. Gandhi has again spoken of a fast, more than once hinted at to reinforce the joint appeal. He says that his signature has imposed upon him the duty of fasting to the death if either Hindus or Muslims descend to the level of savages or beast ... Like many others we have never been able fully to understand these Gandhian fasts. The appeal they make is primarily due to the emotions, to the heart .... once feelings are aroused to a fever pitch, there is no more possibility of subduing them to some other nobler emotion than of curing a rabid dog of his madness by talking gently.
>
> (*The Statesman*, May 12, 1947, p. 6)

This editorial, written in the midst of a communal scare in the city in May 1947, indicates a number of things. First, fasting is now a habitual part of Gandhi's repertoire. Second, the effectiveness of fasting remains in question; while it may be appropriate for something like the communal award in 1932, it's efficacy for more serious issues, such as stopping communal violence, is questioned. This attitude represents a deeper issue with Gandhi and fasting at the time. Gandhi often stated that fasting was meant to "sting" the moral consciousness of people, prodding them into correct actions. Nevertheless, it is clear that even as little as four months before the fast, there was still a significant amount of negative feeling towards Gandhi and his use of the tactic. However, events surrounding the Calcutta fast demonstrate a sea change in Gandhi's favor. In an editorial dated September 3, 1947 (p. 4), *The Statesman* said:

Gandhi and suicide protest in India   35

On the ethics of fasting as a political instrument we have over many years failed to concur with India's most renowned practitioner of it, expressing our views frankly. But never in a long career had Mahatma Gandhi, in our eyes fasted in a simpler, worthier cause than this, nor one more calculated for effective immediate appeal to the public conscious. We cordially wish him unqualified success and trust that happy termination of the ordeal may be speedy.

The reason behind the remarkable change in opinion was in part due to the visible effect of the fast on public order in the city: "[O]n September 3, the second day of the fast, quiet came to Calcutta" (Dalton 1993, p. 155). The fast itself lasted only four days, and considering Gandhi's strict standards about such matters,[23] the fact that he felt tensions had abated enough to actually end the fast demonstrates the power of the tactic in this instance, especially since it occurred within a context of communal tensions tracing back decades and in an area of the country that had been famously ambivalent towards Gandhi and his practices. The previously stated positive reactions to the fast were echoed among the Congress leadership, and even by the British. Alan Campbell-Johnson, Viceroy Mountbatten's press attaché at the time, wrote that Mountbatten felt Gandhi "has achieved by moral persuasion what four divisions would have been hard pressed to accomplish by force (Campbell-Johnson 1953, p. 181).

A comparison of these two fasts allows us to draw some general conclusions concerning Gandhi's practice of fasting, as well as about attitudes towards the act during the time of the Nationalist Movement. First, Gandhi's own philosophical and spiritual traditions were indelibly linked to his practice of fasting. As such, Gandhi's practice evolved as his own theories of *satyagraha* changed over time. The linkages between Gandhi's philosophy and practices also delimit the times and circumstances when fasting would be considered appropriate. Second, we can see a clear shift in when and why Gandhi uses fasting over the course of the movement. Politically motivated fasts give way to fasts aimed at improving the conditions of *harijans* or to stop communal violence. The strategic power of the tactic is subsumed for its "moral" effects. Third, reactions to the tactic remained confused. Gandhi's considerable political and moral power was not enough to create political change; the political context and narration of the events also mattered. As previously described, Indian elites seemed to have an uneasy relationship to the notion of political fasting; even the Calcutta fast was, at least initially, met with skepticism. Finally, and most importantly, we can see a change in the acceptability of the tactic. Gandhi's continued use of it between 1932 and 1948 meant that fasting became an expected, if not always successful, form of protest. Based on a comparison of these two fasts, it's clear that Gandhi was able to change the way that challengers approached protest in India during the Nationalist Movement, to the extent that fasting has now become a habitual protest tactic against the state.

Conclusions

The previous discussion demonstrates the influence Gandhi and fasting had on the Nationalist movement, but what about self-immolation? Based on Gandhi's own writing and actions, I believe that he would have been opposed to the use of self-immolation as a protest tactic, partly because the act does not allow for a dialogue between opponents but also because it would not fit into his strict definition of non-violence. Despite this, I do believe that we can trace the practice and acceptance of self-immolation to a particular unintended aspect of Gandhi's nationalist protests.

I believe that Gandhi's practice of fasting, his lifestyle and his philosophy, helped to create a lasting acceptance of certain forms of self-sacrificing behavior in Indian politics. Gandhi was not the first to introduce the notion of self-sacrifice within Indian politics, but he is one of the first to practice it in the context of gaining a reputation for political success. Gandhi was well aware of the importance of sacrifice within a political campaign. He began to articulate his feelings on the subject during his time in South Africa (CWMG, vol. 4, p. 112). From his earliest political manifestations Gandhi recognized the power that sacrifice could have in a political campaign: "When Gandhi fasted or his followers suffered themselves to be beaten, he and they demonstrated the courage required for self-control rather than self-assertion" (Rudolph and Rudolph 1983, p. 37). For Gandhi physical sacrifice was the natural progression of his theories of *satyagraha*, *swaraj* and *ahimsa* (non-violence). It was an act that could elevate the movement, but only if done non-violently. As Gandhi stated: "[S]acrifice which causes pain is no sacrifice at all. True sacrifice is joy giving and uplifting" (CWMG, vol. 80, p. 436). As with his other thoughts on life and politics, action for Gandhi is multifaceted. Sacrifice, non-violence and political mobilization are intertwined in such a way that it is hard to understand what effect, if any, these theories have had on Indian political mobilization in the contemporary world.

What is clear is that sacrifice was in fact central to Gandhi's approach to life and politics; his adoption and practice of fasting is a direct outcome of that centrality (Bondurant 1988).

Gandhi actively utilized the notion of self-sacrifice in every aspect of his own life. If it is true that suffering is more likely to be effective if practiced by people who lead exemplary lives (Sharp 1973) then Gandhi tried to fit the bill. Fasting is therefore Gandhi's ultimate form of self-sacrifice and suffering. He used it as a way to assert his belief that the physical pain of one could absolve the moral decay of many. This notion is directly linked to a little-studied aspect of political fasting and suicide protest, pain and suffering. Most scholars of these acts focus on the last and most serious outcome, death. But before that moment arrives, suicide protest can also be very painful. Fasting to the death, burning, drowning – all of these are painful ways to die. Fasting, more than any other type of suicide protest, allows for a slow and public mortification of the flesh. By introducing the practice of fasting to the death within

Gandhi and suicide protest in India 37

Nationalist mobilization, Gandhi simultaneously introduced the language of pain and suffering into politics. This language was embedded within his broader theories of nation, freedom and struggle. Gandhi used self-suffering as "a tactic for cutting through the rational defenses which the opponent may have built" (Bondurant 1988, p. 228). By externalizing his pain, Gandhi creates a sense of shared suffering but also a language of sacrifice that has lasted beyond his death.

Notes

1 My use of the term *episteme* derives from Foucault's notion, which describes *episteme* as "the total set of relations that unite, at a given period, the discursive practices that give rise to epistemological figures, science, and possibly formalized systems" (Foucault 1972, p. 191). As such, my term "political idiom," or political *episteme*, shifts from Foucault's focus on the generation and delineation of scientific practice, to that of political practice. Like Foucault I agree that *episteme* is not a static artifact, but is "a constantly moving set of articulations, shifts, and coincidences that are established, only to give rise to others (ibid. p. 192). While I realize that my use of the term *episteme* may raise some questions, I believe it is the right choice here, as I describe the way that political practice and language is constructed and reconstructed in India. My notion of political idiom acts similarly to Foucault's notion of the *episteme*, or Kuhn's paradigm (1962). Political practice and language creates internalized, yet shifting, boundaries. Once those linguistic boundaries exist, new forms of political discourse must either work within those constraints or actively seek to break with them. I understand that my use of this term may enter me into a greater debate, but I don't believe that I need to engage in that debate here.

2 Just because a political practice might be considered "acceptable" or "normal" does not mean that it will necessarily be "successful," as I have outlined in Chapter 1. Clearly the extent to which these practices are a part of the political idiom will be important to success, but it is not a guarantee of the political success or failure of a protest tactic. For example, demonstrations are clearly an accepted aspect of politics in the USA, but not every demonstration ends in a positive political outcome for the movement concerned.

3 The irrelevance of opportunity structures to my overall argument is explored in Chapter 1. For comprehensive discussions on the Political Opportunity Approach see Tilly (2008); Tarrow (2011); MacAdam *et al.* (2001).

4 One could argue that Gandhi's transformation of indigenous acts into political protests was not that dissimilar to the *swadesh* movement that started in Bengal.

5 There are many different understandings of "ritual." I have no desire to enter into that debate. Instead I would direct you to David Kertzer's comprehensive analysis of ritual in politics (1988). Borrowing directly from him I also define ritual as "symbolic behavior that is socially standardized and repetitive (Kertzer 1988, p. 9).

6 I draw a distinction between the use of cultural ritual within politics, and political rituals themselves. While the latter is an important area of analysis and has been used (or transformed) by social movements, this chapter is more concerned with how social and cultural performance can be adopted by movements and politics. For a comprehensive analysis of the causes and effects of political rituals see Kertzer (1998).

7 Clearly there is some degree of dispute regarding the actual volition of practitioners of *sati*, putting the "self" into question.

38 *Gandhi and suicide protest in India*

8 The term *sati* often refers to practice of the ritual, as well as the one who practices it, i.e. the wife of the deceased. The distinction between the practice and the one who does the practice is an important one within the study of *sati*; however, since our concern is mostly for other forms of self-immolation, *sati* will refer only to the practice of widow burning. See, J.S. Hawley's introduction in *Sati the Blessing and the Curse* (1994).

9 I discuss the use of fasting and other acts of suicide protest in other contexts in Chapter 7.

10 This practice is very similar to another practice in Ireland, which I discuss further in Chapter 7.

11 Allen Feldman's examination of the body as a location for the production of violence during The Troubles in Northern Ireland (in his 1991 book *Formations of Violence*) is an innovative example of work in this vein. Feldman focuses on the body as the primary location of political violence. He states (p. 9): "[I]n Northern Ireland the practice of political violence entails the production, exchange, and ideological consumption of bodies." Within the Irish context the body becomes the primary location for political violence and political voice. As a site for violence, the body participates in producing new modes of political, social and cultural discourse. This notion of the body as a site for the production of violence, or other aspects of the social or political, can also be seen in Elaine Scarry's *The Body in Pain* (1985), in which she likens the experience of pain as being linked to the production of imagination. Both these, and other, authors illustrate the constructive potential of the body within political language and mobilization. I discuss the use of fasting by Irish prisoners in Chapter 7.

12 Gandhi was not the first to use fasting for political reasons in India. In fact, another figure in the Nationalist Movement, Jatin Das, fasted to the death in Lucknow Prison in 1929 in pursuit of prisoners' rights. His fast, and death, was a crucial moment for the Nationalist Movement as a whole. Despite previous famous fasts carried out by figures such as Bhagwat Singh, Gandhi has become indelibly linked to the practice of fasting within the Indian context since Independence. Some of this was his own doing as he actively tried to direct and control the use of fasting during the Nationalist Movement. I discuss the Das fast and prison fasts in general in Chapter 7.

13 For an excellent evaluation of the causes and consequences of the Salt March see Dennis Dalton's *Nonviolent Power in Action* (1993).

14 Though Gandhi's fasts prior to 1932 were politicized, they were not seeking to directly change policy. Instead, these fasts were used to draw attention to issues that Gandhi felt were important through his acts of self-purification or meditation. It wasn't until the Yervada fast that Gandhi sought to use the fast as a means for attaining a political goal. Altogether Gandhi fasted 17 times for spiritual and political reasons.

15 See B.R. Ambedkar's *What Congress and Gandhi Have Done for the Untouchables* (1946) for an alternative perspective of the events surrounding the Second Round Table Conference and the creation of a communal award for untouchables.

16 The language of the award was directed to "Depressed Classes"; this is the term that Ambedkar also used. Gandhi referred to untouchables as *harijans*. In this chapter I will utilize the terms predominantly used by the particular speaker.

17 While Gandhi was against untouchability, he was not against the caste system as a whole. Gandhi focused on caste as an occupational not a hierarchical system. In Gandhi's opinion, untouchability was a modern perversion of the caste system that should be abolished (Dalton 1967). However, his approach to dealing with the problems of untouchability was somewhat counterintuitive. Parekh (1989b, p. 211) describes it best: "He did more that any other Indian to undermine

Gandhi and suicide protest in India   39

it [untouchability], yet his attack has a profound weakness. He saw it as a blot on the Hindu religion and made it the sole responsibility of the high-caste Hindus to fight against it. The untouchables themselves, reduced to passive and pathetic symbols of high caste tyranny, were not involved in the struggle for their emancipation, a strange attitude in a man who everywhere else wanted the victims to fight for themselves."

18 Ambedkar gave up the notion of a separate electorate in return for a certain number of reserved seats for his community. The political difference between the separate electorate and reserved seats may come out in the wash, but clearly Ambedkar and Gandhi's conflict was about more than electoral math. At heart, they were fighting about the way to create change for untouchables in India.

19 Many of Gandhi's subsequent fasts were focused on *harijan* issues, such as temple entrance. In Chapter 3 we will see that these fasts were also Potti Sriramulu's first experiences with the practice.

20 Dennis Dalton provides an in-depth analysis of the events surrounding the 1947 fast. I borrow from his descriptions here.

21 The organization of states, and the first partition of Bengal, is discussed in Chapter 3.

22 Calcutta and Bengal were not the only areas in India to suffer violence at the time. Partition had a devastating effect on all border regions. In fact, Gandhi had been urged by political leaders at the time to travel to the Punjab. Gandhi, however, was unwilling to leave the city.

23 For example, Gandhi ended the 1921 Non-Cooperation Movement before it had finished its work – because violence had broken out. This was despite the fact that the movement seemed to be working in pushing the Raj to the brink.

3 Successful suicide

Potti Sriramulu[1] and the question of Andhra

What are the implications of Gandhi's idiom of suffering on post-Independent India? In this chapter I examine a suicide protest event that was able to create long-term policy shifts in favor of the movement – Potti Sriramulu's fast to the death for the linguistic state of Andhra in 1952. This event illustrates my argument that suicide protest can spur political change, but that the tactic must be deployed in particular ways for this to happen.

After India's independence in 1947, the new country was faced with questions regarding the organization of its internal boundaries. Underpinning this issue was the government's desire to mitigate the numerous ethnic and linguistic cleavages that already existed within the state. The British organized India into units known as Presidencies, which eased the Raj's ability to administer the colony. These presidencies were large and often encompassed a number of cultural groups. The most viable alternative to the previous system was to reorganize states along linguistic lines.[2] Faced with the challenge of balancing economic, ethnic and territorial issues, the state initially maintained the British system of administrative control, opting to implement changes gradually. In light of this policy it is surprising that the Government of India conceded to the demand for a linguistic Telegu state, known as Andhra, six years after Independence. The crucial factor in the shift in state policy was Potti Sriramulu's fast to the death in Madras in 1952. This fast was a critical example of how suicide protest can be extraordinarily effective in creating political change.

In order to understand how and why this fast precipitated long-term policy change this chapter closely examines the events surrounding it through the lens of the primary argument; that *how* suicide protest is deployed will play a significant role in its overall effectiveness. Based on an analysis of the events leading to the fast, and the fast itself, I believe that the movement for Andhra was able to achieve successfully high degrees of *tactical depth* and *intensity*, was able to *narrate* the event in its favor, and finally, was embedded within a *politically competitive* environment. These factors contributed to the long-term policy shift made by the state in favor of the movement.

Potti Sriramulu: evolution of a suicide protestor

Sriramulu's fast took place from October 1952, to his death in December of that year, in the city of Madras. Responses to Sriramulu's death were quick and extreme. In the days after the funeral a massive popular action that had not previously been seen on behalf of the Andhra community began to mobilize for Andhra (Murty 1984; Narayana Rao 1973; Sreeramulu 1988). In some instances this action turned violent:

> A wave of hysterical emotion swept Andhra territory. Students, youths and workers ... attacked Indian government property, looted railroad restaurants, hoisted black flags of mourning over government buildings. Police, firing on rioters, killed seven and wounded 40. A 13-year-old boy attempted to halt a moving bus by standing in its path and was run over and killed.[3]

Three days after Sriramulu's death, the central government, led by Prime Minister Jawarlahal Nehru, announced the creation of the Andhra state. At face value the sequence of events described don't seem too unusual. When popular activists die there is often a passionate response from the public. But those responses rarely translate into real political change. What was so different about Sriramulu's case?

Born in 1901, Sriramulu's early life was spent in the Madras presidency, where he was educated and married. After his wife's death, Sriramulu joined the Indian Nationalist Movement (Murty 1984; Sreeramulu 1988), where he first met Gandhi during the Salt March to Dandi in 1930.[4] Afterward he joined Gandhi in the Sabarmati Ashram in Gujarat, where he remained for about three years. During this period Sriramulu was exposed to the ideas and methods of *satyagraha*,[5] which, according to Gandhi, was the only method to gain Independence. It was in this period that Gandhi himself first conducted a "fast unto death" in 1932, to protest the creation of separate electorates for untouchables.[6] Sriramulu was clearly affected by his work with Gandhi. From 1934 to 1947, Sriramulu spent most of his time working for the equal treatment of untouchables, and argued in support of Gandhi's overall agenda. This period was marked by numerous stays in jail, as well as fasts in support of *harijan* temple entry[7] in the Nellore province of Madras in 1946. Sriramulu's association with Gandhi was important in that it introduced him the political tools he would use throughout the rest of his political life: fasting, *satyagraha* and other types of civil disobedience. During this period he was generally supportive of the Andhra Movement, but he was not directly involved in the mobilization for linguistic states until the early 1950s, when he witnessed discrimination against Telegus within Madras.

In 1952, in conjunction with Swami Sitaram, a prominent Telegu activist, Sriramulu had become a leader of the non-governmental side of the larger

42 *Sriramulu and the question of Andhra*

movement for Andhra. They quickly came to the conclusion that constitutional methods had, and would continue to, fail in guaranteeing the creation of Andhra Province (Narayana Rao 1973, p. 246). Sriramulu decided to begin a "fast to the death" in order to speed the establishment of Andhra. With the guidance of Sitaram and others involved in the movement, Sriramulu published a statement before he began his fast, explaining his reasons for the action. In this statement on the eve of the fast he outlines the problem, and then ends with the following:

> I started a fast unto death on 19.10.52 at the residence of Sri Bulusu Sambamurti in Mylapore. I appeal from the depth of my heart to Andhras, Tamils and all others interested in the solution of the future status of Madras city to come to an agreement, so that the will of the people may prevail in the immediate formation of the New Andhra State with Madras as its capital.
>
> (Sriramulu 1952, p. 45)

Except for supportive hunger strikes[8], all other types of mobilization were suspended during the fast (Sreeramulu 1988, p. 200).

The movement for a separate Andhra: tactical depth, intensity, narration and competition

Sriramulu began his fast in a hostile political system. The government was not only opposed to the creation of Andhra, but also opposed to the tactic of fasting. Though there was some historical precedent for the creation of cultural states,[9] this was mitigated by the political, economic and social conditions of the newly independent state. Based on an examination of events leading up to and during the fast, as well as actions taken by the government in reaction to the fast, I argue that Potti Sriramulu's use of fasting was integral to the creation of the Andhra state. This success was not due to any one single factor, but instead was the result of how the movement deployed for the event. As previously argued, I believe that four separate factors influence the likelihood of political success – the tactical depth displayed by the movement, the level of intensity of the act itself, the construction of an emotional narrative, and the competitive nature of the political system at the time.

Tactical depth

Movements that become identified only with suicide protest will rarely be able to transform the use of that tactic into long-term policy shifts on the part of the state. Though suicide protest is shocking and can garner media attention it is not an effective protest tactic on its own; it must work in conjunction with other types of protest. This is due in part to the extremity of the act itself, which can be framed as insane, irrational and dangerous. In order to mitigate the negative connotations of suicide protest, movements must be adept at using other tactics and methods of contestation. Based on this criterion the movement for Andhra displayed a high level of tactical depth, though high levels of tactical depth do not necessarily correlate with the degree of organizational capacity of a particular movement.

The movement for Andhra, though entrenched, was actually a loose confederation of a number of different groups that used a number of different tactics. There was communication between these groups, but they were not a highly systemized organization. Instead, over time, certain individuals and groups became identified with particular types of protest. Throughout the Nationalist Movement, and soon after Independence, Indian politics was characterized by the primary role that political parties had to play. Some "movements" that contested for the creation of Andhra labeled themselves as either regional political parties for which the question of Andhra was their only raison d'être, or sections of national parties that were made up primarily of Telegus and pursued the Andhra agenda within the larger party program. The overarching movement for Andhra consisted of a number of different groups and individuals with different affiliations. Interestingly this structure (or lack thereof) did not hinder the movement, but helped it, especially when it came to the use of suicide as a protest tactic.

Suicide can create strong reactions within the community, and among state actors. Movements that *only* use suicide, or become identified with the tactic of suicide, cannot successfully negotiate with the state.[10] In the case of Andhra, the very fragmented nature of the movement aided in creating a viable negotiating partner with which the government could discuss the creation of the state, since leaders that used extreme tactics were separated from those that did not. The movement for Andhra had three distinct, yet related strategies, which helped in the creation of the Telegu state: legislative contestation, *satyagraha* and suicide protest. The period immediately following Independence clearly shows that the movement for Andhra utilized both a high quantity of, and different qualities of, tactics in response to the state.

Legislative contestation

The years from 1947–1952 were marked by an increasingly mobilized movement contending within an increasingly reluctant state. Though the majority Congress Party officially supported linguistic states, the government's position was unclear. From the outset the government delayed the reorganization of states, and instead commissioned a number of fact-finding committees and reports. Although this was done in part to appease various linguistic groups[11], none of these reports seemed very supportive of the Telegus, or linguistic states. The first commission to examine the question of linguistic provinces was created in 1947. The Linguistic Provinces Commission, which is commonly known as the Dar Commission,[12] published its report in 1948. This document was a blow to the Telegu groups. It signaled the state's worry

44 *Sriramulu and the question of Andhra*

over the implications of vernacular states: "[T]he formation of provinces on exclusively or even mainly linguistic considerations is not in the larger interests of the Indian nation and should not be taken in hand."[13] Reactions to the Dar Report were mixed; most linguistic agitators felt betrayed and sought support from both the Indian National Congress (INC) and other political parties, though the government did heed a number of the report's warnings. Meanwhile the INC commissioned its own report during its party meeting in Jaipur in 1948. This report, known as the JVP Report,[14] was the Congress Party's response to both the Dar Report, and its own members who supported linguistic states. Published in 1949, the JVP Report directly deals with the issue of Andhra and Telegu sub-nationalism. The JVP Report allowed the Congress to rethink its previous support for linguistic organization of states, and its consequences. Citing the upheaval of Partition, as well as the Dar Commission, the JVP concluded that linguistic provinces should be viewed in a new light. According to the report, linguistic states

> would unmistakably retard the process of consolidation of our gains, dislocate our administrative, economic and financial structure, let loose, while we are still in a formative state, forces of disruption and disintegration, and seriously interfere with the progressive solution to our economic and political difficulties.[15]

With regard to a number of previously articulated demands by Telegus, Maratis, Malayalis and Karnatakans must necessarily be accorded different status. The JVP Commission's report cited the longevity and strength of these movements, and felt that the creation of linguistic states could be supported in these cases if particular conditions were met. These included confining new states to well-defined territories so that only those districts with a clear linguistic majority would be allowed to form new units. Capital cities would remain either within the previous state division, or would be made into administrative units themselves, which functionally denied the Telegu claim to Madras city.[16] The report concluded that Andhra must be the first province to be considered before any other.

The existence and conclusions of these two reports gives us an understanding of the political situation at the time. The Indian government not only contended with regional and linguistic groups from outside the government, it also contended with groups from within the ruling party itself, suggesting that the central state was fragmented over the issue of linguistic (regional) states. From 1949 onwards the state, while concerned with the issue, was no longer actively supporting or denying any linguistic claims. Vernacular states were traded off in favor of national stability. Based on these policies it is clear that Nehru was ambivalent about the existence of linguistic states (King 1997; Narayana Rao 1973).

During this period the movement for Andhra progressed on two specific fronts. First, individuals contended on a parliamentary level. The structure of the INC included regional representation from each of the different provinces. Though Telegu communities still rested within the large Madras Province, a number of Telegus were elected to the national legislature. These men functioned as movement leaders within the central state apparatus. These legislators kept the issue of Andhra on the political landscape, and were the impetus behind further explorations of linguistic states and the situation in the south. These men, including Congress Party officials such as Reddy, and P.V. Narayana, worked on the local level to foster Telegu pride and develop Telegu territories. Furthermore, a number of extra-governmental groups began to mobilize in the countryside, using the tactic of *satyagraha* first introduced in the Nationalist Movement. Sitaramasastry, commonly known as Swami Sitaram, used these tools to garner public support as well as to pressure the state. Although these were disparate fronts of attack, the unstructured form of the movement aided in sustaining a level of support for movement goals within the Telegu community, as well as keeping the issue on the political agenda. By 1952 the situation had reached deadlock. The major point of contention was the status of the city of Madras; Telegus claimed the city for themselves, and hoped that it would become the sole Andhra capital, or that it would be a shared administrative city. This desire resulted in the creation of a counter movement by some Tamils, and was an idea generally unsupported by the state. Additionally, in March 1952, after state elections that showed support for Telegu opposition parties, Nehru asked prominent INC leader Chakravarti Rajagopalachari (commonly referred to as C.R.) to head the Madras Congress Party, and subsequently form a government. C.R. was Tamil, known to be less than supportive of the Andhra cause, and was definitely opposed to a change in the status of Madras city.

The social and political context leading up to Sriramulu's fast illustrates the tactical depth displayed by the movement for Andhra. The movement had ample representation within the state. There were Telegu members of the ruling Congress Party, as well as within opposition parties at the time of Independence. In fact, the Vice President of India, S. Radhakrisnan, was from Andhra.[17] These actors utilized their positions in two ways; they kept the subject of linguistic states and Andhra on the agenda, and they brought attention to other mobilizational tactics used by other movement actors such as Sriramulu and Swami Sitaram. Telegu legislators often raised the question of Andhra on the national level. For instance, in July 1952 Andhra Congressman P.V. Narayana brought a resolution before the Rajya Sabha (Council of States) regarding the creation of Andhra. This resolution secured a primary position on the ballot of non-official resolutions, and resulted in two lengthy debates on July 16 and 21.[18] The resolution states:

> This council is of the opinion that the Government should take speedy steps for the formations of an ANDHRA[19] State from out of the existing territories of the State of Madras, giving it the status of a Part A State, and the Bill for the purpose should be introduced by the Government.[20]

46 *Sriramulu and the question of Andhra*

The resolution was clarified further in the debate that followed, P.V. Narayana stating, "[M]y claim is very simple, Sir. According to the Prime Minister, besides one or two disputed items, there is substantial agreement over the Andhra question. What I ask the Government to do is, Sir, to constitute an Andhra Province."[21] Though the resolution to speed the question of Andhra was ultimately defeated in Parliament,[22] the existence of the debate is what is important. Telegu MPs consistently raised the issue of Andhra at the national level. Often Telegu elections were decided on the ability of the member to promote the Andhra agenda among their peers. These Andhra ministers and politicians also served to bring attention to the tactic of fasting within the state. The previously discussed resolution highlighted fasts conducted by Swami Sitaram, a prominent Telegu leader. Once Sriramulu's fast was under way, Telegu leaders used Parliament to highlight the serious nature of the fast, and were able to convey Sriramulu's demands to the government. For example, in December 1952 there were debates in the Lok Sabha (House of the People) regarding Sriramulu's fast, and the state's reaction to it. These debates are the only place that Prime Minister Nehru was forced to respond to the fast in public. On December 8, 1952, the Lok Sabha debated a *Motion for Adjournment* based on the "grave condition of Shri Sriramulu."[23] The House was moved to adjourn proceedings and discuss Sriramulu's fast, and the issue of Andhra. Nehru states:

> Sir, the life or death of any individual is always a serious matter and one should not consider any such subject, that is to say where the life of a person is involved, in a light way, but with all respect to the sentiment. I will say this – that bringing pressure of such a kind on very major decisions would, if acceded to, put an end to the authority of the Parliament and of democratic procedure ... I would appeal to those who are interested in this matter and to the gentleman who is fasting, to try better ways, more legitimate ways. I am very sorry for him.[24]

After some debate, the motion to adjourn was denied. But again, the importance of this debate does not lie in its conclusion, but in the fact it took place. Telegu leaders actively engaged the state and Nehru in discussions about the tactic of fasting, reinforcing and legitimizing its use (to a certain extent) in the process.

These actions allowed Telegu leaders to *cross-promote* the tactic of suicide, while remaining somewhat aloof from it – giving credibility to the tactic while simultaneously distinguishing themselves from its extreme nature. As has been previously discussed, Telegu leaders actively brought the topic of Andhra up in debates in both Houses of Parliament before the fast began. Once the fast was under way, these Telegu leaders turned their attention to Sriramulu and his actions. Specifically, on two separate occasions in the Lok Sabha a request was made to adjourn the regular session in order to discuss Sriramulu, his fast, and his general condition.[25] The motion was denied each

Sriramulu and the question of Andhra 47

time. While in retrospect it would seem unusual if there hadn't been a discussion about Sriramulu and the fast, at the time simply conducting a fast to the death would not have guaranteed state attention. Telegu leaders were able to highlight the lack of state response, and actively tried to shame the government into responding to the fast. For example, in response to Nehru's statement on December 8, 1952, MP Dr Rao from Andhra stated the following:

> The condition of Mr. Sriramulu is very serious – he is practically dying. From the reports coming from all over Andhra, it is evident that this matter is exercising the minds of all parties there. In English papers you may not find much space devoted to this matter. But all the Andhra papers – whether it is Communist or Congress – are giving a lot of space for this matter. In this matter they are all agreed. It is causing a lot of anxiety all over Andhra and the government a [is] showing a callous attitude ....[26]

This statement manages to simultaneously highlight the gravity and widespread reaction to the fast, as well as attempt to shame the government for its lack of response. None of these debates and discussions would have had the same efficacy if Telegu leaders did not practice restraint while talking about and dealing with the fast in general. Men such as P.V. Narayana, R. Reddi, and Rao confined their actions to Parliament and did not attempt to take further actions.[27] There was a clear line of demarcation between those who used extreme tactics and those who did not. The status of Telegu leaders illustrated the crucial role that they played, not only in drawing attention to Andhra and the fast, but also in establishing themselves as viable and reasonable negotiating partners for the state.

Satyagraha

In addition to legislative contestation, the movement for Andhra also utilized agitational tactics in its demand for a separate state. These tactics fall under the rubric of *satyagraha*; a term first coined by Gandhi and one that included non-violent disruptive tactics such as marches, strikes, sit-ins and hunger strikes.[28] As I described in Chapter 2, for Gandhi the use of *satyagraha* entailed more than a simple calculation of which type of protest best fitted the field of action; instead its use could only be legitimate if conducted for "moral" reasons (Parekh 1989b).

The movement for Andhra was clearly influenced by Gandhi's strategy and legacy. After Independence, when the movement was confronted with an increasingly unresponsive state, some turned to the tactics that were made common during the struggle for independence. Spearheaded by Swami Sitaram, a leader of the movement, many supporters of a separate Andhra state began to use non-violent confrontational tactics to promote their agenda. Reports of mobilization started in the early 1950s. Sitaram created and supported cadres of men and women who willingly became *satyagrahis* for the cause of

48 *Sriramulu and the question of Andhra*

Andhra.[29] Campaigns included Sitaram's march through Telegu provinces in 1951, marches conducted by Telegu groups to promote the Telegu language,[30] as well as numerous sit-ins in front of official buildings at the local, state and national levels.

Sitaram also conducted hunger strikes, as did others in the movement. These were used to bring attention to the cause, and were carried out almost up to the moment of Sriramulu's own fast to the death. For example, on August 16, 1952, a young man went on a fast for five days in support of demands for an Andhra state. Newspaper accounts show that this man, T. Amrita Rao, was "under instructions from Swami Sitaram."[31] Sitaram explains the situation thus:

> [H]e (T.A. Rao) came to Madras to fast before the secretariat to impress on the government the need: (1) for the formation of the Andhra State at once, (2) for the carrying on of official correspondence for the administrative purposes in Telegu in so far as the Telegu areas are concerned, (3) for providing full employment for all able-bodied people in the state.[32]

The extent to which Rao was invested in the movement for Andhra is unclear; there is no record of his own thoughts on the subject. Instead, Sitaram was able to convey the message that the movement wanted to promote – that the question of Andhran statehood was more than a simple division of resourced and institutional power, and that the Telegu community was deeply invested in the creation of a state in order to express their own linguistic and cultural identity.

Satyagraha (or civil disobedience) was important for the movement in two ways. The use of non-violent disruptive tactics helped to create the political and social basis for the future state, and inculcated high levels of support for statehood among the general population. Also, the emphasis on linguistic identity by movement leaders helped to cut through (though not completely) previously existing cleavages within the Telegu population. For instance, the young man who went on a five-day hunger strike was an untouchable,[33] a fact *The Hindu* made pointed reference to. Traditional gender divisions were also (at least superficially) mitigated, as women were encouraged to participate in various protest events. This was important in establishing the legitimacy of the demand for the state of Andhra, since mobilization of all Telegus, regardless of economic or social status, would be a more powerful demonstration than only having elite support for the cause.

The presence of multiple tactics was a crucial element in the success of the Andhra movement; its campaigns – legislative contestation, *satyagraha* and suicide protest – worked in concert to create political change. As shown, the tenor of Telegu legislative contestation not only served to bring attention to the cause at national level, but also exhibited the existence of negotiating partners for the state. Telegu leaders on the national and state level were able to successfully convey their demands, while simultaneously maintaining

Sriramulu and the question of Andhra 49

a relationship with the state and Nehru. Meanwhile, *satyagraha* illustrated the high level of support that Andhra enjoyed within the general Telegu population, as well as serving to bring that population together in support of the cause. Finally, while the three types of tactics (legislative contestation, *satyagraha*, and suicide protest) were distinct, a high degree of overlap existed between them. For example, both Sriramulu and Sitaram considered themselves members of the Congress Party, though of course many of their tactics and goals diverged from the party itself. When the fast commenced some leaders in the movement questioned the tactic, but once it had progressed all prominent Telegu leaders were actively affirming the use of fasting, and supporting Sriramulu. The existence of multiple tactics was important to the movement because it demonstrated that the movement for Andhra had viable negotiating partners and leaders who would be willing and able to lead the new state. One of Nehru's concerns over the creation of Andhra was the lack of economic, political and social development in majority Telegu areas, including the lack of viable moderate leaders.

Intensity

Based on Tilly's definition of intensity (Tilly 1978) I investigate the implications of the death of the protestor. What effect does the act of dying have for the movement? Does the number of deaths matter? As discussed in Chapter 1, intensity is important because even though death is the natural end of an act of suicide protest, it is not the inevitable end. Suicide protests can end before death occurs: by force or through the actor's own choice. Examples of this include cases of suicide bombing that were stopped before detonation, or actors who survived self-immolation. The tactic of fasting is a special case as its duration allows ample time for the state or the protest actor to bring an end to the event. The death of the suicide protestor is an important part of the success of suicide protest in that it creates a lever against the state. Also, the death of a protestor will garner more media and public attention than suicide tactics that do not end in death. This is particularly shown in the case of the Andhra movement; the movement utilized fasting[34] multiple times without it ending in the death of the protestor. In order to understand the impact that differing levels of intensity can have on political outcomes I examine two fasts to the death conducted by the movement for Andhra. First, I will discuss Swami Sitaram's use of both hunger strike and fasting in 1951. Comparing Sitaram's use of fasting to Sriramulu's fast to the death showcases the importance of high levels of intensity in determining the success or failure of suicide protest.

A self-proclaimed "Gandhian," Sitaram was the most public proponent of disruptive, or satyagrahic, tactics in the movement after Independence. In June 1951 Sitaram addressed various members of the government claiming that he would begin a fast to the death on August 16 unless an Andhran state was created by Independence Day (August 15) of that year. Hearing no

50   *Sriramulu and the question of Andhra*

response, Sitaram began his fast as promised (Narayana Rao 1973, p. 237). Though the government and Nehru were unmoved (Nehru 1987a), the fast raised public awareness of the issue, and provided an impetus to other segments of the movement. For instance, a resolution of the Andhra Pradesh Congress Committee (APCC) was passed regarding the need to resolve the issue. The fast continued for 35 days and ended when Sitaram responded to an appeal to end it from Vinoba Bhave,[35] a prominent social leader. Ultimately Sitaram's fast yielded no response or concession from the state (Rao 1978, p. 499). Sitaram also conducted a three-week hunger strike beginning on May 25, 1952. This was carried out in conjunction with his *"satyagraha yatra"* (protest journey) through Telegu districts. In response, Nehru (1987b, pp. 26–7) wrote in his *Letters to the Chief Ministers*:

> The question of linguistic provinces has again been raised. Swami Sitaram of Andhra undertook a three weeks' fast, which is, I believe, just over. I confess I do not understand or appreciate this method of dealing with a complicated administrative problem.

This hunger strike also did not result in any specific change on the part of the state. For the rest of the summer of 1952 various followers of Sitaram conducted hunger strikes until Sriramulu commenced his fast in October.

Potti Sriramulu's "fast to the death" began on October 19, 1952, at his friend's house in Madras. He was 51 years old. During the early stages, the fast was not given much attention. *The Hindu*, the major English newspaper published in Madras, first mentions the fast in its October 21 issue on page six. This short mention conveys the level of seriousness that the fast was met with – almost none. As it states: "Mr. Potti Sriramulu a Congressman from Nellore has commenced a fast for an 'indefinite period' yesterday morning."[36] This article was placed alongside notice of another fast that had not resulted in a political outcome,[37] and in no way conveyed a sense of urgency. The state seemed supremely unconcerned about Sriramulu and his fast. In fact it was not mentioned in *The Hindu* again until November. The media and state's indifference can be explained in part by the attitude towards the tactic of fasting in India at that time. Though this tactic occupied an important part in India's mobilizational history, many Indians in power at the time were not supportive of the tactic, inspite (or because) of the fact that Gandhi's use of fasting was carefully constructed to invoke a number of different cultural and symbolic markers that would resonate with a mass Indian audience.

After Independence, fasting was used on numerous occasions, and for a variety of reasons. Most practitioners called themselves Gandhians, and used the fast for social and economic uplift. Sriramulu decided to conduct a fast in an environment where fasting was extremely common, for Andhra and other reasons. Consequently some members of the government did not consider "fasts to the death" to be a serious political tactic. It was simply conducted too many times, and without leading to an actual result for it to be regarded as effective. From the start no one expected Sriramulu's fast would end in his death; either it would be called off because an accord was reached, or it would be called off by the movement itself.

But Sriramulu's fast was not called off, and the government sustained its unwillingness to accommodate the movement's demands. On December 3, 1952, only weeks before Sriramulu's death, Nehru corresponded with the then Chief Minister of Madras, C. Rajagopalachari, regarding the fast. In this letter, labeled "secret and personal," Nehru makes the following statement: "Some kind of fast is going on for the Andhra Province and I get frantic telegrams. I am totally unmoved by this and I propose to ignore it completely."[38] He goes on further to state that regarding the situation in Andhra, though some action should take place, he does "not want to be driven to any reactions."[39] Nehru did not want to accommodate the tactic of fasting, even though he might have been willing to negotiate on the issue of Andhra itself. Sriramulu's fast continued unabated for almost two months. As time went on attention to the fast increased. There were a number of supporting fasts that took place simultaneously with the "fast to the death." As it progressed, both the media and the movement published continual updates on Sriramulu's health and well-being. Meanwhile, there were debates in both houses of the Parliament to determine whether the government should react. By the middle of December Sriramulu was considerably weakened, and unable to function normally. By early December his condition had severely deteriorated, and he was dead by the fifteenth of that month. In the aftermath three days of riots broke out in the city of Madras and its surrounding areas. By December 19 Nehru had declared in Parliament that the state of Andhra would be established by October 1953, and the question of Madras city would be resolved by a joint commission led by a judge.

How does Sitaram's use of fasting compare to that of Sriramulu? Each of these fasts took place in similar conditions and only one year apart. The movement was the same in terms of its organization and personnel. It is clear that Nehru maintained his negative attitude regarding the tactic and practice of fasting in both cases. Both instances of fasting incurred a response from movement and Telegu leaders. In fact, the only difference in terms of context would be that Sitaram was better known as a proponent of Andhra and more active within the movement. Yet Sitaram's fast did not create any real state accommodation in favor of the Andhra state, while Sriramulu's fast did.[40] The only real difference between the two cases is that Sriramulu died and Sitaram did not. This suggests that simply threatening, or even commencing, suicide protest action will not be as powerful or efficacious as suicide protest that culminates in death. Comparatively, Sriramulu's fast was not only able to create solidarity within the movement, it also precipitated measurable policy shifts from the state. The intensity of Sriramulu's act was a lever that not only caused popular reaction, but government reaction as well.

Intensity alone is not enough to engender policy change. Taking suicide protest to its logical conclusion may cause a reaction, but not necessarily a

52 *Sriramulu and the question of Andhra*

positive reaction for the movement. To achieve this movements must construct a positive emotional narrative that attempts to create affective ties between the movement, the event, and the audience.

Emotional narratives

If movements attempt to create an emotional narrative about their use of suicide, then the event will be more likely to result in policy change. I identify two critical audiences towards which the movement will direct their narrative of the event: supporters and the state. Specifically, when movements create a level of familiarity and intimacy between supporters and suicide protest events, the public may feel emotions of pride and sympathy. Also, movements will try to shame the state in pursuit of their cause. Movements start these narratives to engender particular feelings for their group and for the event. The manner in which events are staged and played out will help to establish the type of feelings the movement wants to project. When movements do not try to construct an emotional narrative, they are less likely to create political change in their favor. Suicide protests (like all other types of political action) are emotional, but the emotions that can be aroused during and after a suicide protest event are myriad and changeable. Movements must both harness and create specific emotional responses to acts of suicide through the use of drama and rhetoric. I only examine movement attempts to construct this narrative, not the extent to which these narratives are accepted.

Potti Sriramulu's fast illustrates how movements construct multiple emotional narratives directed at different audiences. Sriramulu's success lies in the way the movement staged the fast as it was happening, as well as the events that occurred after his death. I examine how the movement attempted to create a level of familiarity and intimacy both with the act of fasting and with Sriramulu himself, which would subsequently lead to feelings of pride and sympathy among active and potential members of the movement. Then I examine movement attempts to shame the state into a political response. Elite allies of the movement and the media primarily articulated this emotional appeal towards the state. In this case, shame should be felt as the state fails to respond to democratic contestation.

Pride and sympathy

Feelings of both pride and sympathy depend on a level of familiarity with the object of the emotion (Ahmed 2004; Taylor 1985). The movement staged the fast in such a way that it would generate familiarity and intimacy with both the act and the actor. The duration and staging of the fast served as an emotional appeal by the movement in two ways. First, by linking Sriramulu to Gandhi the public was able to get to know Sriramulu more quickly. Sriramulu's relative anonymity before the fast began was mitigated by the conscious invocation of Gandhian methods, as well as constant reaffirmation of the close bond that

Sriramulu and the question of Andhra   53

Gandhi and Sriramulu shared. Second, the movement re-enacted the fast to the death through the use of supporting and relay hunger strikes, which in turn let others experience the tactic, though on a smaller scale.

The opportunity for the public to identify themselves with Sriramulu and the act of fasting to the death was mediated by the image and legacy of Gandhi. As discussed in Chapter 2, Gandhi was the first person to introduce political fasting into the Indian context; he inculcated the notion of self-sacrificial political action into the Nationalist Movement as a whole. This type of political action is integral to the mythology of the Indian nation and nationhood. Gandhi had numerous detractors both inside and outside the Nationalist Movement, yet it cannot be disputed that he and his image were extraordinarily important in the creation of an independent India. Gandhi's assassination in 1948 cemented his popularity and the reverence many felt towards him. In 1952 his legacy was still very strongly felt within the Indian state; Sriramulu, Sitaram and others in the movement consciously invoked a link to Gandhi, and his type of Hindu spiritualism during and after the fast.

For instance, in his "Statement of Appeal," published before the fast began, Sriramulu very clearly delineated his ties to Gandhi and his long-term commitment to the Gandhian tradition. Sriramulu calls himself a "constructive worker [who does] work on Gandhian lines. (Sriramulu 1952). He goes on to discuss the nature of his work prior to the demand for Andhra, taking care to establish his credibility in terms of his connection to Gandhi. Also, Sriramulu's fast mirrored a number of Gandhi's own fasts that were undertaken during the time of the Nationalist Movement. The fast for Andhra took place in a private residence,[41] like most of Gandhi's fasts. His condition was very closely monitored, and though media attention was slow in starting, those in charge of the fast monitored minute details of Sriramulu's condition and used the media and other sources to relay "weekly bulletins" regarding his condition (Sreeramulu 1988, p. 208). Finally, based on his own statements, above all this was to be a "Hindu" fast (Sriramulu 1952, p. 45). Whether or not this was actually the case is irrelevant to this analysis. What is important is that Sriramulu and others in the movement made a conscious effort to frame this fast within a national and spiritual matrix that would hopefully appeal to more than just Andhras, and would instead invoke memories of the Nationalist Movement and embed Sriramulu into a religious context that was familiar to most of the public.

Events after Sriramulu's death were also staged to create sympathetic bonds between the movement and the public. By the end of his fast various Telegu communities had begun to use the method of the *hartal*[42] against the government in support of Andhra (Sreeramulu 1988, p. 215). Again, by including others in different protests, the movement can create a sense of identification with its goals, and Sriramulu's funeral procession in Madras added to the sense of mourning and urgency regarding the need for Andhra. Sriramulu's death also garnered international attention[43], as it was one of only a handful of fasts that actually resulted in death.[44] The funeral procession, which lasted

54 *Sriramulu and the question of Andhra*

five hours, progressed from the scene of the fast to the Vysya crematorium. Telegu schoolboys and young men carried Sriramulu for the length of the procession.[45] The entire procession chanted terms such as "we want Andhra Rashtra (nation)," and that "no Andhra child will rest content till the Andhra Rashtra is achieved."[46] At the memorial Andhra leader T. Prakasam delivered an oration, praising Sriramulu for having "'done something which is sure to convince us of the potentiality of the fast. He has shown us the ways of god" (Sreeramulu 1988). Also, according to newspaper accounts, Prakasam continued:

> Sriramulu stuck to his principles and ideals, showing tremendous spiritual strength. He scrupulously adhered to Gandhian ways and faced his death courageously. He laid down his life convinced that it would bring good to millions of others. Mr. Prakasam hoped that after Sriramulu's supreme sacrifice, the Andhras would stand united and follow in the footsteps of the great departed soul to achieve what he had fasted grimly and died nobly for.[47]

The spectacle of Sriramulu's funeral highlights the movement's attempts to create affective ties between Sriramulu and the public. First, the funeral served to promote the martyred identity of Sriramulu himself. In fact, his funeral procession was close (though not in number or scope) to Gandhi's funeral that had taken place four years before, simultaneously reinforcing Sriramulu's relationship to Gandhi as well as the similarities they shared. Second, the funeral procession gave Telegu leaders a public forum from which they could showcase the commitment of the Telegu people, and foster a sense of Telegu community that might transcend political, economic and caste cleavages. Sriramulu's funeral was a drama that could engender emotional responses among the public by creating a level of intimacy between the people, the suicide act, and the actor.

Shame

The movement actively attempts to create feelings of shame within the state. This is done through the rhetoric surrounding the event. Shame is linked to norms and moral rules within society. In order to be able to shame a state, movement leaders first had to present the case of a moral collapse on the part of the state. The continued lack of response from the center constituted a break with the moral obligation of democratic states to hear and answer political appeals. Although the state did engage with the movement to a certain extent throughout its history, Nehru's attitude towards Andhra in general and Sriramulu in particular made it possible for the movement to claim that the state was unfeeling and unable to deal with these demands. The ability to shame the state hinged in part on the fact that the movement consistently talked about the fast as its "last resort" (Sreeramulu 1988; Sriramulu 1952);

the notion that the movement had exhausted all possible avenues of influence on the state, leaving suicide protest as the *last* method that might get attention. The movement's shaming attempts were clearly taken up by other Telegus during Sriramulu's funeral, solidifying his role as a martyr and spiritual saint, spurring the Telegu population to act on behalf of this particular demand, and shaming the state for its inaction. Telegu leaders harnessed the emotional resonance of suicide protest in order to further their own cause.

The movement for Andhra attempted to both amplify existing emotions within the public sphere, and create emotions within the state, increasing the likelihood of movement and tactical success. These attempts help to direct the way people view the event and the movement. In constructing emotional narratives of the fast the movement transformed an unusual and unlikely event – suicide protest – into something that seems logical and familiar. The ability of the movement to direct these narratives is crucial in creating a positive response from both the public and the state.

Levels of political competition

The last factor that increases the probability that suicide protest will yield a successful result in favor of the movement is the level of political competition that exists within the state at the time of the protest. Based on work done from a political process approach to social movements (McAdam 1996; Tarrow 1998), I identify high levels of political competition as an indicator for political vulnerability. As the level of viable political competition increases within a state, so too will the likelihood that that state will be willing to negotiate, or at least respond to the use of extreme tactics. States that have viable political parties and competing groups are more vulnerable, and therefore should be willing to engage with extra-governmental groups and institutions in an effort to maintain and increase power. When conducted in a politically competitive environment extreme tactics can attain long-term policy outcomes from the state. Potti Sriramulu's fast illustrates this point.

At the time of the fast India only had one viable national party, the Indian National Congress (INC). The single party structure of the party system indicates low levels of political competition, but the nature and structure of the Congress Party at that time created a situation where the state was forced to deal with numerous competing interests, and was often placed in the position of negotiating with other groups both inside and outside the party itself. This meant that there was a high degree of political competition present at the time of Sriramulu's fast. Competition rested in *intra*-party politics, not *inter*-party politics.

The political history of India is marked by the dominance of the Congress Party at the Center for 30 years (Franda 1962). Though the INC was undoubtedly in power in 1952, and would remain so for quite some time, the federal structure of the state, and the internal structure of the party itself, ensured that the party would have to contend actively with competing forces and

56 *Sriramulu and the question of Andhra*

groups. As with many other aspects of Indian politics, the ascendancy of the INC began during the time of the Nationalist Movement, during which time it coordinated the overall effort. The creation of Pakistan shifted the power of the Muslim League out of India, resulting in the almost-total control of the Congress Party over the transition of power from the British. Though there were other political forces in existence, such as the Communist Party of India, the Praja Socialist Party, the Jan Sangh, and other ethnic and cultural groups, the Congress Party clearly dominated the central state; by the early 1950s there was no other party that had achieved the same amount of popularity and power on a national scale (Weiner 1954). One would imagine that in a system such as this there would be less room for the accommodation of political contestation. This was not the case for India in the 1950s; two factors contributed to the negotiating stance that the Congress, state, and Nehru were forced to take vis-à-vis the movement for Andhra. First, the magnitude of the Congress Party itself made the party vulnerable to factionalism, leading to a high degree of negotiation and accommodation within the party itself. Second, the federal character of both the state and the party strengthened the Andhra cause.

Party factionalism was a primary concern for the INC after Independence. The party's structure mirrored the political system at that time. It was based on regional membership that in turn led to a strong central presence. The widespread affiliation with the INC was as much a result of habit and tradition as it was of ideological loyalty. Within the INC itself there were numerous competing sub-organizations that would press demands on the central leadership of the party based on cultural, regional or economic terms. Party members themselves were often at odds with the central party structure. The INC did not have the political capacity to disregard these demands since the threat of attrition to other parties was a real problem, and could be disastrous for the INC in the long term. This situation held true in 1952; Telegu Congress Party members often attempted to cajole their national leaders to respond to the demand for Andhra. The previous discussion indicates a high level of political competition at the national level, though this did not necessarily mean that there were any strong opposition parties. Instead, the numerous competing interests worked within the ruling party to create political change, and the threat of factionalism within the party made both it, and the state, vulnerable to other political forces.

Also, the political situation within the Telegu community was complex. The Andhra Mahasabha (AM) was formed in 1912 with the purpose of fostering a separate Andhra state. Members of the AM were often also affiliated with the INC. As Independence drew closer two other parties gained hold in the South: the Praja Socialist Party and the Communist Party. Each of these parties also had significant Telegu membership, and many of these men were actively involved in the mobilization for Andhra itself. Each of these parties, and their members, had shifting alliances throughout the early 1950s. The central government was forced to deal with all of these parties and personalities in discussions concerning linguistic states and Andhra, creating an environment that was highly competitive at the regional level, the competitive nature of which, in turn, funneled up to the center.

Finally, the fact that Andhra was a sub-national movement put pressure on the center from other movements that wanted ethnic or vernacular statehood. Though Andhra was the first, it certainly was not the last linguistic group to demand its own official state. In fact the possibility that the creation of Andhra would open the door for a full reorganization of states was one of the reasons Nehru was reluctant to respond to the Andhra community; the presence of such groups also increased pressure on the government to act. Throughout the Independence Movement, and after 1947, both Marati and Karnatakan groups had also demanded a state of their own based on shared language. While these requests were not as entrenched as those for Andhra, the fact that they existed at all kept the issue of linguisitic states alive within the Central Government, even if proponents remained silent on the issue of Andhra or the fast. These linguistic groups would often put pressure on the state in order to guarantee the reorganization of internal borders in cultural terms.

The political situation in 1952 clearly shows a central state that was vulnerable from multiple sources both inside and outside its own power base. The large and fragmented nature of the party, the growth of other political parties, and the sub-nationalist demand made by Andhra, all put pressure on the central state to negotiate with claims of cultural identity and statehood. Though a cursory examination of party politics in the 1950s would suggest that the INC was the only significant party and therefore had no need to negotiate with competing groups, this was not the case. Sriramulu's fast was able to strengthen the political demand for reorganization. Indeed, soon after Sriramulu's death, the committee on the reorganization of the state recommended that states within India should be based upon language (Report of the India States Reorganization Committee, 1953). This came to fruition with the large-scale state change in 1956.

Conclusions

Potti Sriramulu's fast is a critical example of how and when suicide protest can create political change in favor of the movement. Despite Nehru's conviction that his decision to create Andhra had nothing to do with the fast, the timing of that choice suggests an alternative logic. I doubt that the Government of India would have acted on the Andhra question so quickly if the fast had not taken place. What does Sriramulu's fast tell about suicide protest? There were many political fasts before Sriramulu, even within the same movement. Yet these fasts were not able to create the same level of policy shift. Is it simply that Sriramulu died and other practitioners of fasting often survived? Sriramulu's death is an important factor in the event's success, but not the only one. It was the interplay of the political context, cultural and symbolic

58 *Sriramulu and the question of Andhra*

resonance, and movement strategy that created a context in which a fast to death could and did create real political change. The success or failure of suicide protest is not arbitrary or random, but dependent on how well the movement embeds itself within the movement, and society.

Sriramulu's fast illuminates some issues surrounding movements and their use of extreme tactics. Actions such as suicide protest have a visceral power, but that power doesn't often translate into political power. By examining Sriramulu's fast it is clear that suicide protest should be embedded within a larger rubric of protest to create change; but is that enough? In the following chapters we examine two cases that were not able to create the same level of policy changes that the movement for Andhra was.able to achieve.

Notes

1 There are various different spellings of Sriramulu (Sreeramulu, Sriramalu). For clarity I will only be using Sriramulu, which is the most common spelling.
2 There was precedent for linguistic states, starting with the first partition of Bengal along linguistic lines in 1905.
3 "Fast and Win" in *Time Magazine*, December 29, 1952. Accessed from http://content.time.com/time/magazine/article/0,9171,822565,00.html
4 The Salt March to Dandi was a major campaign in the Indian Nationalist Movement. Designed as a protest against the salt tax levied by the Raj, this march mobilized thousands of activists throughout India.
5 *Satyagraha* was a term coined by Gandhi in his writings. Translated by some as "truth-force" *satyagraha* became the word most commonly used to refer to the different tactics of civil disobedience that Gandhi popularized throughout the country. These included short-term hunger strikes, marches, protests, and so on; the difference being that acts of *satyagraha* were conducted with a feeling of non-violence towards all people, including the target of the protest.
6 Though this fast was deemed a success by the press and other political actors, Gandhi himself condemned it for not truly being "non-violent." It is interesting to note that this fast was not conducted to gain a political outcome from the British; in fact, Gandhi never fasted "against" the state, but limited his use of fasting to compel other political actors – in this case the untouchable community in general and B.R. Ambedkar in particular.
7 Untouchables were usually barred from entering Hindu temples as they were seen as polluted by other castes. Abolishing this practice was a cornerstone of Gandhi's and others work for "*harijan* uplift."
8 The practice of others fasting in support of the main fast to the death. These supportive fasts usually had a finite length, and were conducted simply to show support to both the cause and the protestor.
9 In particular the partition of Bengal in 1905 by the British was carried out along religious lines, as was the Partition of India and Pakistan in 1947.
10 This will be discussed further in Chapter 5 and Chapter 6.
11 By this time the Telegu community was not the only language group to be contesting for a state of their own. Maratis and Malayalis were also protesting. The demand for Andhra was much more entrenched.
12 The commission is named after its chairman, S.K. Dar. This tradition holds for most Government of India reports.
13 Government of India, Linguistic Provinces Commission, *Dar Commission Report*, 1948.

14 The official name is the *Report of the Linguistic Provinces Committee of the INC*. It is known, however, by the initials of its three authors, Sardar Vallabhbhai Patel, Dr Pattabhai Sitaramayya, and Jawaharlal Nehru.

15 Indian National Congress, *Report of the Linguistic Provinces Committee*, 1948, p. 9.

16 Ibid.

17 Though Radhakrisnan was a Telegu and had previously supported the cause of the Andhra state, for the most part during parliamentary debates he remained impartial as the presiding member of the debate (*Raiya Sabha Debates. Official Reports*, Government of India Press, 1:16, July 16, 1952).

18 Ibid.

19 Existing emphasis.

20 Ibid., p. 1224.

21 Ibid., p. 1228.

22 *Rajva Sabha Debates*, op. cit., 1: 19, July 21, 1952.

23 *Rajya Sabha Debates*, op. cit., 11: 1–12, December 8, 1952, p. 1823.

24 Ibid., pp. 1823–4.

25 These motions were heard on November 12, 1952, and December 8, 1952.

26 Government of India Press, *Parliamentary Debates, Official Report*, 5:6, December 8, 1952.

27 For instance, in June 1952 an Andhra MLA informed authorities that he would leave the assembly for six weeks in protest against the State's position on Andhra (*The Hindu*, June 25, 1952, p. 4).

28 I differentiate between the terms *hunger strike, supportive hunger strike* and *fasting*. For this book fasting is an act of suicide protest, where the stated purpose is to die. Often these fasts will be called "fasts to the death" as in the case of Potti Sriramulu. On the other hand hunger strikes are conducted for a previously stated finite time span. Supportive hunger strikes take place simultaneously with fasts to death, or some other, larger protest action. These will more often than not also have a previously stated finish point. By this definition, the *hunger strike* does not fall into the category of "suicide protest" as the stated end point of the act will not culminate in the death of the actor. Instead, hunger strikes fall into the larger category of *satyagraha*, as they are both non-violent and disruptive.

29 *The Hindu*, December 18, 1952, p. 6 "'Follower of Gandhiji' Tribute to Potti Sriramulu, Performance of Last rites."

30 Ibid., August 4, 1952, p. 4.

31 Ibid., "Andhra State Demand: Harijan Youth on Fast" August 17, 1952, p. 6.

32 Ibid.

33 In the article Mr Rao is described as a "*harijan* youth," *harijan* being the term used by Gandhi for Untouchables, which translates as "children of God," a somewhat paradoxical appellation as Untouchables were thought to be outside of the *varna* system of categorization. Today the term *harijan* has been mostly discontinued in favor of the term *dalit*.

34 As previously discussed, I define fasts and hunger strikes as two distinct acts. I label all known finite fasts as hunger strikes, while all fasts that are intended to last until death (though may not end with that result) are labeled as fasts.

35 Vinoba Bhave was a contemporary and friend of Gandhi. He was considered by many to be Gandhi's most prominent follower after his death in 1948. While he focused on social causes, Bhave continued to have a relationship with Nehru and other parts of the government. Though he never sought a formal role in the government, he was very influential in both official and unofficial spheres of influence.

36 "Demand for Andhra State Formation" in *The Hindu*, October 21, 1952, p. 6.

37 Fast conducted by two young men to compel Mr Prakasam, a prominent Andhra leader, to take control of the movement. This fast lasted ten days.

38 Unpublished personal correspondence from Nehru to C. Rajagopalachari, December 3, 1952. Archived at the Teen Murti Library, New Delhi, India.
39 Ibid.
40 Though Nehru continued to deny that Sriramulu's fast had anything to do with his declaration the timing suggests something else. This point will be discussed more fully further on.
41 This contrasts with more recent types of fasting that take place in public settings, or outside government property. This change will be discussed later in the text.
42 The term *hartal* originates in Gujarati, and is akin to the act of a strike. During the Nationalist Movement *hartal* came to mean more than simply closing down one sector, and instead was a general shutdown of all private businesses and some public institutions such as schools. Other areas of northern India use the term *bandh*, or closing, to describe this sort of action.
43 *Time Magazine*, December 29, 1952.
44 In India only one person had died from fasting prior to Sriramulu.
45 *The Hindu*, December 18, 1952, p. 6 "'Follower of Gandhiji' Tribute to Potti Sriramulu, Performance of Last rites."
46 *The Indian Express*, December 17, 1952.
47 *The Hindu*, December 18, 1952, p. 6 "'Follower of Gandhiji' Tribute to Potti Sriramulu, Performance of Last rites."

4 Short-term success

The Narmada Bachao Andolan

In December 2005 I attended a rally held by the National Alliance of People's Movements in Jantar Mantar, New Delhi. I had been told that Medha Patkar, leader of the Narmada Bachao Andolan (NBA), and V.P. Singh, former Prime Minister of India from the Janata Party, would be there and I was interested in seeing the crowd's reaction to their presence. The day was cool and sunny as I went to the center of Delhi; people had traveled from all over India to come to the rally and the subsequent march to Parliament. There was a massive group of people sitting in the middle of the street facing a speaker's dais. There were men, women and children present. As I walked through the crowd I heard Hindi, Marathi, Bengali and a variety of other languages. Patkar and Singh were on the dais surrounded by other speakers. The crowd was attentive and enthusiastic. Listening to Patkar's speech and the various reactions to it, it was clear that the people who had journeyed to Jantar Mantar that day supported her and her ambitions of *adivasi*[1] rights, fair rehabilitation for internally displaced people, and reviews of all large state projects. Once the speeches were finished the crowd began to move down the road while shouting "We will fight! We will win!" in Hindi. After crossing a police barricade made of tow buses and ropes, the protestors made it to the Parliament *Thana* (police station), where they occupied the building with tacit permission from the police. Speeches continued for the next hour. Though the police allowed and in fact encouraged reluctant protestors into the station with assurances of safety, there was still a general fear of police retaliation expressed by many of the people I spoke with. Despite the prospect of detention, or worse, the protestors were willing to risk their freedom to participate in a protest event. Risk is an inherent part of protest.

I tell this story to highlight a crucial aspect of political protest – the importance of risk. The readiness of protestors to sacrifice not only time, but also to put themselves in danger of state retaliation or repression is one of the keys to the symbolic and normative power that protest displays. As discussed in Chapter 2, courting arrest and physical harm has been a mainstay of protest in India since the Nationalist Movement. Like other movements before them, the Narmada Bachao Andolan commands a high degree of devotion on the part of its members, who have time and time again risked their material well-

62 *The Narmada Bachao Andolan*

being, and also their lives, to stop the Sardar Sarovar dam in Gujarat and secure fair rehabilitation and resettlement packages for displaced people.

For the past 22 years the NBA and its leader, Medha Patkar, have commanded state and popular attention through their sustained efforts against the hydro-electric development of the Narmada River in western India. The NBA is a key player in the shifting debate dealing with issues of environmentalism, development, displacement and human rights within India. The NBA also extends its presence beyond Indian borders through strong ties with international NGOs and environmental movements, helping to shed light on the consequences of large dam construction and other state-sponsored projects within the developing world as a whole. Both the NBA and Medha Patkar have attained a level of fame within the state and public sphere heretofore rare in India. Despite the high level of influence the NBA has attained within the Indian state, it has failed to reach either of its two primary goals – stopping or significantly changing the development plan for the Narmada River basin, and securing fair rehabilitation and resettlement for displaced people. During the course of its agitation against the state the NBA's tactics have delayed construction on numerous occasions, and were even the impetus behind the World Bank's decision to pull funding from the project. However, with regard to the project itself, the Indian state remains unmoved by the NBA's position.

I analyze 12-years of NBA mobilization from 1988 through 2000. During this period the NBA used the tactic of fasting to the death five times;[2] it also attempted deliberate drowning once. Since 2000 it has diversified its interests to include other areas of Indian policy, such as the effects of development and the environment.[3] In this chapter I closely analyze the first major fast conducted by the NBA, which took place in the winter of 1990 and 1991. This fast lasted for 21 days and was the centerpiece of a number of protests against the dam. I also examine the NBA's attempt to use *jal samadhi* in 1993. Though the NBA continues to use the tactic of fasting, none of its subsequent fasts are very different from the first event.

The controversies surrounding the development of the Narmada River Valley involve a number of different political actors. The particulars of the Narmada Development Plan (NDP) caused conflict among different states and government institutions within India, as well as inciting a long-term popular movement against the state. The issue of Narmada remains one of the most salient environmental concerns for the state today, and the debate surrounding the plan has influenced the way that people approach development, environmental policy, displacement and protest in India today. From the late 1980s onwards the NBA emerged as the most important actor to stand in opposition to the dam. A self-identified non-violent movement, the NBA and other affiliated movements continue to impact the debate surrounding environmental issues, despite losing the Narmada dams issue. The NBA and its protests against the state are a crucial case of anti-state mobilization within India. As one of the most important and programmatic social movements within India today it is essential to study and understand the NBA's use of suicide protest and the impact such protests have on contemporary Indian politics.

The first major fast to death by the NBA

In September 1989 the NBA sponsored a rally held in the small town of Harsud in Madhya Pradesh (MP). Reports claim that 25,000–60,000 people attended the rally: the *National Rally Against Destructive Development*. Sometimes called the "coming of age of the Indian environmental movement," (Baviskar 1995, p. 206) this protest articulated a new conception of development which challenged the notion of progress for progress's sake seemingly proposed by the state. Protestors chanted "*vikas chahiye, vinash nahi*" (we want development, not destruction) (Sangvai 2002, p. 54), indicating a need for the state to look at the possible negative consequences of large projects. After the Harsud protest the NBA had a clear mandate to act on behalf of those living in the 245 villages that faced being submerged upon completion of the dam – and the organization meant to use this mandate. Fresh from the success of the Harsud protest and other rallies, the NBA decided to intensify its agitation against the Central, Gujarat, and MP governments. In December 1990 a large group of activists, *adivasis* and landless laborers began a march from Nimar in MP called the *Jan Vikas Sangharsh Yatra* (march of the struggle for people's development). Their goal was to reach the construction site of the Sardar Sarovar Project (SSP), which was located in the neighboring state of Gujarat. Once there, the NBA hoped to disrupt construction of the dam. Most of the protestors were project-affected persons (PAPs) whose homes would be submerged once the SSP was completed. The march was massive, stretching over two kilometers (Baviskar 1995, p. 207). Having recently vowed to "get drowned if the projects on the Narmada came up and submerged lands, habitats and even lifestyles"[4] the protestors were stopped before they were able to cross into Gujarat. Meanwhile, pro-dam[5] proponents gathered on the other side of the border, determined to stop the procession from entering the state. Every day the 25 volunteers "with their hands tied, symbolizing their non-violent intent ... stepped forward as their names were called and, to the beating of tribal drums, crossed the border" between MP and Gujarat (Fisher 1995, p. 3). Despite their arrest, the NBA continued to send people over the border. Feeling the need for stronger action, seven members of the movement, including Patkar, began a fast to death, calling for the state to stop construction of the dam until a comprehensive review of the project could take place. This fast lasted for 21 days, and ended when counter-movement activists withdrew from the border. Though the Indian government did not directly respond to this fast, the World Bank did cite the fast as a justification for its decision to prepare an independent review of the project.

Is the 21-day fast, conducted over the winter of 1991, a success or a failure for the movement? The fast ended because counter-movement actors were

64 *The Narmada Bachao Andolan*

unwilling to risk the lives of the protestors, and it also precipitated the World Bank's withdrawal from the project. But the state did not respond to the fast in any real way, nor did it stop construction of the dam. Despite the World Bank reconsideration of the project, I do not consider the 1990–1991 fast and its aftermath as an example of long-term success for the movement. Not only did construction of the dam continue during the World Bank review of the project, it took another fast and attempts at deliberate drowning for the Indian state to conduct it's own review of the project. The fact that the 1990–1991 fast was soon followed by other suicide protest events illustrates its inability to provoke a long-term policy shift by the state.

History of the Narmada Development Plan

The Narmada is the fifth largest river in India and touches four western Indian states – Madhya Pradesh (MP), Gujarat, Maharashtra and Rajasthan – forming the border between many of those states. The Narmada forms an integral part of the literal and figurative landscape for those who live around it (Deegan 1995). The river originates, and is mostly located, within MP running westward into the Arabian Sea. The river basin is measured at about 100,000 square kilometers, and extends around the river and into the delta.[6] The Narmada was relatively untouched by the Raj, but did not remain so after Independence. In 1947 the central government commissioned a study of possible development strategies for the Narmada River basin. Conducted by the Central Waterways Irrigation and Navigation Commission (CWINC) this report was the state's first step towards harnessing the river. The CWINC mainly sought to determine the Narmada's potential for flood control, irrigation and expanded navigation on the river. Despite its innocuous beginnings, the CWINC report sparked a number of controversies that pitted different states against one another, and the center. Between 1955 and 1978 all conflicts surrounding the development of the Narmada basin centered on inter-state conflicts between the major players involved in the plan. Popular opposition against the movement was intermittent until the 1980s.

Inter-state conflict: 1961–1978

In 1955 the Government of India commissioned a study to examine the Narmada basin for its hydro-electric power potential. The commission suggested that a single large dam should be built, with construction to proceed in two stages. Administration and benefits would primarily be in the hands of the state of Gujarat, which took over official control of this dam in 1960.[7] Located on the western side of the river, the Navagam dam would fall within Gujarat's borders. In 1961 Jawarlahal Nehru traveled to the Narmada River and placed the first stone of the dam, which would be the only aspect of construction to materialize in 20 years. The biggest obstacle impeding construction was the dispute that quickly arose between the states of Gujarat and MP, which soon grew to include the states of Maharashtra and Rajasthan. Disagreements between these states centered on the particulars and cost of construction, as well as the division of benefits expected from the dam. The Navagam dam was designed to help Gujarat with irrigation and power issues. Other states on the Narmada, especially MP, disputed the singular benefit from the dam and demanded that the river be utilized to the advantage of all states along the basin, the largest of which was MP. The inter-state dispute was soon exacerbated by MP's refusal to ratify the 1963 Bhopal[8] agreement, which agreed to the construction of three dams and divided the monetary responsibilities between MP, Gujarat and the central government. Announcing the plan Dr K.L. Rao, the Union Minister for Water and Power, is quoted as saying: "[I]t [is] unfortunate that the Narmada, with its great flow of water, [has] remained unexploited so far. The proposed exploitation of its resources would prove more economical than any other river."[9] Though the Gujarat government supported the plan, MP was not willing to ratify the agreement. In response to MP's rejection of the Bhopal agreement the central government created a commission whose sole purpose was to create an equitable division of river's resources. The Narmada Water Resources Committee, usually called the Khosla Commission,[10] was created in 1964. According to court documents, the commission was asked to draw up a "master plan of the Master Plan for the optimum and integrated development of the Narmada water resources, the schedule of construction, and finally, to determine the reservoir levels for the dams themselves."[11]

Despite the Khosla Commission's clear mandate it was unable to broker an agreement between MP and Gujarat. However, the Commission did author the first comprehensive development scheme for the basin. The Commission's 1965 report outlined an approach to the problem of Narmada development that included the primacy of national interest over that of separate Indian states and introduced the development of the whole river, expanding the scope of earlier proposals. The Narmada Development Plan was to "provide for maximum benefits in respect of irrigation, power generation, flood control, navigation etc. irrespective of State boundaries."[12] The report suggested that irrigation should be the top priority of water development in India, over that of power, with particular focus on the predominantly arid regions of Gujarat and Rajasthan. The means to this large-scale irrigation project rested in the construction of 12 major dams over the length of the entire river. By default most were located within MP, with the Navagam remaining in Gujarat. The Navagam would be the terminal project and was suggested to be 500 Full Reservoir Level (FRL) about 455 meters in height, creating a *big dam* as defined by international standards.[13] This was seen as the optimum height to enable the highest volume of irrigation to the largest area of land. Big dams create higher water storage levels – a positive for regions that experience cycles of drought. However, the central government's attempt to create a comprehensive plan for the basin was not implemented. In a turnabout of previous events, this time Gujarat would not concede to the plan, claiming

66 *The Narmada Bachao Andolan*

that both MP and Maharastra's use of the river would impede its own ability to exploit the river.

It is striking that throughout the debates surrounding the Narmada's development, the environmental and human impacts of the project were rarely mentioned. None of the relevant actors involved in the development of the Narmada plan officially brought up the issue of how the dams would affect people already living on the banks of the river, other than to mention that individuals who were affected would be provided for. The inquiries into the relative cost or benefits of fewer or more dams, smaller or larger submergence zones, and differing reservoir heights, were relegated to issues of finance and power-sharing. The fact that each of these decisions directly impacted on a number of communities, and would permanently change the ecological structure of the region, seemed to be a secondary consideration for the Khosla Commission and the Governments of India, Gujarat and MP.

In response to the continued failure of MP and Gujarat to come to a mutually beneficial agreement the central government created the Narmada Water Disputes Tribunal Council (NWDTC) in 1968[14] to arbitrate the dispute. The NWDTC deliberated and studied the issue for ten years, handing down its judgment in 1979. The council provided the basic structure of the plan that has subsequently been carried out by the state. The NWDTC award primarily specified the dam height of the Sardar Sarovar Project (SSP), formerly known as the Navagam dam, and the division of cost and benefits between Gujarat, MP, Maharastra and Rajasthan. According to the NWDTC the Sardar Sarovar dam would remain at 455 FRL, which was seen as the optimum height for storage, irrigation, potable water and the production of energy. The cost of the dam would primarily be shouldered by Gujarat, though MP would also bear a part of the financial burden. The NWDTC also requested the creation of an inter-state commission to oversee construction of the dams, the newly formed Narmada Control Authority (NCA) which would monitor state compliance on all aspects of the award. Finally, the award divided both the costs and benefits of the Narmada plan among each relevant state. The allocation of resources was coupled with a large-scale plan for the river basin as a whole, which included 30 large dams, 135 medium-sized dams, and over 1,000 minor dams. The four largest dams were the SSD in Gujarat, the Narmada Sagar (which is now known as Indira Sagar), the Omkareshwar, and the Maheshwar, all of which are in MP. In order to offset costs, India approached the World Bank, which, in 1985, agreed to help fund the project. In return the Indian government would conduct an environmental and human impact report as construction of the dam commenced.

The project was considered to be unquestionably good for the state. The problem of what to do with people living in soon-to-be-submerged villages was a secondary issue. Both the NWDTC and the NCA understood that a rehabilitation and resettlement plan was needed for the project, but did not anticipate much resistance to it. Once the plan was announced the NCA was tasked with considering the practical considerations of displacement. The award stipulated that Gujarat would pay for those displaced within the state of MP, but no particulars regarding resettlement and rehabilitation, such as when and where these people would be moved, were addressed.

Soon after the award was handed down it became clear to the center that questions of resettlement and rehabilitation would not be as easy to deal with as had been previously thought. The SSP is expected to submerge "37,000 hectares of land in three states: Gujarat, Maharashtra, and MP ... Conservative estimates place the number of displaced at approximately 152,000 persons" (Tata Institute of Social Sciences 1997, p. 185). The high number of people in need of rehabilitation raised a number of questions that still concern most parties in charge of the dam. First, what type of compensation was appropriate for individuals within the submergence zone? Would land for land work? Or should the state give a lump sum monetary award? Would continued assistance be a better idea? Second, who would benefit from rehabilitation policy? The Narmada river valley, like many other regions in India, depends on unofficial claims to property. Many *adivasi* groups who had lived for generations in particular areas of the submergence zone had no proof of ownership or any official claim to the land, which disbarred many of these groups from consideration for rehabilitation (Patel 1997, p. 67). Finally, what, if anything, could the state do to mitigate the environmental degradation that would result from the NDP? At the time the centre evidenced a lack of understanding or care regarding the environmental changes that such a large dam project would create. Some common environmental concerns surrounding big dams include soil erosion, salinity and alkalinity, water pollution, the increased silting of reservoirs, seismic shifts, and of course the loss of plant and wildlife in the region (Goel and Prasad 2000, p. 47).

Emergence of protest: 1978–1988

From the early 1980s onwards it became increasingly difficult for the state to ignore the issue of human and environmental impacts of the Narmada Valley project, primarily due to growing opposition to the dam by activists living outside the region. First attempts to oppose the dam were not well organized; this can be attributed to the complex nature of economic, cultural, and caste affiliations within the valley. The Narmada Valley in MP was home to both large and small farmers, a number of *adivasi* groups, landless laborers and competing caste groups. The variegated nature of cultural, economic and ethnic differences hindered the creation of a mass organization that could oppose the state's plan for the valley. Initial actions against the plan were intermittent, though intense. For example, on August 19, 1978, a man jumped off the Khalghat Bridge close to Indore in MP, and into the Narmada River. Eyewitnesses to the suicide stated that the man shouted "that it was better to end the life now than to be submerged under the water when the Navagam dam was constructed."[15] Though shocking, this individual act of suicide did not have any measurable effect on the plan or the state as it was not embedded

68 *The Narmada Bachao Andolan*

within a larger social movement that could exploit it in support of its cause. Subsequent examinations of newspaper coverage following the incident show a complete lack of interest in the incident. In fact, there were no other reported protests against the dam for a number of years.

Four factors hindered the creation of a programmatic mass movement opposed to the dams. First, the complex history of the dam created a lack of awareness about the plan in general. As previously discussed, conflicts over the dam were limited to inter-institutional disputes, effectively leaving the general population outside the debate. Second, the complex ethnic and economic structure in the valley made it difficult for various groups to mobilize together. Third, there was a general lack of awareness inside and outside the valley about the consequences of the project; Amita Baviskar (1997, p. 201) discusses the fact that this was mostly due to a lack of government accountability:

> Although the government plans to drastically alter the lives of so many people with the Sardar Sarovar Project, it has not bothered to consult or even inform them about their fate ... Despite the large numbers of people affected, despite the enormity of the change in their lives, there is *no* government-sponsored system of information that respects the people's right to know. People glean scarce facts from informal conversations with the *patvari* (revenue official) or similar officials when they meet on other business.

Finally, the scope of the project itself hindered the creation of a single movement. The Narmada plan provided for dams in at least two states, and the sheer number of proposed dams made it difficult to identify a focal point for contention. Should the project as a whole be reconsidered, or should groups only oppose the major dams? Should protests occur in Gujarat or MP?

The first and most prominent social movement to act against the dam was the *Nimar Bachao Andolan* (Save Nimar Movement), named after a region located in MP that would be submerged as a result of the plan's implementation. This organization consisted mostly of small land and business owners, and was led by Congress (I) leader Arjun Singh. The Nimar Bachao Andolan did not necessarily want to stop the project, but was concerned with the issue of compensation for landowners. Though this goal would affect others living in the valley, the movement did not try to include different economic and social groups. The leadership of the movement was intimately tied to party politics within MP. Many viewed the movement as simply an attempt by the opposition Congress (I) to destabilize the ruling Janata Dal. This notion was born out as the movement dissipated as soon as Congress retook the state in the early 1980s (Baviskar 1997, p. 202). Besides the Nimar Bachao Andolan a few other groups tried to organize opposition to the dam, but none were able to harness mass support from those living in the valley; these included the *Narmada Ghati Navnirman Samiti* in MP, the *Narmada Dharangrast Samiti* in

Maharastra, and the *Narmada Asargrast Sangharsh Samiti* in Gujarat.[16] The creation of the NBA brought these forces together.[17]

By 1985 the situation in the valley was tense. Gujarat was preparing for construction of the SSP and activists from urban centers all over India were increasingly concerned about the implications of the project. Some activists began to travel to the valley in order to study the situation and help organize concerted opposition; they were active in forming the Narmada Bachao Andolan (NBA), the first organization able to create a sustained and mass resistance to the dam and policy surrounding it. Since its inception the NBA has utilized a variety of techniques in its fight against the dams – including suicide protest – and has had a great deal of short-term success. In fact the NBA was instrumental in forcing the World Bank to review the project, which ultimately led to the Bank pulling out of the project altogether. Despite support from domestic and international sources, and its ability to create short-term change, the NBA has been unable to create long-term policy shifts in its favor. I argue that the NBA's use of suicide protest has been integral in attaining short-term goals, but the manner and method of this suicide protest has hindered the movement's ability to generate long-term change.

The NBA: tactical depth, intensity, emotional appeals and political competition

The NBA is one of the longest running movements in India today. It has forged relationships with a number of environmental and human rights organizations both inside and outside India. In the last ten years it has turned its attention to other large state projects, and has helped shift the discourse on environmentalism and development within contemporary India towards a greater sensitivity to the ramifications of state projects.[18] Over the course of its campaign against the Narmada Development Plan (NDP), the NBA gained concessions from the state and other interested actors regarding the dam but could not accomplish its two main goals: (1) stopping, or significantly changing, the Narmada Development Plan; and (2) ensuring the creation of a comprehensive "land for land" rehabilitation scheme for project affected persons. One of the most dramatic methods that the NBA employs in its fight against the NDP is the use of suicide as a form of protest tactic. From 1988 to 2005 the NBA utilized fasting to the death on seven occasions, and deliberate drowning at least once.[19] Participants in these events include both the leadership and rank-and-file of the movement. Though the NBA's use of suicide has pressured the state into entering negotiations, and has even resulted in certain concessions, in contrast to the movement for the linguistic state of Andhra the NBA's use of suicide protest did not result in long-term policy change in its favor. What accounts for the differences between the NBA and Potti Sriamulu's fast for Andhra? Both of these movements act in similar ways, and in similar contexts, yet the NBA's use of suicide, while not a complete failure, has certainly not been a success. I believe that in this case the

70   *The Narmada Bachao Andolan*

key to the NBA's ineffective use of suicide protest can be traced to the critical issues of intensity and narration.

This book argues that four factors will increase the probability of tactic success: *tactical depth, intensity, emotional narratives*, and *levels of political competition*. As one or more of these factors are not present in the movement, the chances that suicide protest will create a policy shift in its favor decreases, though the state might accede to particular short-term movement goals. Similar to the movement for the linguistic state of Andhra, the NBA exhibits a high level of tactical depth and acts within a politically competitive environment. However, unlike the Andhra context none of the NBA's suicide actions have resulted death, evidencing a lack of intensity. It also constructed diffuse emotional narratives which did not adequately highlight the tactic.

Tactical depth

Tactical depth measures the number and type of tactics utilized by movements during their agitation against the state. Higher levels of tactical depth help to increase the likelihood for movement success. In particular, non-violent tactics are important to groups that use extreme forms of resistance; non-violent tactics will mitigate and moderate the movement's reputation with the state and the general population. Movements need to diversify their tactical strategies in order to walk the delicate line between radical action and serious negotiation with the state. In its long-term opposition to central government and other Indian states the NBA has exhibited a high degree of tactical depth by utilizing a variety of protest action types.

The NBA employs four broad categories of protest action in its movement against the state. First, it uses suicide protest in the form of fasting to the death and *jal samadhi*. Second, it uses direct mass action against the state which takes the form of marches, rallies, speeches and courting arrest. Third, the NBA has brought the issue of the Narmada dams and fair rehabilitation for displaced people to the Indian court system. Finally, the NBA puts pressure on the Indian state through its ongoing relationships with inter- and trans-national environmental movements and institutions. With all of these tactics the NBA has shown a facility for using innovative technologies, like the internet, to create awareness and muster support for separate campaigns and protest actions. The NBA displays flexibility in its approach to protest and the manner with which it uses these four tactics. Perhaps one of the greatest successes of the NBA to date has been an ability to simplify the issues at stake for a lay audience, ensuring that there is interest from the general public on the problems in the valley.

Direct action[20]

From the inception of the movement, direct protest action has been a mainstay for the NBA in its strategy against the Indian state. I define direct action as the mobilization of individuals within a movement in protest against the state or another institution. As such, direct action would include tactics such as rallies, marches, strikes or other forms of protest that are predicated on regular participation by movement members and leaders. Direct action serves three purposes for the NBA. First, events such as mass actions and rallies are designed to disrupt the normal working of the state, including construction of the dams. Disruption is also accomplished by the refusal of some people to leave their homes in the valley, which either hinders construction or provokes a response from the state. Second, direct action invigorates the populous backbone of the movement. Rallies, marches, sit-ins and other types of mass protest are designed by the movement to include both highly and moderately committed supporters. The Narmada River basin has become a highly politicized environment. Large protest events channel ephemeral support for the movement into tangible action. Third, events such as rallies and marches can signal the quantity (if not the quality) of the NBA's popular support. The NBA organized large protests involving people inside and outside the valley in an attempt to pressure the state. Like the movement for Andhra the NBA labels its brand of protest non-violent *satyagraha*, embedding the movement and its tactics within the rubric of non-violent action.

From 1978 to 1985 resistance to the project was fragmented and did not present a cogent challenge to the dam or its attendant policies. The variegated cultural and economic groups impacted by the dam were unable to form a singular response to the state's plan until the formation of the NBA in 1986. The origin and evolution of the NBA directly influences its style of protest. In 1985 social researcher and activist Medha Patkar traveled to the submergence zones located in Maharastra and MP on behalf of the Tata Institute. The lack of government disclosure concerning the details and impacts of the project upon those living within the zone concerned Patkar, who quickly began to gather support among locals (Baviskar 1995, p. 203; Patkar and Kathari 1995). Patkar and other activists moved into the valley to organize comprehensive opposition to the plan by bringing disparate groups together, resulting in the formation of the NBA. Initially the NBA only demanded fair rehabilitation and resettlement packages for people living in the submergence zone. However, the state's lack of response on this issue forced the movement to protest against the construction of the dam itself. Due to the enormity of the project, the young organization focused its attention on the two largest planned dams – the Sardar Sarovar Project and the Narmada Sagar on either side of the river – splitting the attention of the movement between Gujarat and MP.

As the start of construction of the dams drew near, the NBA took advantage of the specific context of the valley, turning everyday events into a form of protest. The most pointed tactic in the movement's arsenal was to have members of the movement continue to live their lives as they normally would, in effect refusing to cede the valley to the state. Those individuals who remained in the submergence zone were the most persistent check to the dams. As Baviskar (1997, p. 205) outlines:

72   *The Narmada Bachao Andolan*

Since 1988, the inhabitants of the submergence area have been demonstrating their determined refusal to move from their land. The last five years have been marked by continuous protest; no survey work related to the project has been allowed to proceed.

The NBA made the act of remaining in the affected area a direct form of protest against the state's policy. The NBA continues to use this practice, to the extent of standing in rising waters during the monsoon season, the so-called *jal samparan*. These acts are considered to be different from *jal samadhi* (deliberate drowning) as there is only a chance that protestors will die, whereas in the case of *jal samadhi*, if the event is carried out to its conclusion, actors are meant to die.[21] *Jal samparan* falls into the category of "courting arrest" since most of the activists taking part in it anticipate that the police will forcibly remove them from their homes. More than any other tactic, this type of civil disobedience would fall under the category of *satyagraha* – the type of protest Gandhi supported and used throughout the period of the Nationalist Movement.

The NBA also uses more traditional forms of direct action such as rallies, marches, *bandhs* (general strikes), *dharnas* (squatting on others' property), boycotts and demonstrations. These tactics have been employed by the movement since 1988, and are often coupled with suicide protest events. As previously discussed, the NBA's first major fast in 1991 was the culmination of a long march, and took place at the center of a sit-in and rally along the state border. Throughout this fast the NBA used symbolic acts to underscore the importance of the movement, the fast, and the consequences of the dam.

The NBA's use of direct action, both civil disobedience and more traditional forms, underscores its desire to be viewed as a traditional social movement organization. That is not to say that it doesn't employ innovative or extreme techniques in its campaign against the state, but those tactics are moderated by the use of non-violent forms of protest.

Court appeals

The NBA also contests within the Indian court system as part of its effort to stop or change the project. In the aftermath of Patkar and Amte's fast to the death in 1991, the World Bank and the Government of India both agreed to conduct a comprehensive independent review of the project. The World Bank complied; the Government of India did not. The Morse and Berger[22] review was released in 1992 and presented a major blow to pro-dam forces in Gujarat, MP and Maharashtra. Morse and Berger's report agreed with the NBA on most major points of contention, including the lack of proper investigation into the environmental and human impacts of the project, as well as the probable inability of the Indian government to provide adequate rehabilitation and resettlement for PAPs. The Bank seemed particularly concerned with popular opposition to the dam, citing the strength of the NBA

The Narmada Bachao Andolan   73

as a reason to pull out of the project as a whole. Pro-dam forces suffered a setback once the World Bank's independent review of the project was released in 1992. This review, which was conducted over 10 months, found that issues of resettlement, rehabilitation and opposition were integral to the project, stating:

> Even though proponents describe the Sardar Sarovar as the most studied and least implemented project in India, we do not agree. The Projects may well be the most talked about in India, but the fact is that their human and environmental consequences have not been studied, and their engineering, design, and operation would profit from further analysis. There is a need to consider Sardar Sarovar in the social and environmental context of the Narmada Valley as a whole, to consult, inform, and involve the people affected by the Projects throughout the Narmada valley ... The opposition, especially in the submergence area, has ripened into hostility, so long as this hostility endures, progress will be impossible except as a result of unacceptable means.
> (*Sardar Sarovar Projects Independent Review, 1992*, p. 356)

The review cited both social and environmental areas of concern regarding the handling of the SSP. With regard to the social costs, the review indicated that the Indian government failed to adequately assess the environmental and human impacts of the SSP, particularly identifying the issue of displacement as a problem area. The review also concluded that the state had failed in its duty to inform PAPs of SSP's implications, which in turn created a high level of public opposition to the project as a whole. The review indicated that India's poor history of policy implementation would be an obstacle for the creation of a timely displacement and rehabilitation plan. The review was also concerned about the environmental impacts of the project, stating that the state had not considered the possible environmental ramifications (Khagaram 2004, p. 128). As a result the Bank requested that both the Indian and Gujarat governments fulfil certain conditions in order for funding to continue, giving both institutions a deadline of March 1993.

It was soon clear that neither the Indian nor the Gujarat governments were going to comply with the Bank's deadline, leading the Government of India to forego the remaining funds allocated to the SSP and other Narmada projects in 1985. The decision to reject World Bank funding caused the Gujarat government to seek out alternative sources of funding for the SSP.[23] Once both the Gujarat and central governments reaffirmed their commitment to the SSP, the NBA began to agitate for the state to comply with correct environmental assessment procedures and a further review of the project itself.

The NBA responded to continued construction of the dam, as well as building support from the international community, with increased agitation against the central and Gujarat governments. In June 1993 the NBA began a *satyagraha* to coincide with the monsoon season, and the possible

74 *The Narmada Bachao Andolan*

submergence of a number of villages affected by the SSP. At the center of this protest was an 18-day fast conducted by Medha Patkar and others. In addition, a number of villagers formed a "save or drown" squad, which vowed to drown themselves in the rising waters of the river if the federal government did not step in and review the project's environmental and human impacts.

The fast, and the possibility of a mass drowning, ended with Water Minister V.C. Shukla's assurance that the state would hold talks with the NBA, and that construction would stop during those talks.[24] The talks resulted in the creation of the Five Member Group (FMG) in August 1993. The FMG would conduct an independent domestic review of the project. The history of the FMG was controversial from the start. Both the NBA and the government of Gujarat were unsure of the FMG's authority, but for different reasons. The NBA was worried about the FMG's narrow purview, and wanted a high level of specificity within the group's mandate. Once these issues were resolved the NBA cooperated with the group's investigation. Meanwhile, "the Government of Gujarat questioned the right of the (central) government to set up the group at all and boycotted the FMG"[25] throughout the process. Later, Gujarat contested the review in the state's Supreme Court. Additionally, the FMG's authority to conduct a review was soon called into question by the Ministry of Water Resources, which stated in Parliament that the tribunal award barred any review of the project until 2024.[26] Despite these attempts to block it, the FMG prepared a report that was submitted to the Ministry of Water Resources in July 1994, and conducted a further review which was submitted to the Indian Supreme Court later that year.

Throughout the duration of the FMG's investigation, construction of the dam continued unabated. The Gujarat Supreme Court barred the FMG's initial report from public dissemination. These two issues, and the project itself, formed the crux of the NBA's appeals to India's Supreme Court in 1994. Based on articles 14 and 21 of the Indian Constitution, the NBA claimed that the Narmada Valley Project interfered with the human rights of PAPs, and that the Indian and other governments had not complied with agreed upon stipulations surrounding the project itself.[27] Court arguments proceeded over the course of two hearings held in 1995 and 1996. In 1997 the court issued an indefinite stay on construction of the dam, though this was ignored by the state. The court made its final ruling in 2000, in favor of the state. Full force construction proceeded, ending in completion of the 455-foot dam in 2007.

International pressure

The NBA is one of the first movements in India to have actively participated in an international network of environmental movements and activists. It has created and sustained ties with trans-national anti-dam and environmental organizations, while also sponsoring anti-Narmada groups in other countries. Finally, the NBA has also made direct appeals to international funding agencies, such as the World Bank and other states, in its effort against the dam. These three strategies have helped to put pressure on the Indian state, as well as international investors in the SSP. The international dimensions to this issue are the result of a growing awareness of environmentalist issues within developed and developing countries, as well as the particular problems that attend the construction of major dams and the development of natural resources. The NBA evolved within an international community of environmental activists and scholars who raised concern over the consequences of large state-sponsored projects and notions of "progress."

After Independence in 1947 Nehru and other leaders decided to implement a series of large development projects that they hoped would change the industrial and economic landscape of the nation. Nehru's oft-repeated statement that "dams are India's new temples" underlines the importance these projects had, not only for the material well-being of the state, but also for the perceived status of the newly formed country. India wanted to be a major player on the world stage, and rapid development would be one pathway to that standing. India was not alone in the desire to attain status through progress.[28] Unfortunately many of these projects, in India and other places, did not prove to be the magical key to respect and power within the international community. Controversies surrounding these projects occurred in conjunction with a rise in environmental awareness in developing countries in the 1970s and 1980s. Patkar and other movement leaders of the NBA forged linkages with similar movements in other contexts. Together these disparate organizations spurred the creation of the World Commission of Dams, in which Patkar participated for a number of years. Concerns over the issue of state-sponsored dams created a worldwide group of activists who shared techniques and scientific research on the issue. The importance of these linkages highlights one basic reality of major state-sponsored projects in the developing world – funding. Most big dams rely on international donors. The Gujarat state government, the Indian government, the World Bank and Japan jointly funded the SSP. The ability to engage and support an international community of activists in opposition to dams was crucial for movements that fought on a number of different fronts. While the NBA was able to engage with the World Bank in India, the reasons behind the Japanese pulling out of the project were in part dictated by international pressures and domestic organizations in Japan. Relations between the NBA and other environmentalist organizations were not just resources for the movement, but were specific tactics used to place pressure on the state. The NBA's ability to be a part of a global anti-dam, environmentalist movement helped to legitimize the movement and its agenda. Part of the state's rhetoric in supporting the dam was to appeal to notions of progress, with the image of Western development as its goal.

Not only did the NBA make concerted efforts to build relationships with existing environmentalist and social justice organizations, it also created corollary anti-Narmada organizations in other states such as "Friends of the NBA," which is based in the USA. These organizations were able to actively pressure the US and Indian governments,[29] as well as provide material and

76 *The Narmada Bachao Andolan*

technological support for the movement. The NBA also reaches out to different organizations that share similar worldviews, or have helped to create related groups in other contexts. These strategies have helped the NBA in its pursuit of an end to the dams. First, by deliberately placing itself into a global consortium of environmentalist organizations the NBA hopes to be viewed as more legitimate. Second, the presence of other NBA groups in the West lends technological and monetary support that it may not have had access to had it only focused on Indian members of the movement. In addition to creating supportive movements in other contexts, the NBA often directly agitated in other countries so that they in turn would put pressure on the Indian government. For example, in 1989 the US Congress called for hearings into the project. Patkar and others from the NBA and the valley testified at those hearings (Udall 1995, p. 211), impacting World Bank policy and raising awareness of the issue in other countries. Since then Patkar and others in the NBA have continued to lecture and testify in other countries, directly shaping the funding options of many investors into large-scale projects.

The NBA's use of direct action, court appeals and links to international organizations legitimizes and energizes the movement in and outside India. High levels of tactical depth are integral to the possible success of suicide protest. The NBA's use of multiple tactics has helped to engender short-term change. However, the presence or absence of different tactics is not the only factor that affects political outcomes. For the NBA, failure can in part be explained by how it chose to utilize suicide protest.

Intensity

Though one might expect death to be a forgone conclusion with suicide protest, this is not always the case. Suicide actions can be stopped before the death of the actor. This is particularly relevant in the case of fasting to the death since death from starvation takes a long period of time. Unlike other movements that use suicide protest, suicide events conducted by the NBA have not ended in the death of the actors. Even when the NBA uses tactics that do not rely on slow death, the event reaches that conclusion. With the case of *jal samadhi* in 1993, the "sacrificial squad" was prepared to die but gave the state a number of days to respond to the threat. I argue that the lack of death, or low intensity, is one of the reasons why the tactic has not led to long-term success for the NBA, though the tactic does aid in achieving short-term goals for the movement. People have died in the course of the NBA's mobilization against the state, but these few deaths were not the result of planned, political suicides, but rather the unintended result of repressive state action or other movement mobilization.

The first question to be asked with regard to the NBA's history of fasting is: are these acts really suicide protest at all? Or, should they be defined as hunger strikes where protestors have no intention of dying? I differentiate between the term *fasting* and *hunger strike* to indicate differing levels of intentionality. Fasting is an indefinite act, whereas hunger strikes have a previously announced endpoint. The NBA uses both hunger strike and fasting in its overall campaign against the state; however, it acknowledges that there is a qualitative difference between the two tactics; for a "three or four day fast – the government will never respond."[30] Simply because an indefinite fast ends before the death of the actor does not mean that the act was not a fast to the death; it is a question of intention. Are members of the NBA actually prepared to die for their cause? Based on interviews with activists who have fasted, and eyewitness accounts (Fisher 1995) of some of those fasts, it seems clear that NBA activists are indeed ready and willing to die. When I asked an informant what it was like when they began a fast, they replied: "In the moment we challenge ourselves, we are committed and want to express our commitment ... the fast is special and must be taken to its end."[31] In deciding whether or not to begin a fast to the death the NBA first decides if fasting is the only option left to it in furtherance of whatever campaign it is engaged in. Then it presents the idea to the larger group, who help to determine the tactic's efficacy at that juncture.[32]

The fast of 1991 was the result of serious deliberation by the NBA at the protest site. Prior to this episode Patkar had only fasted once before, for eight days. He described the reasoning behind this fast in an oral narrative describing the history of resistance in the valley:

> On the one hand, we had to retain the moral plane of our struggle and on the other, to express the ultimate commitment, to also appeal to our own conscious, to carry on and show the necessary perseverance and also appeal to the people of our country and the world. We thought that the important and peacefully moral nonviolent weapon that we could have then was a fast. And so, seven persons fasted for twenty-one full days.
> (Patkar and Kothari 1995, p. 166)

The 1991 fast was a resolute attempt by the NBA to stop construction of the dam through the use of "moral pressure" on the state. The NBA chose seven members to fast to the death: Patkar himself, Shatiben, Laxmiben, Khaja Bhai, Mathur Bhai, Devram Bhai and Meghnath. "The [fasters] lay on mattresses by the side of the road, determined to fast until the government agreed to talks that would lead to a review of the SSP" (Fisher 1995, p. 2). The 1991 fast became a symbol of the NBA's willingness to die in the face of an unresponsive state, and sparked support in and outside the valley. However, the action could not create direct political change in favor of the movement.

The long duration of fasting provides the opportunity for movement and state to engage in negotiations, which makes it distinct from other types of suicide protest. However, the NBA does not only use fasting; it has also used deliberate drowning on at least one occasion. Surprisingly this event also did not end in the death of the actor. As previously discussed, according to the NBA there is a difference between what the NBA call *jal samparan* versus *jal*

78 *The Narmada Bachao Andolan*

samadhi. The NBA uses *jal samparan* on a regular basis, when villages are in danger of submergence due to monsoon floods. In this act, villagers will stand and face the waters, sometimes until it reaches their chins, in defiance of state orders to vacate the area. These events have usually ended with arrest and forcible expulsion from their villages. Though acts of *jal samparan* are dramatic and could end in death for those engaging in it, leaders of the NBA do not consider this to be the same level of sacrifice as *jal samadhi*, which entails protestors throwing themselves into the river.[33]

In 1993 the NBA took part in negotiations with the Center to create a domestic independent review of the SSP – the Five Member Group. However, dissatisfied with Five Member Group's review and the partial submergence of the town of Manibeli in Maharashtra, the NBA stepped up its mobilization against the state; some members of the movement went on a fast in Bombay, and the first *jal samparan* was called in July in Manibeli.[34] However, V.C. Shukla, the Minister for Water at the time, seemed unmoved. The NBA felt the need for a different type of action in order to garner more attention. As one leader of the NBA relates:

> Logically [it] came to that (*jal samadhi*). [The state] was not ready to listen to us. We had taken every challenge, so we decided to challenge [the state] in the valley through *satyagraha*. We accepted [that we might] lose people. There were two [sacrifice] squads, if something happened to the first squad then the second would die. No one could have stopped us, they were completely secret plans, [we] were underground from July 7 to August 6. [We] were completely prepared to die.[35]

Despite their readiness, no members of the "sacrifice squads" actually died. Activists did get as far as standing on the banks of the river, waiting for word from the state; but when this came the action was called off, a disappointing end for the journalists who had traveled to the site.[36] Shukla met with Patkar in response to her demands. I consider this to be an actual attempt to use suicide protest, not simply the threat of possible suicide action, due to the fact that the NBA began the protest action. Instead of a quick action designed to amaze, the NBA proceeded with this *jal samadhi* slowly, allowing the event to gain media and state attention.

Why did both the fast of 1991 and the *jal samadhi* of 1993 fail to create tangible political change in favor of the movement? Like the Andhra movement, the NBA aligned itself with Gandhian techniques and beliefs; it also had the support of a large and dedicated population which supported the use of fasting as a tactic. However, suicide protest has not worked for the NBA. I believe that the lack of intensity is one crucial reason behind the NBA's failure to use suicide protest effectively. At heart, suicide protest is a shock to those who witness it. While it is true that groups using suicide protest must show the ability to rationally negotiate with the state through high levels of tactical depth, the method loses its potency if it is continually stopped before death occurs. After dealing with ten instances of fasting to the death since 1991 the state knows that protestors will stop if small concessions are made. Sriramulu's death was the catalyst for casual supporters of Andhra to become militant; the state does not want to contend with a martyred hero, and the NBA does not provide one.

Emotional narratives

Movements increase the likelihood of successful suicide protest if they can establish resonant emotional narratives regarding their use of the tactic. Movements must direct these discourses towards active and potential members of the movement as well as towards the state. I argue that emotions such as pride and sympathy will result from the creation of intimate bonds with both the act and perpetrator of suicide protest. Movements actively attempt to transmit the emotions of shame towards the state. If movements can direct the type of emotional responses that result from suicide protest then those events will be much more likely to produce political outcomes in favor of the movement.

The NBA does construct emotional narratives, but they do not highlight the importance of the tactic in and of itself, rather the movement as a whole. The particular way in which the NBA uses suicide protest illustrates an important aspect of suicide protest in general: martyrs are important. Though Patkar is synonymous with the NBA and has become a symbol for many people, she is not a martyred hero for the cause. In suicide protest the aftermath of the event can be just as important as the event itself. However, the low intensity fasting used by the NBA undercuts this important moment in the narrative of suicide events. I argue that the NBA's failure to utilize suicide protest for long-term change can in part be traced to a diffuse narrative, and an inability to identify a unique martyr for the movement.

Pride and sympathy

The emotions of pride and sympathy are linked to familiarity with an object. In the case of fasting to death the lengthy duration of the event can help to create a sense of intimacy between the actor and the movement. The NBA used the 1991 fast to familiarize members of the movement with Patkar and other leaders. The fast took place out in the open; Patkar and the others often spoke with reporters and were located at the center of the larger protest action. The setting and location of the fast allowed members of the movement easy access to those people who were sacrificing themselves for it. This is clearly the most direct way in which the movement was able to create affective ties between the fasters and other members during the fast itself. In addition to creating space for activists and other members of the movement to get to know one another, the circumstances surrounding the fast of 1991 provided the opportunity for many people

80   *The Narmada Bachao Andolan*

to directly experience types of starvation in sympathy with those on the fast. During the course of the 1991 fast a number of supporters carried out supportive fasts to share the experience with Patkar, all of which demonstrated to the state a high level of commitment. Though supportive fasts are of finite duration, by using them the NBA can share the visceral aspects of fasting with a large number of people who no longer have to imagine what it is like to starve.

The setting, staging, and media coverage of the 1991 fast allowed current and potential members of the movement to get to know the leaders and the feelings associated with fasting, which was important to the movement as a whole. However, the fast itself was obscured by the immensity of the protest action as a whole. The ritualistic crossing of the border into Gujarat that happened every day (only to be followed by arrests), when added to other aspects of a 21-day rally (songs, chanting, slogans)[37] diluted the message of the fasts. The NBA makes too many emotional appeals, and does not allow the public to concentrate on particular acts. This is in direct contrast to Sriramulu's fast, during which time all other protest actions were suspended. By the time Patkar and others started on their attempt of *jal samadhi* in 1993, intimacy between protestors and other members of the movement was a foregone conclusion; Patkar was the symbol of the movement and many felt as though they already "knew" her. Both the fast of 1991 and the *jal samadhi* in 1993 are clearly acts that are couched in emotional and symbolic terms. Patkar chaining a rock to her feet and standing by a river waiting to throw herself in[38] is an image that will resonate in the public sphere. Unfortunately, while the NBA succeeds in creating a level of familiarity with both the actor and the act of suicide protest, these emotions are sometimes drowned out by all of the other appeals directed towards the public. The more often the movement uses this tactic, the less it seems to mean.

Shame

The NBA, like other non-violent social movements, actively tries to shame the government into negotiation and concession. As with the fast for a separate Andhra, the NBA identifies a failure in Indian democracy as the reason behind the need for suicide protest.[39] The NBA directs this appeal to the state in two ways; first by keeping the decision to conduct suicide protest a democractic one. Before deciding to use fasting or another form of suicide action the NBA will dicsuss the matter openly among members, and come to a decision collectively;[40] a direct contrast to the state's own dealings with the movement. Second, like Sriramulu before, the NBA particularly highlights the fact that these acts are conducted as a last resort.

The weakness in the NBA's emotional narrative lies in the lack of clarity surrounding the events themselves. I believe that there are three reasons for this. First, the movement does not only talk about suicide protest in emotional terms; all aspects of protest are used in this way. Second, the frequency with which the movement uses suicide protest makes the tactic less and less shocking, and therefore less powerful. Finally, lack of intensity makes it impossible for the movement to use suicidal actors as martyred symbols for the cause. In the case of Andhra it was clear that the aftermath of the fast was just as important as the fast itself. The ability of Telegu speakers to use Sriramulu's image as a rallying cry was crucial for the success of the movement. Though Patkar represents the NBA and creates familial ties with the movement[41] she is not a martyr. Suicide protest's power lies in its ability to translate and embody pain and sacrifice within a few individuals. As Gandhi states (1972, p. 174): "[A]ny fast must require some risk, otherwise it has no meaning. It must involve torture of the flesh." The NBA's use of fasting does involve pain and risk; however as it continues to use the tactic the state continues to circumvent the symbolic power of the act itself.

Level of political competition

The final factor that can affect the outcome of suicide protest is the level of real and perceived political competition that exists within the state. I measure competition by determining the number and strength of opposition parties within the government. As the number of viable opposition parties grows states will be more politically open – and possibly more willing to negotiate with movements and factions. If suicide protest occurs within politically competitive environments it is more likely that movements will be able to put a foot in the door and bargain with the state. The case of the NBA is interesting in that the movement contends with two different governments, though they are related to one another: the Government of India and the Government of Gujarat. I argue that despite the fact the NBA was acting within a politically open context, conflicts between the central and state governments mitigated the NBA's ability to access that openness.

The early 1990s was a volatile moment in Indian democracy. At the center V.P. Singh's Janata Party formed a coalition government in 1990, only to see it fall a short time later. Congress, the BJP, the Janata Party, CPI (M) and CPI were all contending to take or share power with one another. Additionally, in 1991 the Congress government decided to pursue a policy of economic liberalization, which would shift the previous 40 years of economic policy. Political parties, social movements, interest groups and Indian states all contended for increased power and resources. The central state was vulnerable to different forces, allowing the NBA the opportunity to negotiate and bargain for concessions.

Meanwhile, the Gujarat government was much less open and competitive, especially when it came to issues surrounding Narmada. At that time Chimanbhai Patel was Chief Minister of Gujarat, a member of Janata Dal, and then later the Congress parties. He, his government, and opposition parties in Gujarat took a hard line position vis-à-vis the SSP and mobilization

82　*The Narmada Bachao Andolan*

against it.[42] Relations between Gujarat and the center were strained over the SSP and implementation of policies surrounding it.

The NBA shifted its campaign away from an unresponsive state government to instead focus mobilization on the national level and on international donors. Though the NBA acted within a fairly politically competitive environment the fact that the SSP was mostly under the jurisdiction of Gujarat made it harder for it to effect substantial change in the project.

Conclusion

The NBA is one of the most powerful environmental movements working in India today. Though it has not been able to create long-term policy change in its favor it has been able to materially affect the Narmada Valley Projects. When asked directly if it felt that fasting was a useful tool in its repertoire a leader of the NBA responded that "the tactic had been successful." Despite this statement it is clear that the NBA has not been able to turn suicide protest into real change. I believe this failure lies in *how* the NBA chooses to use suicide protest, not the fact that they *do* use it. Suicide protest can work, but the public and the state must perceive it in particular ways.

The NBA illustrates an important aspect of suicide protest. Groups that use it must balance between mitigating the negative aspects of the event, often achieved through tactical depth, and highlighting the positive aspects of the tactic through intensity and emotional narratives. Unlike the Andhra Movement, the NBA suppressed the impact of the tactic, which made it less effective. In the next chapter we examine the Anti-Reservations Movement, whose use of self-immolation failed to create any type of political transformation.

Notes

1 The term *adivasi* refers to the tribal population who are settled throughout central India. The so called "tribal belt" includes the states of Jharkhand, MP, Maharastra and others. In this project I will use the terms "tribal" and "*adivasi*" interchangeably.
2 This account only includes fasts that were labeled "indefinite." A number of hunger strikes were utilized during this period, but these are not placed in the same category as fasts to death. Between 2000 and 2005 there were at least three other fasts (Interview with NBA leader, December 18, 2005, New Delhi). Finally, Medha Patkar again fasted in 2006 for fair rehabilitation policies in New Delhi.
3 The NBA acknowledges that it now proposes a more general agenda. In the last two years it has issued alerts on issues such as the proposed Tata Car factory in Singur, West Bengal, and the ramifications of other dam projects in India, while also bringing attention to the issue of Narmada (NBA press releases 2006–07, online, available at: http://narmada.org/nba-press-releases/)
4 Mahesh Vijapurkar, "A March Dammed," Frontline, January 19–February 1, 1991, p. 99.
5 The Chief Minister of Gujarat, Chinambhai Patel, called the SSP "the lifeline of Gujarat," (*Times of India*, April 16, 2012), Gujarat being a region which routinely suffers from water shortages. The NBA's decision to focus attention on the SSP

spurred the creation of intense counter-movements in Gujarat, such as the Narmada Samarthan Abhiyan. This and other movements have been able to bring together a wide range of social and economic groups in support of the dam, and have tried to breach the divide between middle class farmers and *adivasi* groups, though they have not had much success. Pro-dam forces have stated their willingness to "lay down their lives for *mata Narmadey*," (mother Narmada) but as yet have not attempted to do so (Mukta 1990, p. 2300).

6 All figures are from Writ of Petition to the Supreme Court (©) No. 319 of 1994: Judgment.

7 In 1960 Bombay state (formerly Presidency) was divided into the states of Maharashtra and Gujarat.

8 Named after the city where the plan was developed, the capital of the Madhya Pradesh.

9 Times of India, November 18, 1963, p. 1. "Narmada Valley Development: Gujarat & M.P. Reach Accord on Plans."

10 Named after Dr A.N. Khosla, former head of the CWINC.

11 Writ of Petition to the Supreme Court: 3, op. cit,

12 Ibid., p. 4.

13 FRL stands for full reservoir levels, and indicates the height of the dam. As the FRL increases so too does the size of the potential reservoir of water produced by the dam. According to the International Commission of Large Dams a "large" dam measures at least 15 meters in height, while a "big" dam would be 150 meters in height. Based on this classification the SSP is considered a "big" dam. But I have seen it referred to as a major dam as well.

14 Members were not appointed until 1972, and comprised mostly jurists from around the country and some technical experts in the fields of hydrology, agriculture and engineering.

15 *Times of India (Bombay)* August 20, 1978, p. 1 "Man Ends Life Over Award."

16 One other prominent group was the Arch-Vahini, located in Gujarat. While this organization has worked with the NBA, it was not incorporated into it. From the early 1990s the NBA and the Arch-Vahini have not worked together due to differing approaches to the issue of the dam (Patkar and Kothari 1995, p. 162).

17 Tehelka, December 17, 2005, p. 22. "Ma Rewa Tera Paani Amrit," Shivani Chaudhry.

18 Interview with Ramaswamy Iyer, December 16, 2005.

19 Interview with NBA leader, December 18, 2005.

20 The types of protest I place into the category of direct action would fall into the rubric of *satyagraha* as utilized by Gandhi during the Nationalist Movement. In fact, the NBA often discusses these acts using that term. However, unlike Sriramulu's movement for Andhra, the NBA protests are distinct enough for it to be a mistake to label them as *satyagraha*.

21 According to my interview with a prominent leader of the NBA the terms *jal samparan and jal samadhi* are often confused by the media and scholars. Despite the similarity of these two acts, the NBA does not put them in the same category (Interview with NBA leader, December 18, 2005).

22 Titled after the two main authors of the text, Bradford Morse and Thomas Berger.

23 For example, the government of Gujarat began to actively seek donations from Gujratis living abroad, affording non-resident Indians (NRIs) one of the first opportunities to invest in Indian projects (Khagaram 2004, p. 131).

24 Interview with NBA leader, December 18, 2005.

25 Interview with Ramaswamy Iyer, member of the FMG New Delhi India, December 16, 2005.

84 *The Narmada Bachao Andolan*

26 Government of India, August 1993.

27 Writ of Petition to the Supreme Court: 1–2, op. cit.

28 Khagram (2004) discusses conflicts over big dams in China, South Africa and Brazil, all of which used these projects as stepping stones towards achieving heightened international status.

29 See Keck and Sikkink's (1998) description of the boomerang effect.

30 Interview with NBA leader, December 18, 2005.

31 Ibid.

32 Ibid.

33 Ibid.

34 Manibeli's submergence came about as a result of the dam, which at that point was 60 meters high, and the monsoon season. Twenty-seven villagers from Manibeli were arrested after their attempt at *jal samparan*. It was reported: "When the flood came, Keshubhai's family, like the inhabitants of 15 other houses in this part of Manibeli decided to carry the NBA slogan 'Doobenge par hatenge nahin' (we will drown rather than shift) to its logical conclusion. The police, convinced that people would start running uphill the moment water entered their houses stood by for some time. It was only when the villagers stood in groin deep water that they intervened forcefully" (*Frontline*, September 10, 1993, pp. 106–9. "The Sardar Sarovar Project, Manibeli Revisited," R. Padmanabhan.).

35 Ibid.

36 Frontline. August 27, 1993. "The Sardar Sarovar Project, Beyond the Deadline," Praveen Swami.

37 Interview with NBA leader, December 18, 2005.

38 *Times of India* (Bombay), August 7, 1993, p. 1 and 13 by Meena Menon "Medha Calls off 'Jal Samparan'."

39 Interview with NBA leader, December 18, 2005.

40 Ibid.

41 From my observations, many members of the movement call Patkar "*didi*," or "older sister."

42 Frontline, September 10, 1993, pp. 106–9. "The Sardar Sarovar Project, Manibeli Revisited," R. Padmanabhan.

5 Failure of the tactic
The Anti-Reservation Movement

In 1990 over 100 young people killed or attempted to kill themselves throughout India. These students were protesting the adoption of expanded reserved spaces for low castes in public sector jobs, a move which many of the protestors felt was a direct attack on their own future livelihoods. Despite the relatively short lifespan of the movement, these students and their supporters caused much damage and disruption in a number of major cities throughout India. In many ways they fulfilled a primary consideration for a number of social movements; the ability to disrupt normal life so that people will pay attention to the issues surrounding the movement. However, unlike other movements we have discussed, the students of the Anti-Reservation Movement (ARM) were not able to parlay their disruptive tactics into actual policy change in their favor. In this chapter[1] I examine ARM's use of suicide protest and in doing so I explore the nature of social movement "failure." ARM demonstrates a number of necessary, but not sufficient, conditions of the tactical approach to movement success. While active it deployed over 130 acts of suicide protest[2] (Kumar 1992). Despite (or possibly because) of the high number of actual and threatened deaths, student protestors lost their fight against Mandal's implementation.

ARM's failure to transform their use of suicide protest into either short-term or long term success can be attributed to an interplay of different movements and political issues. Through the lens of the tactical approach, it can be seen that ARM only demonstrated one of the four significant factors for movement success discussed in this book– intensity. The emphasis on the death of these suicide protesters, coupled with a lack of emotional narration and a comprehensive agitational strategy served to focus attention more on the method of mobilization, suicide, than on the cause itself. A case of missing the forest for the trees. The movement's failure is not simply due to the fact that they did not demonstrate tactical depth, but that its specific lack of this was coupled with very high levels of intensity and few attempts at construction of an emotional narrative in a politically complex arena. This chapter reveals how the four critical factors of the tactical approach are interdependent and layered, and may work together to make suicide protest a hindrance, not a help, for movements. Most important, the failure of this series

86 *The Anti-Reservation Movement*

of self-immolations reveals the ways that suicide protest can become synonymous with violence and extreme action, in contrast to the other instances of suicide protest we have already discussed.

Before I begin my analysis of the issues and events surrounding the 1990 Anti-Reservation Movement, I discuss the inclusion of this case in this book and why it is important to study movement failure. Defining movement failure can be just as problematic as defining movement success. As discussed in Chapter 1, there are a number of competing understandings of what can constitute both the success and failure of social movements and protest. For the purposes of this book I treat the inability of the movement to achieve its stated goals as failure. ARM, while effective on some levels, was unable to capture direct policy change in its favor. It is important to include an analysis of this negative case for a number of empirical and theoretical reasons. First, ARM was a very well-known and dramatic case of suicide protest in India. Second, it has been relatively under-examined within literature on movements in general. Finally, this movement is important for understanding the limits of both suicide protest and the tactical approach to movement success. The relative success of suicide protest is dependent on four crucial factors, which means that it may fail more than it may succeed. To understand the power of suicide protest we need to truly dig into how it can fail as a tactic. The inclusion of this case exposes the ways that suicide protest may be a detriment to movements, especially regarding the importance of intensity in suicide protest.

Caste and reservations in India

The political history of caste and reservations in India is complex. In the next section I briefly analyze the development of caste-based reservations within the Indian Constitition and the deployment of those reservations within the Indian polity. The caste system in India has traditionally been seen as a system of categorization for people that somehow can be viewed as simultaneously rigid and fluid.[3] The importance of caste affiliation varies from region to region in India. Despite the fragmented nature of the practice of caste, caste identifications have become one of the most important within Indian politics. The origins of that salience began early on. Under the Raj, caste groups began to organize politically in order to gain access to resources. The British were the first to implement reservations for schedule castes (*dalits*) in an effort to overturn traditional group-based discriminatory practice. Though their attempts to change cultural practices through economic shifts were not very successful, the concept of reservations was not forgotten. The untouchable community was largely ignored at the start of the Nationalist Movement. However, as I discussed in Chapter 2, under the leadership of Dr B.R.Ambedkar, *dalits* began to agitate for a larger role under the British and within the movement.

After Independence, Ambedkar's position on the Constituent Assembly made it clear that the new state was serious about finding a solution to the problems of caste discrimination. The Preamble and Article 14 of the Indian Constitution states:

> Inequality ill-favors fraternity and unity and remains a dream without fraternity – so also the other objectives of the preamble cannot be realized without affirmative action to reduce inequality ... Among others, the concept of equality before the law contemplates minimizing the inequalities in income and eliminating the inequalities in status, facilities, and opportunities not only amongst individuals but also amongst groups of people ... including in particular the Scheduled Castes and Scheduled Tribes and to protect them from social injustice and all forms of exploitation.[4]

Thus, the Indian Constitution codified the need for the state to redress historical forms of inequality within political and social life. One method that was implemented was the creation of reserved spaces for dalits within public education and employment. Despite its good intentions the reservation system has been met with controversy from all sides of this issue.

By the early 1950s the state realized that structural inequality was not only relegated to Scheduled Castes and Tribes. In 1953 the Government of India set up the first Commission to Study the Other Backward Classes (OBCs). Known as the Kalelkar Commission,[5] the report identified 2,399 backward castes and communities who were distinct from Scheduled Castes and Tribes. The report recommended a 70 percent increase in reservations for the new category of OBCs[6] but the government did not enact it. In 1979 the state again sought to incorporate OBCs into the reservation scheme, creating the Second Other Backward Classes Commission, known as the Mandal Commission after its chairman. The Mandal Report was published in 1981. It concluded that 52 percent of the population should be classified as OBCs, which, when added to the number of Scheduled Castes and Tribes, would mean that over three-quarters of the population should be eligible for reservations. "But the Supreme Court has rules that reservations cannot exceed 50 percent of the jobs, so the commission ... reluctantly recommended only 27 percent of jobs for OBCs" (Kumar 1992, p. 291). Responses to the report were mixed, leading the government to ignore most of the recommendations made by the committee. It wasn't until 1990 that the report was again placed under consideration.

The political context of the Anti-Reservation Movement

Nine years after the Mandal Commission Report was published, Prime Minister V.P. Singh went before Parliament with the following statement:

> I am happy to announce in this august house a momentous decision of social justice that my Government has taken regarding socially and educationally backward classes on the basis of the report of the Mandal

88   *The Anti-Reservation Movement*

commission. Honorable members are aware that the constitution which we gave to ourselves 40 years ago envisages that socially and educationally backward classes be identified, their difficulties removed and their conditions improved. It is a basic negation of our constitution that until now this requirement was not fulfilled.[7]

Singh went on to state that the government would enact the Mandal Commission report on August 13, which would result in an increase of reservations in public sector jobs for OBCs to 27 percent, adding to the exisiting level of reservations. In the wake of this announcement both north and south India witnessed a wave of violence opposing the decision. For about a month after the announcement high caste individuals and other sectors of the urban middle class protested through strikes, rallies, blocking traffic and the destruction of government property. Protests quickly turned violent. During the first month events were scattered, though intense.[8]

On September 19, the agitation against Mandal was invigorated when Rajiv Goswami attempted self-immolation on the north campus of Delhi University. Goswami did not die as a result of his action, but his shocking act precipitated a series of similar events in north India. Over 100 students attempted suicide, and at least 60 died. Violence and repression rose dramatically throughout UP, Bihar, Punjab and Andhra. In Delhi the government shut down all schools and colleges for one month, and ordered the removal of glass panes from all buses. Other cities faced similar issues. The violence culminated with a riot at the Boat Club in Delhi on October 2.

Increasing levels of violence helped further to destabilize an already unstable government. By late November, the left front coalition government fell once the BJP withdrew its support after ten months in power. The protests surrounding the implementation of Mandal clearly contributed to the decline of the Janata Dal in 1990. However, despite the fact that the Mandal protests helped to topple the government, the Anti-Reservation Movement failed in its attempt to promote its own stated short- and long-term goals. The movement's inability to create positive policy change can be attributed to a number of factors. By tracking the movement's use and misuse of suicide protest, as well as the particular political context of the time, I reveal certain weaknesses of the tactic and its deployment.

The political situation in 1990 directly contributed to the sustained and uncontrolled violence in the wake of the Prime Minister's announcement. The National Front, a coalition government of the Janata Dal and other parties, came to power in 1989. The government had parliamentary support from the Bharatiya Janata Party (BJP), a Hindu party, the Communist Party of India (CPI), and the Communist Party of India – Marxist (CPM). The Janata Dal's election seemed to be more an indictment of the Congress Party and less a mandate for the National Front (Sission and Majumdar 1991). Coming to power in January 1990, the new government was forced to contend with a number of pressing issues. First, there were three distinct separatist movements active at the time – Punjab, Assam, and Jammu and Kashmir. Early in the year, President's Rule[9] was declared in both Punjab and Kashmir. Second, the state was dealing with increasingly strident protests from the NBA and other social movements. And third, there was a steady increase in Hindu chauvinism, often supported by members of the government. Overlaying all of this was the notion that the National Front government had been elected in part because it promised a "government sensitive to the popular pulse and reflexive to the complex popular will" (ibid., p. 103). By the summer of 1990 a variety of tensions and pressures were starting to show in the ruling coalition. In the midst of growing discontent from a number of different political and social actors, V.P. Singh announced the implementation of Mandal.

The Anti-Reservation Movement: tactical depth, intensity, emotional narrative and levels of political competition

ARM was an ad hoc movement, created solely to fight the adoption of Mandal into state policy. It is more correct to view the movement as a loose confederation of a variety of caste-based student organizations. Some were peaceful, other were not. High caste students feared that they would be shut out of public sector jobs once the increases went into effect. On college campuses throughout the north and south, groups began to mobilize. The most affected areas were in UP, Bihar, New Delhi and also Hyderabad. These cities were shut down for a few weeks as riots and violence continued unchecked.

After Goswami's self-immolation on September 19, a wave of students replicated his suicide bid, either with fire, like Goswami, or in some cases by hanging themselves. The movement's use of suicide as a protest tactic became an emblem for the cause as a whole. Despite the drama and passion behind these acts, the movement was not able to use suicide protest to gain its primary goal. In the middle of the protests, opposition forces approached the Supreme Court to order a stay on the government, which was granted. But I do not think that the Supreme Court's actions should be considered a short-term success for the movement as the students themselves had no direct involvement in agitating for that decision. They certainly had an indirect influence, but the tenor of their movement precluded the use of the courts as a valid avenue for change. And so, the Anti-Reservation Movement is the only case of complete failure out of the four cases that I examine. Why was this movement unable to gain any type of political outcome, or create internal movement coherence, through its use of suicide? Because it only exhibited one of the four factors that increase the probability of movement success – intensity. Though it was acting within a politically competitive context, I believe that the movement's relationship with opposition parties hindered its ability to create policy change, which indicates a much more closed political environment than the level of electoral competition might suggest. In order to understand ARM's failure I closely examine the duration of the protest action as

90   *The Anti-Reservation Movement*

well as the relationship between it and other political parties. Though student organizations were active in various locations, I concentrate my analysis on New Delhi and other major cities. Based on this analysis, I show that very high levels of intensity can actually have diminishing returns for movements.

Tactical depth

Tactical depth measures the number and types of protest used by a movement. Non-violent tactics are particularly important as the presence of mundane forms of contestation can mitigate a movement's reputation for extremism. Higher levels of tactical depth will increase the possibility of a movement's success since the presence of other types of political mobilization allows some movement leaders to be viewed as moderate forces. Based on the above criteria, I claim that the Anti-Reservation Movement had very low levels of tactical depth. Though the students did use strikes and rallies, these tactics were soon overshadowed by the movement's use of violence and suicide protest. Over the course of their agitation against the state the students utilized self-immolation (and other types of suicide action), collective violence and direct action in the form of strikes and rallies. However, the preponderance of violent tactics weakened any moderating effects that non-violent protests may have had on the movement.

Direct action

Almost immediately after V.P. Singh's announcement, students began to mobilize on campus to protest against the adoption of Mandal. No single student group took a dominant position within the movement, "but the closest thing to an umbrella organization guiding the stir is the Anti-Mandal Commission Forum based in Delhi University, which has forged links with other ragtag student groups in a few states."[10] Class, caste and political divisions within the larger student community hindered the creation of a large organization, leading instead to a variety of groups that replicated those structural cleavages. Despite these conflicts, protest actions by a majority of high caste students seemed to support the larger protest actions.[11] In their approach to protest the students were unable or unwilling to sustain their use of non-violent direct action, in contrast to the movement for AP or the NBA. Often, demonstrations or marches that began non-violently, would end in violence against property or people. For example, rallies in New Delhi quickly became an excuse for protestors to destroy government property. A rally in Bihar resulted in the death of five protestors after police opened fire on students when they began to riot.

> An air of death and desolation hung over Patna after police firing on a procession of anti-reservation agitators on September 4, which left at least five dead and 50 injured. Bodies lay in pools of blood amid the

debris of brickbats, smashed barricades and wire-netting and burnt vehicles. Bailey Road, the scene of the police firing and violence, resembled a battlefield.[12]

The shooting occurred after a protest rally turned into a battle between police and students. These types of events did damage to the movement's reputation as a whole; either the movement was unable to control its supporters, or it didn't want to control them. Regardless of the truth of the situation, ARM's use of direct action not only failed to show the state that it could be a trusted negotiating partner, but actually reinforced violent perceptions of it.

Collective violence

In addition to their sporadic attempts at non-violent forms of direct action, the student movement also engaged in collective violence, which erupted as soon as the announcement concerning the implementation of Mandal was made. The timing of this type of collective violence is significant for two reasons. First, by resorting to violence from the start, the students could not claim that violence was a natural escalation of protest borne out of the inactivity of the state. In other words, violence was clearly *not* a last resort for the students. Second, the timing of collective violence inextricably links the students with a violent reputation; as discussed in previous chapters a violent reputation can make it very difficult for states to justify negotiating with movements, even if their use of violence is unplanned.

Students in Delhi and other cities began to stage violent, and public, events to gain media and state attention.[13] For example, in Hyderabad, "in a spontaneous manner the anti-reservationists took to the streets venting their ire on the State transport buses, deflating tires and smashing windscreens and hijacking them at will. Girls formed human chains to block traffic."[14] The levels of violence were so high they were discussed in Parliament. On September 4, 1990, A.G. Kulkarni, an MP from Maharashtra, made an appeal to students during a Rajya Sabha debate:

> Madam, may I request you and through you, the Government and the whole House that we, the Members of the Rajya Sabha, should request the students to shun violence and to apply their minds to the real aspects of the Mandal Commission [sic].[15]

The government was aware of the rising tide of violence, and was worried about it. The number of riots and other types of violent action carried out is hard to calculate, but what is known is that most major universities throughout the north were shut down due to fear of the violence escalating. The levels of spontaneous violence employed, without any attempt at negotiation, suggests that the students were unwilling to negotiate with the state and instead wanted to be recognized in a very public way.

92   *The Anti-Reservation Movement*

While court cases and other types of protest came later, for the most part ARM resorted to violence in the pursuit of its goals. As a result the movement was unable to mitigate or moderate its radical reputation, strengthening the possible negative effects of suicide protest. In the next section I examine how the lack of tactical depth in the movement was exacerbated by high levels of intensity.

Intensity

Intensity measures the number of deaths that occur as a direct result of suicide protest. Death is an important part of the success of this tactic as it illustrates to the state and other actors the commitment level of the movement. High levels of intensity are also important as they can be used as leverage against the state. ARM demonstrated high levels of intensity vis-à-vis its use of suicide protest, but this intensity was not enough to create political change in its favor. In fact, the increasing number of deaths may very well have had diminishing results for the movement as a whole.

The first suicide protest event by Rajiv Goswami occurred on September 19. Goswami was a 20-year-old student at Deshbandhu College in Delhi. He came from a middle class family and was involved in student politics. Accounts are unclear on whether Goswami's intention was to die or simply to maim himself. One report of the event states:

> Tempers were running high after a nine-day hunger strike, which the students believed hadn't received adequate attention. Frustrated, Rajeev and his friends came up with the idea of self-immolation. Yet Rajeev retained an element of sanity. The night before, he called his mother and reassured her: "*Hum sirf tamasha karne ja rahe hai*" (we are staging a drama). But in an atmosphere charged with emotion, the initial plan of a mock self-immolation went awry. Having previously come with only his legs doused in kerosene, Rajeev then poured kerosene all over his body. And when he lit that matchstick, he was at the back of the crowd, and his friends, detailed to douse the fire, were not around.[16]

Goswami was hospitalized and ultimately survived his attempt; though in 2003 he died as a result of his burns. Regardless of Goswami's intentions, in the following weeks at least 130 students (both male and female) followed his example, and the death count reached 63.

One young woman inspired by Goswami's act was Monica Chadha, who at "19 slipped out of the one room apartment in South Delhi where she was watching a video with her mother and five sisters, went out to the terrace, and set herself on fire."[17] This was not simply an act of suicide, it was a suicide protest. An hour before the event, when she had told her mother that she wished to self-immolate, her mother had responded by saying " 'Go to V.P. Singh's house and tell him what you feel. Death is not an answer.' "[18] Chadha's quiet act stands in contrast to another self-immolation conducted by a student named Surinder Singh Chauhan, aged 22. Chauhan became involved with the movement after Goswami's self-immolation. "On September 24, he torched himself in full view of by-standers, sustaining 98 percent burns. His suicide note read: 'The responsibility for my death lies with those who consider reservation a vote bank, people like V.P.' "[19]

These stories are but a few examples of students who were willing to end their lives in protest at Mandal policy. The Anti-Reservation movement displayed a high level of intensity in its use of suicide protest but its leaders failed to translate the demonstrations of their commitment into favorable political change. There are a number of reasons why ARM failed. But if we focus on the effect of intensity in isolation, I believe that this movement illustrates a possible flaw in the deployment of suicide protest – too much of it may not be a very good thing. The high frequency of student self-immolations pushed such acts into the background and they became an indistinguishable and even anticpated part of the overall movement. Though each event was dramatic and surprising in itself, the fact that another was likely to take place a few days later meant that each individual act did not have time to cause an impact. In this particular case the high numbers of suicide events (especially when combined with a lack of emotional narrative, which I discuss in the next section) transformed these events into background noise. Each individual event still matters, but will have lessening effects as time goes on.

The negative effects of intensity were heightened by the inability of the movement to deploy non-violent or constitutional forms of protest. Low tactical depth and high intensity makes it possible for the movement and its cause to be framed as violent or extreme. While these types of movement can be successful, it is rare. The previous analysis demonstrates the ways in which these factors interplay, and demonstates that they are layered and complex. Lack of tactical depth may not be enough for a movement to fail, but when combined with high intensity failure seems much more likely than success. Finally, the negative aspects of the movement and its use of suicide protest were qualitatively affected by the fact that it did not attempt to construct emotional narratives of pride and sympathy around the use of suicide protest.

Emotional narratives

The ability of the movement to craft emotional appeals aimed at both the state and its own members will increase the possibility of success. I identify four emotions that, if engendered, will not only help to create solidarity within the group but will also aid in attaining the movement's goals. These emotions are pride and sympathy towards the movement, and shame or fear towards the state. Based on its level of intensity, one might assume that the Anti-Reservation Movement would use these protests to craft a number of different emotional narratives directed towards a variety of audiences. While the student protests were very dramatic and emotional, ARM did not create

94 *The Anti-Reservation Movement*

specific emotional narratives, instead allowing other actors such as the media and political parties to construct those narratives for them. There were a number of ramifications of this type of abdication. The students were unable to explain their own reasons for using suicide protest effectively. Moreover, the explanations that did exist rarely utilized the rhetorical forms of language that had already proved effective for other suicide protests in India in the past; by this I mean the active invocation of Gandhian ideals and tactics. The use of self-immolation was considerably weakened as the students allowed others to narrate their use of the tactic.

Pride and sympathy

Pride and sympathy are the products of intimacy between the actor and the event. Movements that use ritual and celebration to highlight acts of suicide will be more likely to create these feelings among their members. In the case of ARM, the instinctive emotional reactions to self-immolation events were not directed into support of the movement. After Goswami's self-immolation a number of supporters gathered at the hospital and named the crossroads in front of the building *qubani chowk* (Sacrifice Square). Students repainted street signs with the name "Goswami Marg."[20] But other than these symbolic acts there is no indication that the movement used the event to create emotional ties. That is not to say that the movement did not utilize these events – it did – but suicide protest was only used as a rallying point, not as an attempt to create affective ties between the movement and its constituents. Though the lack of emotional narratives towards the movement may be seen as an outcome of its brevity, I believe the opposite is true. After violence died down and V.P. Singh's government fell, the issue of Mandal was still on the table. Though the Supreme Court was deliberating, there was still ample opportunity to impact the issue of reservations in the public sector and universities. Why wasn't the Anti-Reservation Movement able to sustain itself? One reason may be that while the movement was active, it did not create strong bonds with its membership. There was no internal cohesion or attempt to establish structures that could survive a change in the debate. In order for movements to survive they must be able to engage in a dialog with their members; the Anti-Reservation Movement was unable to do this. By failing to create affective ties between the movement and the community at large, the students missed an opportunity to appeal to related groups and individuals who could have pressured the state. This was particularly detrimental because the high intensity of the group made it particularly important to carefully narrate its use of the tactic and allow individual stories to be distinguished from the white noise.

Shame

Similar to fasting to the death, the act of self-immolation can be used to inculcate a sense of shame in the state. Both the movement for Andhra and the

NBA successfully fashioned emotional narratives designed to make the state feel shame. Whether or not people in government actually feel shame does not matter, what is important is that the movement attempts to signal to the state that it should. Both the NBA and the movement for Andhra justified suicide action by claiming it was their "last resort." This type of statement suggests that the state is unresponsive to the needs and concerns of its own people. The appeal is made stronger by the movement's suggestion that the use of suicide protest demonstrates India's participatory democracy has failed in some way. While students also tried to use this type of language, it was drowned out by their anger and the explosive nature of the movement and its mobilization. I am not suggesting that the narrative of state shame did not exist within the movement, rather it was often obscured or badly delivered – in contrast to both the NBA and the AP movements.

In the case of the ARM there was never any attempt to create a sustained and effective dialog with the state, or vice versa. Though members of the government were certainly worried about the issue and the movement, that worry was not reflected in policy change, or even negotiating for one, Official documents suggest that the government's concern was limited to the frequency and tenor of the protests, not with what the protestors were trying to say. For example, during a Rajya Sabha debate on October 1, 1990, S.B. Chavan, an MP from Maharashtra, brought up the issue of the recent self-immolations:

> Let me at the outset on behalf of my party and myself offer condolences to the members of the bereaved families of the girls and boys who have sacrificed their lives. Of course the government didn't even bother to find out for almost 10–12 days as to what it was that was agitating their minds.[21]

Comparing this language to that used in the aftermath of Potti Sriramulu's death is illuminating. After Sriramulu died in 1952, Parliament issued official notices regarding his death, expressing sorrow. Though Chavan does attempt to compare the students with Sriramulu in an earlier statement, it is clear that he is more interested in scoring points against the government than pointing out the sadness of these acts.

In this section I have laid out the ways that the students failed to construct relevant and applicable emotional narratives. The movement did not take the time to familiarize the public with suicide actors, a failure that was probably in part due to the rapidly changing events surrounding the protest. But whatever the reason, the lack of familiarity contributed to the "white noise" effect of the protests. The drama of suicide protest is key, but it can also be easily buried as more and more people engage in the act. Also, the inability or unwillingness of the movement to narrate its own use of the tactic allowed competing explanations to emerge for the use of suicide protest, ultimately challenging any possible non-violent connotations the movement might want to make for itself. Not only this, the movement did not embed its use

96 *The Anti-Reservation Movement*

of sacrificial suicide protest within the larger Gandhian context in a manner that both the NBA and the movement for Andhra had done. All of this goes a great distance towards explaining why and how the movement came to be painted as purely violent and extreme, making the tactic and the movement itself much less effective overall.

Levels of political competition

In 1990 India was fairly democratic. Elections in 1989 showed that there was an entrenched oppositional force within the state. Logically, one would assume that this division would help the students in their cause. However, with regards to the Anti-Reservation Movement, strong oppositional forces hindered its ability to be an effective negotiator. Over the course of the movement different political parties used the students' agitation in order to further their own positions vis-à-vis the government. Thus, while structural levels of political competition existed within the state, these did not actually translate into a reality for ARM. I argue that the movement was at least partially captured by a political party, and one consequence of this was the lack of emotional narratives from the movement as I discussed in the previous section. Another consequence was that the movement was unable to take advantage of the complex political context and instead was limited in its ability to leverage parties against one another. This type of phenomenon is similar to the effect discussed by Piven and Cloward in their seminal work on poor people's movements in the United States (1979).

Two major parties are known to have worked with anti-reservation groups: the opposition Congress Party and the BJP. Neither of these parties pledged explicit support of the movement or its goals, as most political parties were unwilling to alienate OBCs. However, both the Congress and the BJP used personal connection and individual presence to signal support of the movement and its methods. Though the Congress Party did not formally support the goals of the movement, a number of its officials joined and led various student organizations, providing physical and, at times, material support. Similarly, individual members of the BJP assisted anti-reservation movements by joining in protests and providing resources. Moreover, though movement leaders generally refused to negotiate with the government, they did meet and negotiate with leaders of both the Congress and the BJP. Though students resisted the sponsorship of these parties, in some regions student protests began to look startlingly similar to party conflicts. The movement did not have enough internal cohesion to withstand attempts by parties to co-opt its agenda. In the case of the students' Anti-Reservation Movement, the highly competitive political system did not create space for the movement to press its demands. Instead, the demands were co-opted and finally discarded by the opposition.[22]

The effects of close movement party interactions are varied, in some cases movements may very well be able to use these types of interactions to further their own agendas. However, this was not the case for the Anti-Reservationists.

Party co-option weakened the movement overall. But, does this case fit into my overall argument regarding the need for political competition, or does it contradict that theory? I believe that the nature of the movement–party relationship actually made the political context less competitive for the students as they attempted to change these policies. Thus, the level of political competition is not simply a concrete structural variable, but also indicates the perceived ability of the movement to take advantage of any political openings and conflicts. Comparing the students to the NBA explicates my take on this situation as both movements were active in roughly the same time period. Unlike the students, the Narmada Movement used political fragmentation and spatial fragmentation to its advantage. It was able to do this in part because it remained independent enough to play competing political forces against one another. By allying themselves so closely with opposition parties, the students functionally limited their ability to utilize the existing countervailing forces within the state. As such, I argue that the students existed in a less politically competitive environment than other groups. This limitation added to the failure of the movement to deploy suicide protest in an effective way.

Conclusion

While the protests played a part in the failure of the National Front government, the anti-reservationists were unable to create lasting political success as defined in this book. This chapter reveals some ways that suicide protest not only fails to engender positive results, but may also be a great weakness for movements as a whole. As described in the chapter, the Anti-Reservation Movement was marked by its use of suicide protest, but unlike Potti Sriramulu or the NBA that aspect of the movement ultimately proved to be a detriment. Why didn't suicide protest work for the students in 1990? Based on my analysis of the movement it is clear that the students did not deploy the tactic very well. In fact, their deployment of the tactic not only didn't work, but in the long run worked against the students and their interests.

The anti-reservationists reveal how the four conditions of the tactical approach can work together to hinder movement mobilization. As discussed, as the movement gathered support and began to mobilize it demonstrated low levels of tactical depth, especially when speaking of non-violent forms of protest. In concert with this, the movement also created very high levels of intensity, though with little or no attempt to build supportive and positive emotional narratives. Finally, the movement's relationship with various political institutions limited its ability to take advantage of the level of structural political competition within the state. The layering of these factors ensured that the movement would become synonymous with suicide protest, but unlike Potti Sriramulu or Gandhi, this characteristic seemed more negative than positive. What this tells us is that all four of these factors are important, not on their own, but in how they can work together to create movement success and failure.

98 *The Anti-Reservation Movement*

Of course, there may be many other reasons why the students weren't able to pressure the state with regard to its policy stance. Clearly the political context was unstable at that time. However, one might think that political instability would be the perfect background in which to deploy suicide protest. The student movement illustrates why purely structural explanations of movement success and failure are not enough. Movement entrepreneurs play a crucial role in how they deploy and narrate their use of extreme tactics.

Finally, my analysis of this case also illustrates a possible flaw of regarding the effectiveness of suicide protest. Despite the drama and trauma of suicide protest, intensity is not enough to create positive political outcomes. In fact, too much intensity, especially when it is coupled with low levels of everything else, is actually a serious detriment to movements. Does this mean that intensity isn't important at all? I don't think so. My analysis of both Sriramulu and the NBA reveals the importance of intensity as suicide protest is deployed. What the anti-reservationists show is that intensity can also distance the public from the use of suicide as a protest tactic. This aspect of suicide protest can also shed light on other forms of extreme tactics and political violence. Violence can garner a lot of attention, but it must be embedded within an organized and comprehensive movement to be successful. Based on this, we can see how the tactical approach may be applied to other cases of extreme tactics. In order to explore this further, I extend my analysis to examine a crucial case of suicide bombing, a tactic that can be considered a cousin of suicide protest, in the next chapter. To what extent can the tactical approach help us to understand the deployment of suicide bombing and other tactics in politics?

Notes

1　This chapter is primarily based on archival research of newspapers and government documents. Due the controversial nature of the topic in India I found that most respondents did not want to engage in discussion about the anti-Mandal riots and their aftermath.

2　The exact number of students who killed themselves for this movement is unknown, in part because most people only remember the first instance of self-immolation, but I have seen numbers vary from 25 to 200.

3　There have been many different scholarly examinations of caste. Its political history is implicated by the cultural and social aspects of caste in India. I draw from Beteille's examination of caste in 1997. Beteille states (1997, p. 74): "The caste system is characterized by several levels of differentiations: the larger units are divided into smaller ones and these are subdivided on the basis of fairly enduring cleavages. The divisions and subdivisions either merge with one another or are placed in opposition, depending on the context. In a given context, a unit of lower may lose its identity through the merger with an adjacent unit, in another it may reappear as an independent entity. Thus the system as a whole retains a degree of continuity over time. The segments themselves are differentiated according to styles of life ... One caste differs from another in matters of dress, diet and other habits, while within a caste there is a consciousness of community." This understanding of caste, as a complex system of social relationships and hereditary divisions, demonstrates the insidious power of caste and its ability to withstand delegalization and redressive policies such as the reservation system.

The Anti-Reservation Movement 99

4 Indian Supreme Court Cases, Indira Sawhney v. Union of India, 1992, pp. 6–7.
5 As with all Government of India commissions, this one was named after its chairman, Kaka Kalelkar.
6 Government of India, *Report of the First Backward Classes Commission*, 1955.
7 *Rajya Sabha Debates*, August 7, 1990.
8 There may be some dispute as to whether these disparate events were a social movement or a loose set of similar campaigns. While it was clear that there was regional diffusion, these protests were somewhat coordinated between different groups within cities. Thus, I believe it is appropriate to consider these protests as part of a larger movement.
9 President's Rule specifies that the central government can declare any state government void if it is not fulfilling its duties. During President's Rule the central government retains administrative control of the state.
10 Pachauri, Pankaj with Farzand Ahmed and Dilip Awasthi "The Ragtag Warriors," *India Today*, October 31, 1990, p. 31.
11 Bhaumik, Saba Naqvi, with bureau reports. "A Spreading Stir," *India Today*, September 30, 1990, p. 36.
12 Upadhyaya, Ramesh. " Battle in Bihar," *Frontline*, September 15–28, 1990, p. 31.
13 Badhwar, Inderjit. "Mandal Commission Dividing to Rule," *India Today*, September 15, 1990, p. 98.
14 Rao, D. Kesava. "Student Ire in A.P.," *Frontline* September 15–28, 1990, p. 34.
15 *Rajya Sabha Debates*, September 4, 1990, p. 251.
16 Kalra, Nonita. "Rajeev Goswami Act of Desperation," *India Today*, October 15, 1990, p. 27.
17 Baweja, Harinder with N.K. Singh and Kanwar Sandhu. "Mandal Commission fall-out: Pyres of Protest," *India Today*, October 31, 1990 p. 22.
18 Ibid.
19 Ibid.
20 Kalra, Nonita. "Rajeev Goswami Act of Desperation," *India Today*, October 15, 1990, p. 27.
21 *Rajya Sabha Debates*, October 1, 1990, p. 6.
22 Mandal was finally implemented under a Congress government.

6 The tactical approach and suicide bombing in Sri Lanka

In the summer of 2005, I traveled to Sri Lanka for the first time to start field research for this book. I arrived six months after a tsunami had devastated both the northern and southern regions of the country. The morning I landed, then President Chandrika Kumaratunga signed the Joint Mechanism that would allow the Sri Lankan government to share the 3 billion dollar tsunami relief fund with the separatist movement, The Liberation Tigers of Tamil Eelam (LTTE, also known as the Tamil Tigers). The President's action was met with swift resistance from the supporters of the People's Liberation Front Party (JVP), culminating in the announcement of an indefinite fast by a small number of Buddhist monks. Though the fast abruptly ended a few days later, at the time I was surprised that the monks seemed to have no hesitation about using suicide protest, especially in the aftermath of the tsunami, an event which killed thousands of people within a very short time – wouldn't life be more precious after such a large-scale event? As I traveled though the country and met more Tamils and Sinhalese, I realized that the casual reaction to suicide protest could in part be linked to the habitual use of another tactic in Sri Lanka: suicide bombing. Between 1987 and 2005 the LTTE had deployed over 200 suicide bombers throughout Sri Lanka and the rest of South Asia. In many ways suicide bombing had become a mundane part of life; tragic, but also inconvenient. As I stated in the introduction, I don't believe that suicide bombing is the same as suicide protest. Yet the two acts share some characteristics, making suicide bombing a particularly strong test of my approach to understanding the effectiveness of particular tactics on movement success and failure. More importantly, analyzing the separate act of suicide bombing reveals some interesting aspects of suicide protest and its use. Based on my analysis, I argue that the LTTE's use of suicide bombing led to short-term success for the movement. Its ultimate failure lies in part in the high stakes of civil war politics, and the ways that the movement utilized the tactic itself. The LTTE was one of the first and most frequent purveyors of suicide bombing; as such, it is a perfect case to push the boundary of my approach. My analysis sharply delineates some of the limits of both suicide bombing and suicide protest while identifying areas where it may be important to conceptually stretch the argument.

Suicide bombing in Sri Lanka 101

In this and the next chapter I consider different types of suicide protest and other related tactics. This chapter is primarily concerned with the LTTE's use of suicide bombing from 1987 until the ceasefire in 2002, as well as events leading to the end of the ceasefire in 2008. In the concluding section I will briefly examine the last war and the LTTE's defeat in 2009. The LTTE is an interesting counterpoint to other organizations that use suicide bombing. Unlike Hamas or Hezbollah, the LTTE was not a religious organization, but instead advanced a virulently chauvinistic nationalism based on linguistic and cultural identity. Furthermore, unlike other groups in conflict, the LTTE was able to gain de facto control over the Tamil population and is the only viable representative of Tamils in the north today. The unique nature of the LTTE before the end of the ceasefire in 2007 vis-à-vis other militant nationalist groups allows us to understand the conditions under which suicide bombing may result in success or failure. Finally, the LTTE was the first group to have used suicide bombing in the South Asian context.

Why suicide bombing? Theoretical explanations for the tactic

The tactic of suicide bombing is a relatively recent one, and because of this there is some conceptual confusion regarding exactly what can and cannot be considered suicide bombing. Recent discussions of suicide bombing typically refer to one type of action: the human bomb. The image of a body transforming itself into a detonation device through the use of a vest packed with explosives is common on the news and in fictional depictions of suicide bombing. Despite the preponderance of human bombs in action movies and television shows, another iteration of suicide bombing was the first to gain international attention. These were no-escape missions, where terrorists became the delivery system for bombs but did not carry those bombs on themselves. Primary examples of this would be the Marine Barrack Bombing in Lebanon in 1981, or more recently the terrorists who attacked the World Trade Center in 2001. In these cases the terrorists did not directly transform their bodies, but nonetheless clearly carried out suicide missions. Both of these actions are examples of suicide bombing, but human bombs have been much more common in the last 20 years. The existence of different types of suicide bombing illustrates another issue concerning how social science deals with this tactic. Under my description of no-escape missions, Japanese kamikaze pilots could be considered suicide bombers but they are generally left out of this category since they acted within the bounds of war. This exclusion is a function of the strong linkage between the tactic of suicide bombing and instances of terrorism in both scholarship and in the media. When a group uses suicide bombing it often clears up the muddy divisions between terrorism and other forms of contention like guerilla warfare or insurgency, labeling suicide bombing as an act of terror. To put it another way, not all terrorists use suicide bombing, but all suicide bombers are terrorists, at least in the minds of a large percentage of the media, social scientists and policy-makers.

102 *Suicide bombing in Sri Lanka*

I don't mean to belabor the point, certainly bombing is intimately linked to how we view terror, but I do feel that the automatic linkage between suicide bombing and terrorism raises certain issues regarding how we approach the topic. By treating suicide bombing as a completely unique form of political violence, we limit the ability of states to construct comprehensive and holistic polices to contain and stop the threat. We also limit ourselves in the tools we use to analyze the phenomena. I argue that we must place suicide bombing on a continuum of violent or extreme tactics; when we do that we can begin to compare the tactics and their efficacy.

Like other types of political violence, suicide bombing was initially described as a type of mental illness; these theories were quickly disabused as scholars began to recognize the organizational dimension behind the tactic. I don't deny that the decision to utilize this tactic may involve individuals who have psychological problems, but that is not what I, and most others, are really concerned with. I focus on why *groups* choose to deploy suicide bombing. As with other types of political violence, the majority of work on suicide bombing tries to discern the possible causes for this tactic. There are three broad schools of thought on the motivations for suicide bombing; economically motivated, culturally motivated, and strategic.[1]

Scholars applied Gurr's theory of relative deprivation (1970) as a possible reason for suicide bombing. The underlying assumptions of this theory would indicate that suicide bombers themselves should come from relatively poor, uneducated and vulnerable populations. But deprivation theories are not borne out by the empirical evidence. Rather than being poor, isolated and uneducated, the profiles of many suicide bombers seemed to indicate that they hailed from an educated and usually middle class background[2] (Pape 2005; Laqueur 2004; Brym and Araj 2006). Moreover, these individuals were deeply embedded within the organizational matrix of the terrorist group. In fact, in a 2006 study Brym and Araj concluded that the educational level of the bomber was crucial to the tactic's success (they define effectiveness as the level of destruction resulting from the event).

Cultural explanations for suicide bombing generally pinpoint a form of hyper religiosity as the main motivator. This reasoning stems primarily from the assumption that all suicide bombings have taken place in the Islamic world. While it is true that a preponderance of suicide bombings have occurred within the Middle East, these phenomena have in no way been limited to that region. The LTTE in Sri Lanka deployed the tactic over 200 times once it started using it. Moreover, it has been used in Europe and other parts of Asia. Finally, there are instances where suicide bombing has been used in the Islamic world, but not for religious reasons, such as by the PKK in Turkey. The theory that religion in general, or Islam in particular, is the cause of suicide bombing is clearly not supported by the empirical reality of when and why suicide bombing is used.

In reaction to the weaknesses of cultural and economic theories, scholars cited the strategic nature of the act, for both the individual actor and the group. Scholars such as Pape (2005), Bloom (2005), and others, systematically examined the possible causes and consequences of suicide bombing, citing issues such as the need for media attention and control of the cause as some possible motivating factors behind it. According to these scholars, suicide bombing can be "successful" especially within democratic contexts. However, these theories don't adequately explain why suicide bombing is used in non-democratic contexts (which have a low chance of success) or in the face of continued repression and resistance by the state.

Contemporary scholars of the tactic (Hafez 2006; Brym and Araj 2006; Abufarha 2009) believe that a comprehensive and holistic approach would better explain the complexity of suicide bombing. For example, it may be prudent to disaggregate the audience when trying to understand what suicide bombers are trying to communicate. Moreover, we should disregard the notion that strategy is bounded by cultural connotations, that suicide bombing is strategic precisely because it reconstitutes cultural breakages and norms.

Theories on suicide bombing don't spend too much time on its success or failure. Pape (2005) points out that the tactic is most successful in democratic states but while that structural argument is empirically borne out, I don't think that regime type is an adequate explanation for suicide bombing's efficacy. As such, the tactical approach that I have outlined presents a better way to understand the impact of suicide bombing.

I identify four criteria can help to create political change: tactical depth, intensity, emotional narratives and political competition. By stretching my approach to examine suicide bombing I have found some subtle differences in how these factors worked for the LTTE. In particular, I examine shifts in the type of emotional narrative that are more appropriate for suicide bombing. This case also demonstrates the diminishing returns of intensity, setting a limit on that factor and how it affects suicide protest as well as suicide bombing.

I argue that the LTTE had low levels of tactical depth. Based on my analysis, I show that though the LTTE used other tactics the movement was marked by its use of suicide and militaristic tactics. This reputation was emphasized by the sometimes creative and daring examples of LTTE military operations.

The organization did, however, display very high levels of intensity. Though there have been some suicide bombers who have not detonated themselves,[3] the LTTE was mainly known for its ability to perpetrate the tactic of suicide bombing, even if the mission has failed. For many in and outside Sri Lanka, the Black Tigers symbolized the entire organization. The LTTE also actively created and disseminated emotional narratives both towards the state and towards active and potential members of the movement. Through the use of ritual and celebration, the LTTE fostered a high degree of identification with the Black Tigers among its own population. Finally, though Sri Lanka is a democratizing state, I argue that the LTTE worked within a context of low levels of political competition (a result of deep political divisions between

104 *Suicide bombing in Sri Lanka*

north and south), causing most Tamils to have "opted out" of democratic processes before and during the ceasefire.

High levels of intensity and emotional narratives helped the LTTE to garner short-term goals from the state – such as negotiations with the government – but these ultimately ended in failure. Through an analysis of the historical evolution of the conflict, and an investigation of the LTTE's use of suicide protest, I aim to explain the role that suicide bombing played within the organization before the end of the ceasefire.

Suicide bombing, suicide protest and the LTTE

On July 5, 1987, a young military officer in the Liberation Tigers of Tamil Eelam (LTTE) army drove a truck full of explosives into a Sri Lankan Army camp, killing himself and at least 40 others. This moment marked the first time that the LTTE used suicide bombing, but not the last. Since that moment the LTTE has used suicide bombing on land and sea for a variety of reasons, including assassination, destruction of military targets (both human and material), and the destruction of non-military government property and persons.[4] It seems strange to compare a military organization, such as the LTTE, with social movements like the Narmada Bachao Andolan and the movement for the linguistic state of Andhra. As a military organization, the Tamil Tigers operate differently from other social movements. However, fundamentally, the LTTE was a group attempting to gain an outcome from the state. Thus, while the LTTE, NBA, and other social movements may use different tactics to approach the state, they all fall under the rubric of contentious politics.

History of the conflict: the pre-colonial and colonial eras

The civil conflict in Sri Lanka centered on the ethnic and geographical divisions between two groups: Tamils in the north and Sinhalese in the south. Despite modern rhetoric to the contrary,[5] relations between these two ethnic groups were relatively peaceful in pre-colonial times (Nissan and Stirrat 1990, p. 19). While conflicts occurred, for the most part they did not run along ethnic lines but centered on religious affiliations and cultural practices (de Silva 1983; Ghosh 2003). Additionally, conflicts between Tamils and Sinhalese were rarely nationalist in nature (Nissan and Stirrat 1990).

However, under subsequent waves of Portuguese, Dutch and British colonization, Tamils and Sinhalese slowly began formulating ethno-nationalist identities. Sri Lanka, rich in spices and other natural resources, was a tempting prize for many European states heavily invested in the spice trade. The Portuguese were the first Europeans to settle in Sri Lanka in the sixteenth century; though their rule was short, they used a system of direct control over their territory, particularly Jaffna, which effected traditional practices and relationships.[6] Dutch settlers helped drive the Portuguese out of Sri Lanka, and then took control for over 100 years (1668–1796). According to Gosh (2003, p. 45), Dutch control relied on pre-existing administrative structures and did little to disturb the cultural practices of Tamils or Sinhalese. The longest European presence on the island was British; they took control at the end of the eighteenth century. As a British colony, Sri Lanka was reorganized into a number of easily controlled administrative units (similar to India). Ethnic identities gained more salience as groups vied with one another for greater access to legislative power, education and religious dominance. Ethnic competition was exacerbated as the British began to shift large numbers of Tamils from south India in order to expand the workforce. Tamil workers from India resided close to the center of the island, on tea plantations, in the midst of the Sinhalese majority. While British colonization established the adversarial relationship between the Tamils and Sinhalese, during that period there is no indication that these ethnic identities evolved into a chauvinist ethnic agenda.

Constitutional cleavages: 1948–1970

The conflict between Tamils and Sinhalese did not significantly escalate until after Independence in 1948. Unlike its closest neighbor, India, Sri Lanka (or Ceylon, as it was called until 1972) had a relatively peaceful period of nationalism. Power shifted from the British and into the hands of a mostly Sinhalese elite with little or no bloodshed (Ghosh 2003). However, within 10 years of Independence, ethnic and cultural cleavages became pronounced and virulent. The conflict started over one central question: what kind of nation would Ceylon be? Secular or religious? Unitary or federalist? Culturally exclusive or inclusive? The ruling Sinhalese community's answer was clear; fundamentally, Ceylon was to be Sinhalese. Communal conflicts grew as Tamils and Sinhalese alike came to terms with these issues. The Sinhalese elite promoted Sinhalese nationhood in two ways; first, Ceylon was declared a Buddhist state, in fact the only official Buddhist state in the world. This was supported by a nationalist rhetoric that was, and often still is, self-consciously couched in religio-nationalist terms and symbols. Thus, within the Sri Lankan context, Buddhism has become an actively nationalist religion. The construction of a "Buddhist nation" has included the use of violent and repressive measures against the Tamil minority in northern Sri Lanka, who are predominately Hindu, Christian or Muslim[7] (Tambiah 1992). Second, and more importantly, the predominantly Sinhalese government began to enact a series of policies designed to disenfranchise the Tamil population.

For instance, in 1948 and 1949 the government created the "Citizenship Acts," which made it more difficult for Indian Tamils to retain Sri Lankan citizenship. These acts "distinguished between citizenship by descent based on a two generation connection with Sri Lanka, which required no proof with respect of inhabitants. And citizenship by registration, which required documentary proof of past residence and present means" (Ghosh 1999, p. 30). Changes in citizenship laws were soon followed by changes in language

106 *Suicide bombing in Sri Lanka*

policy. In 1956, President Bandaranaike's Sri Lanka Freedom Party (SLFP) government adopted the "Sinhalese Only Act," making Sinhalese the only official language of the state. This effectively marginalized most, if not all, of the Tamil population in the north, who were primarily educated in Tamil or English. Unsurprisingly, reactions in the north were unsupportive of the new law. Sinhalese instruction was immediately suspended in all Jaffna schools, and students and other Tamil elites began to organize political opposition against the state. Retaliation by the Tamil community provoked the first instance of Tamil–Sinhalese ethnic violence in 1958: the "anti-Tamil" riots. These riots ended quickly, but the use of violence as a means for ethnic competition took root in the north and east. From 1956–1960, the conflict centered on electoral politics; hoping to gain power, Tamils in the north formed the Tamil Federation Party (TFP), which stood in parliamentary elections. It was soon clear to most Tamils that the increasingly hard-line Sinhalese majority would circumvent any attempts to claim democratic power.

Violence erupts: militant Tamil resistance and the genesis of the LTTE

The 1970s witnessed the shift in Tamil mobilization from non-violent democratic opposition to violent separatism. This change was spurred by the inclusion of Tamil youth into the overall movement, as well as Tamil frustration over increasingly discriminatory state practices. By 1970, Tamils had given up on the notion of equality within a unitary state, and began to agitate for devolution of power to a federal system. The newly formed Tamil United Front (TUF)[8] actively promoted a federalist agenda in the north and south. While there was deep resentment of the Sinhalese state, Tamil reactions remained relatively non-violent.

Hostility against the state increased for two reasons. First, in 1970, the government introduced the "Standardization Act," which reserved public university seats for students from "backward" regions, measured by the level of English language training available in any area. Since English had remained the de facto language of educational institutions, those areas that had not benefited from English language training would gain the highest number of seats. Historically, Tamil regions had the highest number of English speakers. This plan effectively cut down the number of places that Tamils could take at university. Also, during this time, the state began to regulate contact between Sri Lankan Tamils and Tamils from India by banning the import of Tamil literature and other media to the island.

These two policies mobilized Tamil students. A variety of organizations were created, including the People's Liberation Organization of Tamil Eelam (PLOTE), The Eelam People's Revolutionary Liberation Front (EPRLF), The Tamil Eelam Liberation Organization (TELO), and the Tamil New Tigers, led by a student named Vellupillai Prabhakaran. The Tamil New Tigers morphed into the LTTE in 1976. All of these groups operated out of the north and, at the time, got along with one another.[9] The LTTE, along with other organizations, carried out raids and an anti-government agenda. By 1980, these groups had transformed into paramilitary organizations, arming themselves by raiding police stations and military barracks and fighting what they considered to be a guerilla war against the government.[10] Many members of the LTTE, EPRLF and other organizations left Sri Lanka for south India. There they trained in guerilla tactics, with some cadres joining the growing international network of terrorist organizations which included groups such as the PLO and IRA, with which they trained.[10] The collaboration between different Tamil groups was short-lived as infighting began to affect the make-up and leadership of the groups. Though for a time Tamils maintained the hope of negotiated settlement through its political wing, The Tamil United Liberation Front (TULF), by 1983 the many Tamils in the north clearly supported a violent solution to the problem.

The popularity of paramilitary groups was compounded when the state passed a new constitution in 1972 that reaffirmed Sinhalese as the national language, and did not leave any room for an autonomous Tamil area within the Sinhalese nation. The 1972 Constitution, coupled with the death of prominent Tamil moderates (Ghosh 2003), spurred the general Tamil population to support the violent tactics espoused by youth organizations. By the end of the decade, hope for a non-violent solution was waning, and what little expectation there was abruptly ended after the anti-Tamil riots that took place in the Colombo area in 1983.

In 1983 the LTTE carried out an attack on a military convoy outside Jaffna, killing 13 soldiers (Hopgood 2005, p. 48). In response, riots broke out in Colombo and other areas in the south. Though there had been a number of riots since Independence in both the north and south, none approached the level of violence seen in 1983. This violence was not only targeted at disadvantaged Tamils; the perpetrators actively sought out and killed Tamil elites. Many Tamils, including the LTTE, believed that "the commencement of the riots reportedly revealed a hitherto absent element of organization and instigation in [the] attacks on Tamils and their property in Colombo" (Kearney 1985). Reactions in the north were predictably violent. Various paramilitary organizations, including the LTTE, began to train forces in India and declared war on the Sri Lankan government. Relations between north and south rapidly deteriorated after the riots, and in 1987 the Sri Lankan government asked for military aid from India which resulted in the occupation of the north by the Indian Peace Keeping Force (IPKF), causing further erosion of relations between the opponents. From 1983 to 2001, the LTTE and the Sri Lankan Army (SLA) fought three different "wars." In the course of these wars the LTTE emerged as the only viable representative of the Tamil community in the north, actively incorporating or eradicating all other Tamil groups.[12]

Negotiations facilitated by Norwegian ambassadors led to the complete cessation of military violence between the Sri Lankan state and the LTTE in 2001. The northern half of Sri Lanka was opened to the public and the A9

108 *Suicide bombing in Sri Lanka*

highway, the main artery that connects the north and south, was reopened, enabling distribution of international aid and the prospect of economic development. Though Sinhalese and Tamils alike had great hope for this ceasefire, relations worsened after the tsunami in 2004. Elections in 2005 returned a hard-line government to power, and both the LTTE and the government withdrew from negotiations; the ceasefire ended in 2008. Violence escalated from sporadic skirmishes between the SLA and LTTE in the north and northeast, to unrestrained military engagement. The north was once again closed off to the public, and war declared. By 2009 the LTTE had been pushed into a small corner of the island. Prabhakaran's death was a major blow to the organization, which was defeated by the government soon after.

The gradual change in Tamil resistance from non-violent electoral contestation to extreme militarization illuminates two key characteristics of the LTTE. First, the continued and systemic discrimination of Tamils by the Sinhalese majority solidified widespread dissatisfaction with the state by the general Tamil population. This resulted in the creation of a nationalist Tamil identity and agenda that exploited linguistic and cultural differences between the Tamil and Sinhalese populations. The LTTE reconstituted and reaffirmed this identity. Second, the LTTE justified its use of violence on the previous failure of the Tamil community to attain any political accommodation from the state through non-violent methods.[13] For some in the north, violence was one of the only means through which Tamils would be able to achieve either equality with Sinhalese or an independent Tamil state.

The Liberation Tigers of Tamil Eelam: tactical depth, intensity, emotional appeals and levels of political competition

During the ceasefire the LTTE was the only viable representative of Tamils in the north. Its ascendency was accomplished through a combination of violent repression of other Tamil voices, and its ability to provide social and humanitarian services in its territory.[14] Unlike other separatist or terrorist organizations, the LTTE established itself not only as a military force, but also as an entrenched social and civil organization that had complete authority over the territory known as the Vanni (north from Vavuniya to the southern end of the Jaffna district). Organized into a number of different units that controlled specific areas, the LTTE created a de facto Tamil state in its territory. It levied taxes, ran schools and hospitals, and, until the ceasefire ended, negotiated with international NGOs and other international institutions for aid.[15] The LTTE also supervised the booming economic and social development of its capital, Kilinochchi, and the surrounding areas. Despite its organizational capacity, the Tigers could not engender a long-term settlement with the Sri Lankan state.

Though the use of suicide bombing initially led to policy outcomes and negotiations it did not engender a lasting peace. Why didn't suicide bombing lead to long-term political change in the Sri Lankan context? I contend that four factors will increase the likelihood of political change: tactical depth, intensity, emotional appeals and levels of political competition. Though the LTTE's use of suicide protest demonstrated high levels of intensity, and though the group drew up salient emotional narratives to accompany acts of suicide, low levels of tactical depth and political competition hindered the tactic and the movement.

Tactical depth

In order to measure the tactical depth of an organization I identify the different number and types of ways it contests the state. Groups that only use violent or extreme protest will be less likely to create change since states will not view them as a negotiating partner. The presence of non-violent tactics is particularly important for extreme groups, as these types of tactics more readily mitigate the extreme nature of suicide violence. Though the LTTE used diplomacy in its conflict with the state, I do not think that its attempts at non-violent negotiation were strong enough to counteract the negative connotations of suicide bombing with either the government, the public, or the international community. Also, I believe that the organizational structure of the LTTE contributed to the problem. In the course of its agitation with the state, the LTTE used suicide bombing, suicide protest, military engagement and diplomacy. The small number of tactics employed, coupled with a fragmented organizational structure, relegates the LTTE to a low level of tactical depth.

Military engagement

Since 1983, the LTTE used military force against the Sri Lankan state, and has engaged in at least four wars with the Sri Lankan Army.[16] The first war sparked the anti-Tamil riots of 1983 and continued for four years. The level of violence in that war caused Sri Lanka to invite India to become involved in the situation. In 1987, India's Prime Minister, Rajiv Gandhi, agreed to President Jayewardene's request for military assistance in dealing with the LTTE and other militant groups. Gandhi and Jayewardene's accord created the Indian Peace Keeping Force (IPKF), which was mandated to maintain peace in the north and east of the island. The motivation behind this agreement was to aid in

> Nurturing, intensifying, and straightening, the traditional friendship of India and Sri Lanka and acknowledging the imperative need of resolving the ethnic problem of Sri Lanka, and the consequent violence, and for the safety, well-being, and prosperity of people belonging to all communities in Sri Lanka.
>
> (Government of India, Indo-Lanka Accord, 1987)

Despite the fact that a number of Tamil parties agreed with the accord, including the EPRLF, PLOTE and the ENDF (Eelam New Democratic Front), the LTTE was not consulted prior to the agreement being made. The Tigers' exclusion from the process proved to be problematic since the IPKF

110 *Suicide bombing in Sri Lanka*

was meant to police war-torn Tamil areas in the north and east (Ghosh 2003, p. 138). According to Prabhakaran the Tigers felt that the accord was biased in favor of the Sri Lankan government, as it did not acknowledge the legitimacy of Tamil claims of ethnic nationalism. The mandate also demanded that only the LTTE and other Tamils give up their arms, and not the SLA.[17] The LTTE began to target IPKF forces, which responded in kind. By 1988 the LTTE had shifted its diplomatic and military concern from the SLA to the IPKF, deciding to negotiate directly with the Indian government in the hope that India would broker a deal with Sri Lanka on the LTTE's behalf. The IPKF remained in Sri Lanka until March 1989. By that time it was clear that the LTTE held a dominant military position in the north and east.

The second war between the LTTE and the SLA began in 1990, after a series of peace talks had broken down between the relevant parties. The second war lasted four years and was again followed by peace talks that collapsed after four months. The third war lasted from 1995 until the ceasefire in 2001. Over the course of these wars, both Tamils and Sinhalese suffered heavy casualties. Most of the fighting took place in the Vanni and Jaffna province, the area where both the LTTE and SLA sought territorial control. In the last war, before the ceasefire, the SLA pushed the LTTE out of Jaffna province and into the Vanni. The frequency and intensity of these wars created a high level of hostility between Tamils and Sinhalese, but also increased the isolation of the north from the south. Jaffna Airport was closed, as was the A9 highway. Despite territorial losses in the third war, the Tigers seemed determined to win at any cost. For instance, when the SLA recaptured Jaffna for the last time in 1995, the LTTE forced all Tamil residents out of the city. An LTTE press release explains the reasons behind the edict:

> The mass exodus of Tamils from Jaffna peninsula has dealt a severe blow and signaled a political defeat to the Chandrika administration. It has made meaningless the political objective behind the Jaffna invasion. The mass exodus has clearly demonstrated the collective resentment and opposition of the Tamil people towards the strategy of military takeover of Jaffna.
>
> (Subramanian 2005, p. 27)

Events such as this illustrated the level of commitment the LTTE had towards its cause. The use of military action highlighted the LTTE's violent nature and contributed to the group's label of "terrorist" organization by Sri Lanka, the USA, the UK and Canada.

Suicide protest

The LTTE also used[18] the tactic of fasting to the death, but directed that act towards the Indian government rather than the Sri Lankan state.[19] On August 15, 1987, Thileepan, leader of the LTTE political wing, began a fast to the death in the north. The target of the fast was not the SLA or the Sri Lankan state, but India. Thileepan protested the IPKF's presence in the north and

Suicide bombing in Sri Lanka 111

northeast. According to a representative from the LTTE, the organization felt "that India, the land of Gandhi, would be more likely to understand this tactic" (fasting).[20] The fast took place outside "the Kandaswamy Temple at Nallur in Jaffna to press five demands" (Ghosh 2003, p. 140), which included: the release of Tamil prisoners; the creation of an interim Tamil government; and the withdrawal of SLA forces from Tamil areas.[21] Thileepan and the LTTE decided that since India was involved in the fight, it could influence the SLA to comply with these demands. Thileepan died from starvation on September 26, 1987. His death sparked a large demonstration against India in the north, and is often seen as a catalyst for subsequent LTTE anti-Indian sentiment. Though Thileepan's fast to the death was able to move certain segments of the population, this particular form of suicide protest was rarely repeated by the LTTE.

Diplomacy

Even as the LTTE battled with the SLA, it tried to maintain diplomatic relations with the Sri Lankan government. As the LTTE consolidated its power in the north, the state had no option but to deal with the organization.

Throughout the 1980s and 1990s, the moderate political party TULF continued to negotiate with the government on behalf of the Tamils. However, the efficacy of these negotiations is in question. Despite progress made by the two groups, the LTTE's growing dominance and legitimacy in the north vitiated any negotiations carried on in its absence. By the third war, the Sri Lankan government had started to conduct serious peace talks with the LTTE while supporting other Tamil institutions. President Kumaratunga wanted approval for a devolution plan which would put some control of the region in Tamil hands. Though the 1995 peace talks failed, as did many others, the Tigers were now in a dialog with the state. Talks continued intermittently throughout the third war, ending when the Norwegian government joined in as a neutral facilitator. With the Norwegians' help, the LTTE and the state were able to negotiate a ceasefire, which lasted from 2001 to 2006.[22]

Overt diplomacy served the LTTE in two ways. First, the Tamils were able to gain concessions from these talks and the subsequent ceasefire. For example, until the ceasefire, LTTE territory had no resources or access to public works. Most of the fighting took place in the north, resulting in a devastated infrastructure. By the time I traveled into LTTE territory in 2005, the capital city of Kilinochchi was flourishing. Bombed buildings stood next to new internet cafes and satellite phone stores. Though reports suggest that this prosperity has changed since the ceasefire ended, it is clear that the LTTE gained something from the ceasefire, if only the ability to maintain its region. Second, diplomacy helped the Tigers gain legitimacy from Sri Lanka and other states. The LTTE was labeled a terrorist organization by Sri Lanka, India, the USA, UK and Canada. This was particularly problematic for the LTTE, as a large percentage of its income stemmed from donations from Tamils living abroad. In most of these countries it is illegal to give monetary or technical support

112 *Suicide bombing in Sri Lanka*

to terrorist organizations, which cut off the LTTE's access to foreign funds. Though Sri Lanka and other states continued to place the organization within the "terrorist" category, they were much more willing to negotiate with the LTTE as a viable and valid representative of the Tamils when it was necessary to do so in this period.

The fact that the LTTE engaged in negotiation with the state is important to the organization and perceptions of it. However, diplomatic efforts were not enough to mitigate the LTTE's reputation as a violent and coercive organization. I contend that the inability of the LTTE to overcome its reputation can partially be blamed on the organizational structure of the group itself. The LTTE created a highly efficient structure for its organization, which relies on separate knowledge and power. The Tigers relied on a number of different cadres, or units, each of which is responsible for different aspects of the organization. The different units of the LTTE included but were not limited to the political unit in charge of peace negotiations, the Tamil Rehabilitation Organization (TRO), which was in charge of social and civic development, and, of course, the military unit. Within each of these units exist smaller subsets that controlled particular areas of concern. While these units worked together, a lack of transparency characterized their relations with one another. The military unit of the LTTE was further divided into specialized divisions including the Black Tigers, who used suicide bombing on land, and the Sea Tigers, who used suicide bombing at sea. Both of these units worked under a veil of strict anonymity. Prabhakaran headed the military division, and oversaw all other units.[23] Though the division of labor and lack of clarity made the LTTE very efficient in its ability to conduct war with the state, it did not help to burnish their reputation within the Sinhalese population. By separating out the military from the diplomatic side, the LTTE attempted to simultaneously maintain its revolutionary status within the Tamil community as well as its diplomatic credentials in the south. Though Tamil negotiators enjoyed success in their peace efforts, the primacy of Prabhakaran's military operations remained the main thrust of the LTTE agenda (Ghosh 2003).[24]

Despite attempts to equalize its military and diplomatic personas, the level of violence that the LTTE utilized made it very difficult for the state to justify continued negotiations with the organization. Social movement scholars often cite the power of disruption and violence (Gamson 1975; Piven and Cloward 1979) in creating political change; but violence on its own may not be effective, it must work in concert with other actions that demonstrate the movement's willingness to negotiate with and be a partner to the state. Though it tried, the LTTE couldn't maintain its diplomatic image in the face of the violence employed.

Intensity

Intensity measures whether or not the actor dies as a result of suicide events. This is an important factor, as part of the shock value of suicide protest depends on the fact that someone has died by his or her own choice for a political cause. Though one would assume that suicide bombings would always end in death that is not necessarily the case. Police, or others, sometimes stop suicide bombers before they can reach their targets. Also, the bombers themselves can change their minds before they detonate themselves. Though some Black Tigers failed or changed their minds, the majority who were deployed did carry out their missions. It would be impossible to discuss all the different Black and Sea Tiger missions, so I concentrate my discussion on the following suicide events: the first suicide bombing by Captain Miller, and Thileepan's fast to the death, both in 1987. These acts set the stage for all other uses of suicide bombing conducted by the LTTE. I also provide an overview of the different types of suicide missions carried out since then.

Suicide bombing

On July 5, 1987, a young LTTE soldier drove a truck filled with explosives into a SLA camp located in the Jaffna peninsula. Captain Miller, as he was called, died in the resulting explosion along with at least 40 members of the SLA.[25] After the truck exploded, the LTTE overran the camp, taking supplies and arms as they left. Though there is some dispute about whether or not Captain Miller was meant to die in the explosion (Hopgood 2005, p. 50), the LTTE clearly considers this event its first[26] use of suicide bombing. The decision to use it as a tactic stems from an escalation of the war, which had begun in 1983. The SLA had taken control of parts of the Jaffna peninsula and threatened to move south into the Vanni, the LTTE's stronghold. The SLA's offensive into the Vanni, called "Operation Liberation," was the army's best hope for bringing a decisive end to the war (Hopgood 2005, p. 51). According to an LTTE representative, the first suicide mission evolved out of the LTTE's weaker position vis-à-vis the state. "Tamils had no power with regards to the SLA. No power with regards to the military. The members [of the LTTE] were ready to sacrifice their lives in any way needed."[27]

Miller's attack was considered a success by the Tigers; they claim it helped stop the advance of "Operation Liberation." However, Miller's mission fulfilled an even more important role within the LTTE – it was the template for future suicide actions. According to one LTTE website (eelamweb.com), between 1982 and 2004 263 deaths resulted from Black Tiger missions. Of those, 194 suicide missions were conducted by men and 69 by women. These missions were divided between land and sea. Black Tiger missions came at huge material and human cost for both Sinhalese and Tamils. What effect did the high number of suicide missions have on the LTTE? Similar to the Anti-Reservation Movement, the frequency of suicide protest in the movement weakened the symbolic power of the act over time. Suicide missions accomplished certain goals, such as removing an opponent, but as they became a commonplace act their power diminished.

114　*Suicide bombing in Sri Lanka*

The LTTE's use of suicide bombing highlights one of the issues inherent in high intensity protests – are there diminishing returns for the act? In other words, can there be too many deaths, and at what point does the number of deaths begin to adversely affect the movement? Unlike acts of suicide protest, suicide bombing is rarely carried out in isolation but rather is embedded within a long-term campaign against the state. In Chapter 5 we saw that the student activists' protests began to lose power as more people engaged in suicide protest; the same could be said for suicide bombing. The detrimental effect of too many suicide bombings plays out in a few ways. First, as suicide bombing outstrips other tactics, those tactics lose their ability to counterbalance extreme tactics. Second, as the number of events increases they lose their ability to shock and disrupt, an integral aspect of movements and protest. Finally, a high number of suicide bombings limits the potential to construct strong affective ties with the actor. Intensity is a necessary, but not independently sufficient, condition for tactical success.

Emotional narratives

The most important distinction between suicide protest and suicide bombing is that movements cannot narrate these acts in the same way. Whereas suicide protest tries to evoke feelings of pride, sympathy and shame, suicide bombing excludes shame and instead tries to engender fear in the state. This does not mean that the LTTE did not attempt to shame the Sri Lankan state, but that suicide bombing could not be used to convey that message. The LTTE constructed a number of emotional narratives to explain its use of suicide bombing, both to members of the movement and to the state. Emotional appeals are important for groups that use suicide protest since they provide a guide for how these acts should be situated in the movement narrative. I identify two audiences and four emotional states that movements must try to create. First, the movement attempts to inculcate pride and sympathy towards the suicidal actor through the use of celebration and ritual. These emotions are directed towards potential and active members of the movement. Second, in the case of suicide bombing, the movement will direct fear towards the state. If the movement makes an effort to create these emotional reactions, then it is more likely the tactic will be a success.

Pride and sympathy

The LTTE actively crafted emotional stories regarding its use of suicide bombing. First, it celebrated suicide bombers on Black Tiger Commemoration Day – July 5. This was the anniversary of Captain Miller's mission. Each year on this day, Prabhakaran gave a speech honoring the LTTE's "martyrs," which appealed to the audience to feel pride in, and sympathy for, the Black Tigers. Some of Prabhakaran's speeches and poems concerning the Black Tigers were published in the 2004 *Black Tiger Commemoration Day Pamphlet*. One notable poem, by an unspecified author, follows:

The century started by Black Tigers
Began today.
On the earth and sea,
Mingling with air as air
And with waves as waves,
Filling our hearts
Are the Black Tigers.[28]

This poem conveys how the LTTE wanted its members to think of the Black Tigers as martyrs whose acts permeate everyday life. Another poem, by Prabhakaran, reads:

We will reach the path of the leader
Who sacrificed himself totally
We will, as the tigers are known
For self-sacrifice.
We will rise as wave after wave
Looking for a day-break for us.
To reach that goal, we will
Sacrifice our lives.
And become exploding bombs.
We will tread as Black Tigers
And attack the enemies
We will climb the battle field and
Live to see the flowering Eelam.

This poem not only illustrates the significance of Black Tigers within LTTE mythology, but also the ability of suicide bombing to get what the Tigers wanted – a state of their own. These pamphlets were published every year for Black Tiger Commemoration Day, and include pictures of the Black Tigers, as well as information regarding their deaths. The veneration and celebration of Black Tigers on a yearly basis allowed members of the movement to know these actors. Through this sense of knowing, members of the movement could feel pride in the Black Tigers' actions and sympathy for their fate. Unlike fasting to the death, suicide bombing does not have a long duration. The LTTE utilized the aftermath of these actions to construct emotional appeals to the movement.

Fear

The LTTE used suicide bombing to strike fear into the state. This tactic can best be seen by looking at the manner in which the Tigers deploy suicide bombs in the south. For the most part, each Tamil war took place primarily in the north and northeast where the state and the LTTE vied for contested territory; the LTTE did not make any claims on majority Sinhalese areas and so fighting did not spread to the south. However, in the 1990s the

116 *Suicide bombing in Sri Lanka*

LTTE began to attack government and military installations in and around Colombo. Fear depends on proximity to the object of that feeling.[29] It is more difficult to be afraid of something that is distant; by bringing the war to the south the LTTE signaled that it wanted the state to fear it and its abilities. The act itself, not the rhetoric surrounding the act, becomes the emotional appeal.

The construction of fear is a common trope used by terrorist organizations. Groups that use suicide bombings seem to maximize this fear for a few reasons. The unpredictability and damaging nature of the tactic is clear, but many forms of violence can be unpredictable and cause a lot of damage. Still, suicide bombing seems to inculcate more fear than other types of political violence. I don't know why this is, but I suspect that it is what the act says about the movement as a whole. Suicide bombing demonstrates a very high level of commitment within organizations; maybe that's what scares people – the notion that there is no end in sight to the conflict.

The delimited type of emotional narrative illustrates the ways that suicide bombing and suicide protest differ. Whereas movements that only use suicide protest can make a case that the state should be ashamed by its behavior, this appeal to guilt doesn't work with suicide bombing. Movements that use suicide bombing have a difficult time claiming the moral high ground, which in turn limits their ability to narrate events in different ways.

Levels of political competition

The political structure of institutions can affect the success or failure of tactics and movements. If the state has high numbers of viable opposition forces then it will be more willing to negotiate with movements. Though Sri Lanka had become increasingly democratic with regards to the LTTE, there remained a low level of political competition within the state. The reason is twofold. First, the LTTE opted itself out of democratic practices in the south. Second, opposition to the Tigers hardened in the south. Though people wanted peace, many in the south did not want it with the LTTE.

From early on, the LTTE decided that there could be no political solution to the issue of Tamil nationalism. Though Tamil parties like TULF and the EPDP (Eelam People's Democratic Party) stood in elections, the LTTE usually refused to participate.[30] For example, in 1998, elections were held in Jaffna for the first time in 15 years. Five Tamil parties participated in those elections, but the LTTE condemned the elections and those Tamil parties that participated. They actively discouraged other Tamil parties from engaging in state elections through intimidation and assassination. For example, in 1999 a human bomb killed Tamil academic and politician, Dr Neelan Tiruchelvam, outside his office in Colombo. Tiruchelvam was a vice-president of TULF, the moderate Tamil political party. Though the LTTE denied involvement in his murder, it was openly attributed to them. Actions against moderate Tamils discourage participation of all Tamils in Sri Lankan politics.

In addition to the LTTE's own attitudes towards democratic politics opposition to the organization grew in size and intensity in the south. If we return to the issue of the joint mechanism mentioned at the beginning of this chapter, we can see some of the fault lines that existed within Sinhalese politics. President Kumaratunga from the United National Front (UNP) signed an order that would share relief funds with the LTTE. This and other perceived pro-LTTE actions helped lead to the UNP's defeat in the Fall 2005 elections. The situation regarding Sinhalese attitudes towards the LTTE is similar to the relationship between the NBA and the Gujarat government. By 2008 the state was committed to a military solution, successfully destroying the LTTE apparatus in 2009.

Conclusion

The LTTE was one of the most powerful purveyors of suicide bombing in the world. Since its inception, the group has established a powerful military force, and has the capacity to provide for people living under its control. More importantly, the LTTE established strong ties with its members who in turn are willing to die for the organization.[31] Yet the LTTE was not able to gain an ethnic Tamil state in the north, no matter what method it used. The Tigers deployment of suicide protest helped to create affective ties between the movement and the community, but did not engender long-term policy change in its favor. I argue that part of the LTTE's failure lay in the group's over-reliance on the tactic of suicide bombing, as well as the political context of the state. Despite efforts to come to a solution though negotiation, the LTTE's own tactics branded it a militant organization. The LTTE was an example of a violent movement that needed to show its ability to use non-violent tactics.

I chose to engage in a discussion on suicide bombing for a couple of reasons. First, suicide protest and bombing are related to each other and work in similar ways. It makes sense to try and apply my approach to both tactics. In this chapter I showed that the tactical approach to movement success and failure can and should be applied to other types of extreme political action, though the theory must be adapted. My analysis of suicide bombing identifies some areas where this approach changes because of the nature of the tactic, especially with regards to the types of emotional narratives the movement can construct. This stretching doesn't make the approach unrecognizable, but simply underlines that tactics in and of themselves work differently within movements and should be studied individually and not simply be deemed as interchangeable social movement actions. Second, to be perfectly candid, in a post-9/11 world it is hard to make an argument about suicide protest *without* dealing with suicide bombing as well. Finally, established theories of suicide bombing and its ability to impact the state rarely look at the internal mechanisms of the movement and its deployment of the tactic, an area of study which needs to be explored further.

118 *Suicide bombing in Sri Lanka*

Notes

1 For a comprehensive examination of these schools of thought see Brym and Araj (2006).
2 These studies focus on suicide bombing in the Middle East, but based on observation this demographic profile seems to hold true for Sri Lanka as well.
3 This is rare, if only because of retaliation by the LTTE against suicide bombers who changed their minds.
4 The LTTE claims "they try to avoid civilian casualties" (Interview with LTTE representative, Kilinochchi, Sri Lanka, July 7, 2005). However, the movement's definition of "civilian" is unclear. The LTTE often does not take credit for suicide events, though most assume that it is responsible. A good example of this would be the Central Bank Bombing of 1996.
5 Both Tamil and Sinhalese activists have begun to search for the historical roots of this conflict (Nissan and Stirrat 1990).
6 For instance, according to de Silva (1983, p. 128), the Portuguese had a "record of religious persecution, coercion and mindless destruction of places of worship that were sacred to other faiths [that] was unsurpassed in its scale and virulence."
7 The Muslim community is primarily located in the north eastern part of the country. Though most are ethnically Tamil, as the conflict worsened they took on a distinct character based on their religious identity. They are either incorporated into the larger Tamil population, or separated from them depending on the politics of the time. In the early history of Independent Ceylon, the Muslim population was fully part of the Tamil minority.
8 TUF was the combination of all major and minor Tamil political parties at the time (including the TFP), which decided to collectively bargain with the state and stand in elections.
9 Interview with unnamed member of the EPDP, Colombo, Sri Lanka, July 12, 2005.
10 Interview with media source, Colombo, Sri Lanka, June 29, 2005.
11 Interview with unnamed member of the EPDP, Colombo, Sri Lanka, July 12, 2005.
12 See Bloom 2005 for a description of the outbidding process in Sri Lanka and other contexts.
13 Interview with LTTE representative, Kilinochchi, Sri Lanka, July 7, 2005.
14 For example, Douglas Devananda, the leader of the Eelam People's Democratic Party (EPDP), has had 19 separate attempts made on his life. EPDP headquarters in Jaffna is a bunker surrounded by barbed wire and armed guards. The last suicide bomb to detonate in Colombo before the ceasefire was an aborted attempt on his life. Furthermore, in 1986 the LTTE allegedly killed over 150 members of TELO, decimating the entire organization (Ghosh 2003; Bloom 2005).
15 It was clear that the LTTE had good relations with a number of relief organizations when I went to Kilinochchi in the summer of 2005. However, during wartime the LTTE was particularly careful to maintain good relationships with international organizations such as the UNHCR and UNDP. One UN worker told me about an instance when both the LTTE and the SLA stopped a pitched battle to allow UN vehicles to drive through the area; neither side was willing to risk the death of an international aid worker. Once the vans were through the battle restarted.
16 Some scholars consider the conflict between the LTTE and Sri Lankan government to be one long war, which simply had three different phases (Ghosh 2003). For clarity's sake I discuss them as related but distinct military engagements.
17 Bobb, Dilip and Anita Pratap, with S.H. Venkatramani and Mervyn De Silva. "Sri Lanka: Accord Discord," *India Today*, August 15, 1987, pp. 52–56. Also see

Pratap, Anita, "Pirabhakaran 'We reviewed out stand'", *India Today*, August 15, 1987, pp. 54–55.

18 There was another instance of fasting, but this was not conducted by a member of the movement, though it did adopt the act as its own retroactively.

19 When I asked why the LTTE used fasting my informant replied that it was assumed the country of Gandhi's origin would be more amenable to this tactic, but it wouldn't work for Sri Lanka.

20 Ibid.

21 Ibid.

22 The ceasefire has not officially been ended, but the escalation of violence since 2005 clearly shows that peace has ended in the country.

23 Interview with LTTE representative, Kilinochchi, Sri Lanka, July 7, 2005.

24 Until recently the two men in charge of talks were A. Balasingham, Prabhakaran's spokesman, and Tamilselevan, head of the political wing of the LTTE. Both men recently died.

25 The exact number of casualties is unknown. Different sources state that between 39 and more than 100 deaths resulted from this attack (Hopgood 2005, p. 50).

26 The LTTE claims that the 1987 bombing was the very first suicide bombing in any context. There is some dispute about this, as car bombs were used in Lebanon in 1983. However, those attacks could be defined as no-escape attacks. Captain Miller's attack was more in line with the traditional reading of suicide bombing.

27 Interview with representative of the LTTE, Kilinochchi, Sri Lanka, July 7, 2005.

28 LTTE, *Black Tiger Commemoration Day Pamphlet*, 2004, p. 2. All translations from Tamil by M. Jesudasan.

29 See Chapter 2 for an in-depth discussion of fear.

30 Officially, the LTTE claims that elections in the north are invalid. However, at times LTTE supporters have been elected from the north.

31 All members of the LTTE had cyanide capsules sewn into their collars in case of capture.

7 Suicide protest from a global perspective

This book is principally concerned with the impact of suicide protest in South Asia. My decision to concentrate on that region was driven by empirical, theoretical and practical concerns. It should be clear from the previous chapters that India has been witness to a significant amount of suicide protest in the twentieth and twenty-first centuries. Moreover, the variation in type and outcome of suicide protest was crucial in helping to build a theoretical framework to support my analysis of movement success. Finally, my scholarly training has predominantly been on South Asia and that training was crucial to my ability to conduct in-depth qualitative field research. I believe that embedding my book within the South Asian context was both valid and necessary. But I also recognize that that decision effectively curbs my ability to engage with the wide variety of forms and contexts of suicide protest. In this chapter I give myself room to explore the practice of suicide protest outside South Asia. Incidences of suicide as a form of political mobilization have occurred in Europe, East and South East Asia, the Middle East and North America. While certain acts like self-immolation are less common in Latin America and sub-Saharan Africa, the practice of fasting has been adopted within a number of different contexts in those regions. According to a database collected by Michael Biggs, there were 533 suicide protest events worldwide between 1963 and 2002 (Biggs 2005). The global scope and frequency of suicide protest ensures that the tactic has been practiced in a number of different locations and for many disparate reasons. In order to make sense of the variety of cases recorded I have chosen to edit the types of suicide protest I discuss in this chapter down to two specific areas. First, I examine two cases of suicide protest within repressive regimes. Next, I look at suicide protest conducted by single actors.

I begin by investigating the impact of suicide protest within repressive institutions. Embedding this book in India limits the type of political context in which these suicide events take place. Since Independence India has adopted and, for the most part, inculcated democratic institutions, the result of which has been a relatively high tolerance of political mobilization and protest.[1] Even Sri Lanka is officially labeled a democratic system.[2] Nonetheless, politics in India has at least been marked by the desire for, if not always the application of, democratic norms, which influences the forms and outcomes of mobilization. In this chapter I turn away from democratic contexts to examine the use of this tactic in authoritarian regimes. What might suicide protest look like in these places? How effective might this form of mobilization be in regimes that have no need to listen or be moved by citizenship participation? I begin to answer these questions by briefly looking at two cases of suicide protest within repressive regimes or institutions.

I also limited the scope of the core cases in the book by only including instances of suicide protest that were part of a larger organization. In fact, the existence of an organizing mobilizational structure is a cornerstone of my definition of suicide protest. It is the presence of a social movement organization that makes these acts suicide *protest*, and not simply emotional or personal suicide. I continue to maintain that approaching this topic through the lens of organizations is correct. Yet there are a number of instances where suicide has clearly been used by people for a political purpose, but not planned by a larger movement. In other words, there are many different types of suicide protest, ranging from an individual who self-immolates in front of a municipal building without clearly articulating his purpose, to the type of organized suicide protest conducted by the NBA. In this chapter I investigate the possible effectiveness of individual suicide protest; these events may have a lot of dramatic potential, but can they engender policy change without an organization to back them?

To understand the effectiveness of suicide protest within other regions, I focus on four significant cases in the Middle East, Europe, China and the United States. Each of these suicide protest events stretch my theory either empirically or theoretically. I have chosen to assess my approach in this way for three reasons. First, as previously discussed, suicide protest has increasingly become a worldwide phenomenon. The global scope of suicide protest needs to be analyzed, though of course this is much more easily said than done. I have devoted a great deal of space in this book to arguing for a context-dependent approach to the study of suicide protest. I still believe in the richness of that style of analysis. But it is very difficult to conduct thick description on a global scale. To that end, this chapter is an initial attempt to conduct a cross-national comparison of suicide protest. Of course, this is a superficial examination at best; I am not an expert in any of these regional contexts. However, I believe that it is necessary to start investigating suicide protest as a global issue and a global concern.

Next, this chapter allows me to examine the influence that different organizational matrices may have on the effectiveness of suicide protest. My model is designed to examine this tactic when it is embedded within a larger social movement.[3] However, suicide protest has been deployed in a number of different ways, including seemingly spontaneous individual acts. Sometimes these acts seem to have long-lasting effects, and at other times they are rarely discussed; what explains the difference? This chapter allows me to present initial conclusions regarding the application of the tactical approach on single acts

122 *Suicide protest from a global perspective*

of suicide protest. Of the four cases under discussion in this chapter, two had little or no initial organizational backing. Despite this similarity, the impact of these two cases varied significantly. Thus, this chapter allows me to engage with another type of political suicide protest and compare and contrast its effectiveness.

Finally, beyond broadening the empirical scope of this book, this chapter also helps to test the theoretical limits of the tactical approach. To what extent can my argument be applied to other cases? Is the approach generalizable to other contexts and types of suicide protest? In Chapter 6 I stretched my method to examine suicide bombing in Sri Lanka, a different type of tactic within the same region. In this chapter I do the opposite, looking at the same tactic – suicide protest – within different regions and political contexts. I believe that my work has implications for how and why it may result in successful or failed mobilizations in other places, though not in quite the same way as I have shown in the rest of the book. This chapter raises more issues than it resolves, but I do reach some tentative conclusions that point to possible theoretical and empirical areas of future concern.

Cases

In order to extend the empirical and theoretical scope of my approach, I examine four significant cases of suicide protest in a global context; these four cases are regionally distal and exemplify particular differences within types of suicide protest acts. I divide these four cases into two pairs that focus on different spheres of concern. The first pair of cases focus on the use of suicide protest within repressive regimes or institutions. I start by looking at a common type of suicide protest – the prison fast. Over the course of the twentieth century hunger strikes and fasts have become a common form of protest within institutionalized settings. Prisons fasts have occurred in all parts of the world, with varying consequences. In particular I apply the tactical approach to the series of fasts which took place in the Long Kesh Prison (also referred to as the Maze) in Northern Ireland in 1981. Conducted by members of the Provisional Irish Republican Army (IRA), the fasts at the Maze are justly regarded as being among the most prominent examples of suicide protest in general, and prison fasts in particular. I then compare this series of fasts to the recent instances of self-immolation by activists in and outside Tibet. The Chinese government is not known for its tolerance of protest, but it seems particularly ill-disposed towards suicide protests, especially within Tibet. In this section I explore the possible consequences and effects of suicide protest within institutions that allow little or no space for mobilization. What impacts, if any, can suicide protest have on these contexts?

Next, I compare two cases of individual self-immolation. I examine the history and impacts of Malachi Ritscher's protest against the Iraq War in 2006 in Chicago to the self-immolation of Mohamed Bouazizi in Tunisia in 2010, an act that helped to spark the series of democratizing events in the Middle

East known as the Arab Spring. Despite superficial similarities between these acts, each self-immolation engendered very different political impacts. Both of these cases are good examples of individual acts of suicide protest. In contrast to organization-based suicide protest, or personal suicide, individual acts have the potential to be either ignored or, conversely, impactful. What are the factors that can guarantee the latter and not the former? Can an individual act really change public policy? In examining these four cases I find that my approach can shed some light on extreme protest and movement outcomes.

In the rest of this chapter I utilize secondary sources and media reports to briefly consider and compare the four cases. Based on this investigation I hope to not only expose some strengths and weaknesses of the tactical approach, but also see how suicide protest plays out in disparate contexts around the world. One concern I would like to raise with my analysis in this chapter is the unequal amount of information available about the four cases covered. The duration and importance of the Irish case cannot be disputed; that reputation and legacy has resulted in a lot of secondary material and analysis. The other three cases are either too recent, or too little-known, to have produced as much secondary information. Sometimes that lack of information itself, however, is indicative of the status of these protests within the public consciousness.

Suicide protest in repressive contexts

In deciding to explore different types of suicide protest, I felt it important to begin my analysis within less democratic, or repressive, institutional settings. Each of the three cases of suicide protest I examine within the Indian context is set in relatively democratic space. In this chapter I look at two types of suicide protest performed in repressive contexts. I first look into the circumstances and events of the Long Kesh Prison fasts in Northern Ireland in 1981. Next I investigate the ongoing self-immolations of Tibetans in China and neighboring countries in 2011. I compare these two cases by using the rubric of the tactical approach. Clearly there are differences in the actions and implications of a repressive regime versus a repressive institution. However, I feel that the comparison between the prison fasts in Northern Ireland and the self-immolations against the Chinese government make sense in that both contexts exert similar types of control and disincentives to protests by individuals who reside within them.

Repressive states and institutions

Despite evidence to the contrary, the presence of dissent within a democracy remains counterintuitive to some observers; there is a notion that democratic institutions provide space to express discontent institutionally or through elections. If we follow through on this logic, protest *should* only occur in repressive regimes, where it is likely there will be higher levels of social and

124   *Suicide protest from a global perspective*

political dissatisfaction but no avenues to express it. In fact, democracies are much more likely to create the framework for mobilization as groups seek to shift public policy, making democracies a much more welcoming place for mobilization (Goldstone 2004).

Social movements, small and large, are much more highly controlled and repressed within authoritarian systems. Because of the high levels of regulation, contention can look very different within repressive or closed regimes. The notion of mobilization as "a last resort" may have more meaning when more institutionalized forms of dissent are delegalized or met with repression.[4] Not only may protest look different in repressive contexts, it may engender very different political outcomes. Borrowing once again from the suicide bombing literature, Pape (2005) suggests that the tactic is more effective in democracies because public opinion can pressure the state to accommodate extreme forms of protest. This conclusion can be adapted for other types of protest. As mobilization increases, democratic states are vulnerable not only to movements, but also to public opinion and electoral cycles (Giugni 2004) which can have crucial effects on the ultimate outcome of the movement. Authoritarian and repressive regimes do not have to worry as much about negative public opinion, or about their prospects in an election. I do not mean to suggest that protest and mobilization cannot be effective in less democratic contexts. However, not only might these movements face a rougher terrain in their pursuit of political change, success in these regimes could look very different to the way it does in democracies.

Based on my analysis of the fasts in the Maze, and of the Tibetan self-immolators, I find that suicide protest can have an effect in repressive regimes – but not necessarily in the form of forcing a policy shift. Instead, the positive effects of suicide mobilization are more keenly felt within the movement itself, making such actions more symbolically successful as compared to the more practical understanding of success that I utilize in the core analysis of this book. In other words, suicide protest within repressive regimes may not win groups their stated goals, but can help to create a powerful narrative and hagiography of struggle and resistance, which may indirectly lead to political success in the long run.

Prison fasts[5]

In 1929 Jatindra Nath Das, a Bengali revolutionary, was the first person to die of a fast in Lucknow Prison. This was a political fast conducted in order to create better conditions for Indian prisoners. His death earned respect from other activists and people throughout India, and Das was hailed as a hero of the movement. Das's fast was famous at the time, especially since Bhaghat Singh, another well-known revolutionary, was fasting with him. But the use of protest fasts to change prison conditions fell out of favor within the Nationalist Movement as a whole, though Gandhi and others continued to use prison as a setting for other fasts. Much of the unpopularity of prison

Suicide protest from a global perspective   125

fasts as a way of advancing prisoners' rights can be attributed to Gandhi's own attitudes towards these events, which I discussed in Chapter 2. Despite Gandhi's disapprobation of this type of fast in India, the tactic continues to be popular throughout the world. Similar to Das's fasts, other prison fasts often focus on the conditions and treatment of prisoners, though there may be a larger political issue concerning the underlying reasons behind the imprisonment of those individuals involved. Prison fasts have become a common, if not habitual, practice in the twentieth and twenty-first centuries. Based on this high frequency of use we should examine how, when, and why prison fasts may be effective. I separate these fasts from other fasts for one crucial reason. Generally speaking, prison fasts take place within a much more repressive, coercive and monolithic environment.[6] Unlike states, democratic or not, prisons have fewer points of competition and, therefore, compromise, than other political institutions, even if the state gets involved. The coercive nature of prisons should be self-explanatory; however, there is one area where, depending on the context, the prison environment can influence suicide protestors more than the state and other institutions – I am speaking of the issue of force-feeding prisoners.

Unless activists are held in prison, fasts to the death rarely end in the forced feeding of the protestor. In the early twentieth century, suffragettes and Irish nationalists in the UK and the United States have often been force-fed as a response to their actions.[7] Force-feeding continues to be carried out as states attempt to control these types of protest, despite international agreements to the contrary (World Medical Association 2006). For example, when I was writing this chapter at least ten detainees in Guantanamo Bay naval prison were being force-fed by the American government.[8] There are numerous reasons why states may choose to respond to a fast by force-feeding activists: to prevent publicity or further actions in and outside the prison, to demoralize protestors, to prevent death, and many others. But clearly this is a drastic measure and one that presupposes prisoners have no entitlement to take ultimate control of their own bodies, a situation that suicide protestors outside prison must rarely face. The process of force-feeding is often painful and invasive[9] and clearly indicates a high level of coercive power within the institution (Anderson 2009; Anderson 2010). Moreover, not only does force-feeding sometimes not save the life of the activist, it can also serve to simply extend the duration of the fast.[10] In Chapter 2 I discussed the construction of a political idiom of self-sacrifice and pain in India. That idea rests partially on the understanding that actors have control over their own bodies and can therefore proactively choose to transform their bodies into a location of protest. Within a context like prison, where the institution controls every aspect of life, using the body for protest may be the only option available, and yet, in the end, even that power could be taken away. That level of domination demonstrates the coercive and repressive nature of the institution of prison with regard to suicide protest.

Fasting has become a common method in many parts of the world for prisoners to try and assert their rights within a coercive and closed system. Goals

126 *Suicide protest from a global perspective*

for these acts of suicide protest range from asserting prisoners' rights, to disputing prison status, to raising attention about imprisonment, let alone the underlying reasons that may have led to a protestor's imprisonment in the first place. With this in mind, I believe that despite the fact prisoners in the Maze were opposed to *democratic* Britain[11] and its policies, it is appropriate to include their fasts as examples of suicide protest within a repressive institution, i.e. prison.

Northern Ireland and the Maze fasts of 1981

In the following section I briefly discuss the history of the discord in Northern Ireland between the IRA and the British government. The political, economic, social and cultural causes and impacts of this conflict have been well researched by a number of scholars (Bew *et al.*, 1979; Bishop and Mallie, 1987; Irvin 1999). I begin with a brief examination of the IRA as an organization, followed by a discussion of the circumstances leading to the fast. I analyze the setting and staging of the fasts within a comparative analysis of suicide protest in Northern Ireland and China.

The Provisional Irish Republican Army (IRA) has been active in different forms since the late nineteenth century. First formed as a violent nationalist movement in the eighteenth century, later iterations have been labeled as a militant terrorist organization. Initially formed to agitate for Home Rule against the British, early versions of the IRA were able to spur the formation of an independent Irish Republic, after which it split into two broad groups. The IRA of that period was known for its use of violence, as well as other tactics, and seemed to be part of an international wave of similar organizations (such as Narodnaya Volya in Russia) that existed throughout Europe and utilized new technology to deploy violence. Though the IRA was not by any means the only organization working for Home Rule, its use of violence placed it in a position of primary importance. After Independence, the split in the state was echoed in the group; some members were satisfied with a divided Ireland while others wished to continue to agitate for a free Ireland that would encompass the whole island, leading to a short civil war (Whittaker 2012). Thus, the new Provisional Irish Republican Army shifted its focus to Northern Ireland; its popularity waning and then waxing as relations between Catholics and Protestants deteriorated. As before, the IRA was labeled a terrorist organization; its tactics, inventory of weapons and use of tactical training methods reinforcing this conclusion. Despite the presence and leadership of a violent organization, the movement also contained nonviolent and constitutionally minded elements; the IRA was intertwined with the political party Sinn Fein, which ultimately negotiated the ceasefire with the British government in 1975.

Meanwhile, escalation of the conflict in Northern Ireland is a story not too dissimilar to the evolution of the war in Sri Lanka. Mobilization for an Independent Ireland began in the 1800s and ended with the creation of the

Independent Republic of Ireland and the province of Northern Ireland, officially part of the United Kingdom. Partition was motivated by demographic, i.e. religious, differences; the six counties that were shifted into Northern Ireland were majority Protestant and did not want to be part of a free Irish state. These social, cultural and economic fissures were not magically healed after partition, but actually got worse. Between 1922 and 1960 tensions remained high in the new Protestant-majority Northern Ireland, with minority resident Catholics feeling an increasing sense of economic and political marginalization in the new province, until finally the existing fault lines erupted into widespread violence, a time known as "The Troubles." The IRA and other groups mobilized quickly, functionally making Northern Ireland a warzone. The IRA modified tactics it had used in the early twentieth century for the new conflict, including riots, car bombs, bombings and assassination. The conflict escalated as peaceful protests were met with violence, and British law appeared to shift away from democratic norms with regard to the situation in Northern Ireland. Moreover, the violence of the 1960s was aided by the fact that large-scale fighting between Catholics and Protestants had taken place only 40 years earlier, meaning that there were still people alive who not only remembered, but most likely also participated in that violence (Feldman 1991, p. 23). The memories of previous actions created a sense of ongoing history, which helped to embed the fight much more deeply; individuals could draw on a living history to help create a mythological story about the war. It was within this fraught political context that a number of prisoners in the Long Kesh (Maze) and Armagh prisons began to protest their status as political prisoners, a standing that had been revoked by the British. These protests ended in the fast, and the death of ten men in 1981.

The decision to start a series of prison fasts in 1981 was not an impromptu one, but the culmination of deeply rooted cultural, social and political praxis, as well as the escalation of previous body-centered prison protests. Culturally, fasting and mortification of the flesh has been a component of Christian practice (Bell 1985), which in turn may have strongly influenced attitudes towards such customs.[12] Socially and economically, fasting was used in Ireland as a tool for resolving disputes or bringing attention to unjust debts – very similar to the practice of *dharna* I described in Chapter 2. Like a *dharna* the actor would fast on the doorstep of his opponent, which made the dispute public and forced action from the opponent as it would be a matter of social shame to allow someone to die at their door (Beresford 1989). This tradition suggests the relational and emotional context of fasting within Irish culture. Moreover, it makes economic or political motivations for fasting acceptable. Fasting was given a direct political component in the early twentieth century; as I described in Chapter 2, many groups began to use fasting in their political campaigns, and especially within prisons. British and American suffragettes and Indian nationalists, all of whom used the prison fast as a form of civil disobedience, joined Irish activists. For the Irish, initial uses of the prison fast had fatal consequences – at least six men died in prison. As with other groups,

128 *Suicide protest from a global perspective*

prison fasts at this time were concerned more with the treatment of prisoners rather than the underlying conflict itself; but of course these motivations become conflated as activists die, making these fasts important not just for prisoners but the movement as a whole.

Finally, the fasts of 1981 were also the climax of a series of protests regarding prisoner status and prison conditions. The government criminalized IRA members in the late 1970s, overturning an earlier decision to treat them as political prisoners. The change in status was a crucial one, not only because criminals were treated very differently to political prisoners but also because it commented on the merits and morals of the movement itself. In response, IRA prisoners began with the Blanket protests, in which men refused to wear the prisoner uniform choosing to wear instead a blanket or nothing at all. This was followed by the Dirty protests; these actions, carried out by men in the Maze and women in Armagh Prison, consisted of prisoners refusing to wash or use prison facilities, often spreading their excrement and menstrual blood on the walls of their cells.[13] The core goals of both these campaigns was to ensure the application of the "Five Points," which advocated for the application of particular rights of political prisoners in Northern Ireland.[14] By 1980 these protests had been going on for some time with no positive response, leading to a 53-day fast by a number of prisoners. The fast ended when the British government agreed to implement the Five Points. Unfortunately, that promise was not fulfilled and in 1981 Bobby Sands and a number of other men began a second series of fasts to the death, resulting in the death of ten men. Right until the very end, the Margaret Thatcher government remained unmoved by the protests.[15] Despite the cultural and political significance of the fasts they did not result in the type of success that I describe in this book (i.e. policy shifts in favor of the movement), but these actions did help the movement in other, less tangible, ways.

Self-immolations in Tibet

In contrast to the IRA, the self-immolations in Tibet are ongoing, with no end in sight. Despite its claims to the contrary, it is safe to say that China is not a state that tolerates protest and mobilization. The brutal repression during the Tiananmen Square protests in 1989, which included a number of fasts, has served as a warning to activists within the state regarding the possible ramifications of protest within the country.[16] With this history in mind it is doubly surprising that there continues to be such a high level of resistance against the Chinese presence in Tibet. Despite the possible consequences of political mobilization, Tibetans around the world and within China continue to agitate against the takeover, resulting in a series of continuing self-immolations that started in 2012.

China's history in Tibet remains controversial and tragic. The invasion in 1950 by the newly established People's Republic of China (PRC) was a reassertion of control that had been lost in the early part of the twentieth century.

Suicide protest from a global perspective 129

Beyond the violence of the invasion itself, the takeover in 1950 also seeded a long-standing social and cultural conflict between the Buddhist Tibetans and the newly atheistic Chinese state. Despite the claim of Tibetan Buddhism's "non-violent" nature[17] at the time of the invasion the state met armed resistance both in 1956, and then again in 1959, ultimately leading to the Dalai Lama's flight to India. Since 1969 the Chinese government has established highly repressive policies within Tibet including the destruction of numerous monasteries, the resettlement of non-Tibetans in the region, and the reorganization of parts of its territory into already-existing Chinese provinces.

Since 1960 the status of Tibet has remained a major area of contention in China, Tibet, India, Nepal, and, due to a very organized movement, internationally. The Chinese invasion of Tibet has been an international issue from the moment it occurred. The organized opposition to the invasion has utilized the best resources it could have, given the lack of concerted military attack, which was to turn a territorial expansion into a global human rights issue. The movement is somewhat divided, though leadership is generally attributed to the Dalai Lama; groups such as the Free Tibet Movement and the International Campaign for Tibet seem to work in cooperation with each other.[18] These organizations work on a number of fronts; within India the Tibetan leadership must help to resettle and guide the exiled population and negotiate with the Indian and other governments. On a global scale the movement, led by the Dalai Lama, not only educates people regarding the issues, but also raises funds. The movement has been successful at utilizing the same sort of international triangulation that I described in Chapter 4, as used by the NBA – though without the same results. In this case the movement tries to convince or persuade citizens in other states to pressure their own governments into putting Tibet on the agenda – the Free Tibet Movement has made a relatively good job of this. While the movement has not been as effective as the NBA in transforming its interests into political change, the fault doesn't only lie with the organization, but also in the fact that the PRC remains entrenched in the region and generally refuses to discuss the matter. That, coupled with China's economic power, makes it difficult for other states to exert any pressure on it.[19] The PRC has labeled Tibet as an Autonomous Region, which theoretically provides for certain levels of local control.[20] But the government has also instituted an aggressive campaign of resettlement of the Han population in Tibet, as well as interfered with the practice of Tibetan Buddhism. But despite the presence of the regime, Tibetans continue to agitate, and recently they have begun a campaign of self-immolations – though they are not the first to do so within China.[21]

The use of self-immolation in Tibet has historical precedents; though carried out by a different Buddhist group, the first political self-immolations of the twentieth century were conducted by monks such as Thich Quan Duc in protest at their treatment by the Vietnamese government. Quan Duc was followed by other monks, but this should not be taken as an indication that self-immolation is a practice common within Buddhist scripture. In fact, there are

130   *Suicide protest from a global perspective*

distinctly negative feelings towards suicide within Buddhism; what *is* viewed as positive is the notion of self-sacrifice (Thurman 1997, p. 16).

The tactical approach in Northern Ireland and Tibet

Comparing these two cases using my approach reveals some problems in the usage of suicide protest within repressive regimes. In order to complete this comparison I apply each case to the four crucial variables outlined in my argument. Of course, the situation in Tibet is ongoing, so it is a bit unfair to compare this case to such an iconic instance of suicide protest. However, based on the history of the region I believe that it is fitting to make some tentative speculations regarding outcomes. My analysis of these cases demonstrates a lack of policy change and social movement success, but despite this I believe that these events can be powerful in a different ways. The strength of suicide protest in repressive regimes lies more in its ability to communicate narratives within the protest community in general, and within the movement more specifically, not in its ability to create policy change.

Tactical depth

As I have previously discussed, high levels of tactical depth indicate the level to which movements use a comprehensive approach to the issue at hand. In particular, I believe that the presence of non-violent tactics helps to mitigate the extreme nature of suicide protest, allowing the state to find a negotiating partner within the movement. Looking at the two cases in Ireland and Tibet, it is clear that their campaigns take very different approaches.

The tactical depth of the IRA's prison fast is difficult to discern for a number of reasons. First, should we only include the prison protests, or the IRA as a whole? If we do choose to analyze the larger movement against the British, then should all groups be included? In other words, what is the level of analysis? In analyzing the IRA I examine the movement as a whole. Though the prison fasts were primarily concerned with prisoners' rights, it is clear that both the causes behind the mobilization and the responses of the British were mediated by the larger religious and political conflict. Would the Thatcher government have reacted, or not reacted, in the same way to a prison protest not linked to a larger issue? Second, though there were a number of different groups working throughout the conflict, the IRA was perceived by the British to be the strongest representative for Catholics at the time. With that in mind, to what extent did the IRA demonstrate tactical depth? I argue that there was a medium level of it for the IRA. Once again, I believe that a comparison between the IRA and the LTTE is apt. Though both used other, non-violent tactics, the severity of the violence that they used mitigated the moderating effects of those tactics. Within H-block of the Maze itself, clearly the prisoners used other forms of protest, but I would argue that the extreme nature of those body-centered protests did little to calm the authorities. Thus, the

Suicide protest from a global perspective 131

extreme forms of violence and protest deployed by the IRA were not positively affected by the moderating presence of political parties, non-violent groups, or even engagement in non-violent forms of protest.

In contrast, I argue that the movement for Tibet demonstrates a high level of tactical depth, though this claim must be qualified. Studying the movements for Tibet presents a slight sense of schizophrenia as one navigates between the domestic and international campaigns. This disjointedness is a reflection of the fragmented goals and issues at the heart of the movement. Of course, the overwhelming goal is for greater autonomy within China and the return of refugees. However, the community is also concerned with the status of Tibetans outside China. In addition to the previously described split, the goals of the movement internationally – to have citizens of other states pressure their own governments and international organizations – and the goals of Tibetans in Tibet – to openly agitate against the Chinese government – differ in the extreme. Thus, there is a sense of strong non-violent values on the international front, coupled with the increasingly risky and extreme protests that take place within Tibet. The issue at hand regarding the Tibetan case is that an international observer may claim a high level of tactical depth, which can be seen in the numerous demonstrations, boycotts and letter writing campaigns started by the movement. Simultaneously, the PRC could (and does) assert that Tibetans are highly confrontational and tend to use extreme forms of protest. This thorny issue of multiple areas of mobilization and perceptions limits the potential power of movements that use many types of tactics. Thus, while the movement for Tibet does actually utilize many different forms of mobilization, it doesn't necessarily do this *within* Tibet. Of course, by the same token, whatever amount of protest it does engage in within China is subject to harsher forms of punishment. That said, the domestic movement has been known to use demonstrations, boycotts and letter writing campaigns in addition to international political persuasion.

Intensity

Both the IRA and the Tibetan protestors exhibited high levels of intensity. Bobby Sands and other protestors utilized the method of relay fasting (which is extensively used in India for hunger strikes) during their mobilization, which means that as people succumbed to death, other activists would begin to fast. This served to prolong the duration of the fast as a whole and demonstrated the depth of commitment to it. Altogether 23 men from the IRA and the Irish National Liberation Army (INLA) started to fast, with ten men dying as a result of starvation-related illness. Bobby Sands was the first to start the fast on March 1, 1981. He died on May 5, 1981. Sands's death was followed in short order by Francis Hughes, Raymond McCreesh and Patsy O'Hara, all in May of that year. A second group of six protestors began to die in July and August 1981, they were; Joe McDonnell, Martin Hurson, Kevin Lynch, Kiernan Doherty, Tom McElwee, and Mickey Devine. The fast began to break

132 *Suicide protest from a global perspective*

apart when Paddy Quinn's mother decided to intervene in his fast (Beresford 1989, pp. 275–9). The deaths were not only tragic, but also well documented. Death from starvation is a long and drawn out process. Protestors waste away as the body literally begin to it eat itself in order to survive.

Tibetan protestors also have demonstrated a high level of intensity. According to newspaper reports and the Free Tibet website, at least 100 people have self-immolated since 2011 in and outside Tibet. Protestors include Buddhist monks and nuns, as well as a teenage boy and others. While not as organized a resistance as the IRA, the movements in support of Tibet have been able to account for all of the individual protestors on different websites and new articles. Since this is an ongoing campaign it is hard to speculate if the immolations will continue and whether or not we will see the same type of "suicide protest fatigue" that I described with regard to the LTTE and the students of the Anti-Reservation Movement, though that sense might be mitigated by the continuation of political reprisals against protestors by the state.

Emotional narratives

As I previously discussed, the differences between fasting to death and self-immolation are distinct when discussing the creation and deployment of emotional narratives of pride, sympathy and shame. The duration of a fast allows the protestor to communicate with the public directly, which is much less likely to happen in the case of individuals who self-immolate. However, both the IRA and the Tibetan Movement clearly attempted to create emotional narratives regarding their use of suicide protest.

I claim that movements endeavor to familiarize constituents with suicide protest actors in order to aid in the creation of affective ties of pride and sympathy. Movements will also try to direct a sense of shame towards the state. Attempts to create a sense of familiarity between Irish Catholics and the IRA activists were not difficult. An ongoing narrative was the idea that these prisoners could have been anyone. Moreover, Bobby Sands and others actively communicated with the public through representatives, and with their own words. Sands published poems and an autobiography, highlighting why he engaged in the fast and introducing the notion that he was just like everyone else living in Northern Ireland. Later on his diary at the start of his fast was published. In it he describes the day-to-day-reality of his prison fast (Sands 1997). Sands's poetry and writings, as well as the public statements made by protestors, helped to direct the way that the IRA and INLA wanted the fast to be discussed. In addition to written and oral testimonies, Sands also ran for a vacant parliamentary seat. His subsequent election helped legitimatize his cause and protest, but also aided in creating a sense of knowing him. The emotional narratives of the fasts in the Maze have lasted beyond the death of Sands and the others. People still celebrate and commemorate their actions throughout Northern Ireland.

Suicide protest from a global perspective   133

The Tibetan case is ongoing, so it is a bit unfair to compare their protest to the completed suicide protest action in Northern Ireland. However, it is clear that the movement is trying to narrate these events internationally as well as within Tibet, though less so to the government of the PRC. The Free Tibet Movement website (freetibet.org) has a list and short biography of each person who has self-immolated. There have been numerous articles and editorials published about these protests. The movement is doing this, in part to mitigate the effect of a campaign against the self-immolations started by the PRC. Despite actions by the Chinese government, the movement has actively tried to establish affective ties between actors and potential constituents of the movement.

What seems most interesting is the seeming lack of narrative towards the state. Of course the IRA and other groups were in negotiations with the government to end the fast throughout its seven-month duration. But the descriptions of the fast seem to focus much more on what the fast might mean to the movement as a whole and less on the fast's ability to create a strategic lever against the state. The situation in Tibet is even more acute as protestors routinely disappear or are jailed or tortured. The notion that protests can be a means of communication with the state seem secondary to the attention these suicide protests can bring to the issue.[22] This is one area where we may be able to make a distiction between the deployment of suicide protest in democratic and repressive regimes.

Level of political competition

I claim that both the IRA and Tibetan protestors work within repressive institutions. That said, to what extent is there an actual (or perceived) politically competitive environment? Before I begin to look at the movements themselves, I would like to examine the differences between the level of political competition and the level of coercion within political space, as I do not believe that these things are synonymous. The level of political competition cites the actual and perceived ability of movements to take advantage of shifts or fragmentation within the state. In India, this occurred within a single party when that party internalized different ideologies, or describes the conflict between central and state governments. Meanwhile, movements may also be unable to recognize this competition, as was the case for the Anti-Reservation Movement students when that movement was co-opted by a political party. Thus, there may be different levels of political competition within a single political institution. Considering the levels of political competition within repressive regimes I find that there can be scope for competition within these systems. However, the repressive response of the state when dealing with protest makes this variable much less important in trying to understand the effects of suicide, or indeed any type of protest.

Based on my analysis of the IRA's fast in 1981, I contend that the movement was working within a moderately competitive political context, but that

134 *Suicide protest from a global perspective*

Table 7.1 A comparison of the IRA and Tibetan protestors

	Tactical depth	Intensity	Emotional narrative	Political competition	Outcome
IRA	Medium	High	High	Moderate but repressive	No policy shifts
Tibet	High	High	High	Low and repressive	No policy shifts

this was functionally nullified by the repressive attitude of the state towards the movement as a whole. The situation in Northern Ireland was an example of a repressive regime and institution working within a relatively competitive environment. For example, not only were elections held during the fast, Bobby Sands was able to use the process to win a parliamentary seat. But success through electoral competition was not enough to shift the state or the prison's stance regarding the fast. The best example of the state's attitude is the fact that it stripped IRA prisoners of their political status. By criminalizing the protestors the state effectively forbade them from claiming any type of rights-based reparations or consideration from the state. They were criminals, and like other criminals they should be punished. This type of attitude is a not uncommon background for many examples of prison fasting. Not all prisoners that fast are incarcerated for political reasons, but the standing of "prisoner" then becomes of paramount importance.

In comparison, the Tibetans are mobilizing within a regime that is both repressive and uncompetitive. The effect of this is that protest itself becomes much more risky and less likely to move or change state opinion. The nature of political protest in contemporary China reveals that while protest routinely occurs, it is small in scope (Perry 2009, p. 206), indicating a lack of willingness to contend with the state regarding fundamental state institutions, political practices or over its authority. The Free Tibet movement is attempting to change this.[23] Accounts regarding the high level of repression in Tibet include those of people who are tried and jailed for being suspected of inciting self-immolation. I argue that this type of repression ensures that these actions will be less able to shift state policy, in which case, once again, the level of political competition seems less important than it would within a democratic context.

Is it simply the case that suicide protest cannot be effective within repressive contexts? The answer is yes, but only if we consider the very narrow definition of movement success that I have chosen to utilize in this book. The inability or failure of movements to effectively communicate to the state by means of their suicide protest actions makes those events less able to clearly engender policy change. However, while events described in Northern Ireland and Tibet did not create political shifts, it would be wrong to think that they were totally "ineffective." The picture changes if we begin to think of outcomes not in terms of policy shifts, but of internal movement concerns. In another article (Lahiri 2014) I discuss the motivations for suicide protest and focus on the

Suicide protest from a global perspective 135

ability of movements to use this method to speak in certain ways to their own supporters, arguing that movements use suicide protest to increase support, drive recruitment and engender cohesion. In many ways these are the same goals as an emotional narrative, as I have described here. The difference of the effect of suicide protest in democratic and authoritarian regimes is that movements may place a primacy on increasing support over actually attaining their stated goals. In other words, my analysis of these movements suggests that we may need to unpack the notion of "success" when speaking of suicide protest in different contexts.

Individual suicide protest events

Protest is most often associated with groups and mass action. The preoccupation with organizational and collective forms of dissent makes sense, since these are events that are most readily discerned and are most likely to attract attention. Even though it is rational to focus our attention on the theoretical and empirical implications of social movements, protest is not only limited to the large scale. Indeed, quotidian forms of protest not only exist, but they may have crucial implications for the development of collective action and the articulation of claims as movements grow. Unfortunately, individual acts of protest are very difficult to research, precisely because of their size. A single person standing in front of Parliament with a sign might garner some attention and questions, but that single protestor is unlikely to attract media attention or a reaction from the state. The ability to ignore single person protests diminishes once the actor chooses to deploy suicide, though not always. The more important question, however, is can those single suicide events have any lasting impact on policy and politics? Based on my analysis of two such cases I claim that suicide protest can have an incredible influence on politics and protest, but the level of impact is contingent on how, when and where the event is deployed, more than the underlying cause or the presence of supporting movements.

There is little work in social movement literature on individual protests. In fact, the literature seems to be moving in the opposite direction by focusing on how social movements are embedded within a political or mobilizational field – broadening, not narrowing, the scope of analysis (Koopmans and Statham 1999; Fligsten and McAdam 2011). Individuals could be a part of a social movement field, but their actions and impacts have not really been studied. There are empirical reasons for this lack of analysis; it is hard to trace and track these types of actions. But that difficulty does not mean that single or non-movement acts of suicide protest are rare. Based on the 482 events of suicide protest coded in my database, at least 130 were not reported as being linked to any larger movement. While not the majority, this still leaves a significant number of cases that need to be investigated.

To understand the implications of individual level suicide protests I examine two events that have occurred this century. First, I describe the self-

136 *Suicide protest from a global perspective*

immolation of Mohammed Bouazizi, a Tunisian fruit vendor. Bouazizi's self-immolation is credited as the impetus for the "Arab Spring" and is now considered to be a crucial moment in the development of anti-government mobilization in Tunisia. In contrast, Malachi Ritscher, an American musician who immolated himself in Chicago in 2006, received little to no media attention. His protest is mostly forgotten, if it was ever known at all. These two cases demonstrate the importance that staging and setting have on the deployment of protest, as well as emphasizing the consequences of emotional narratives or lack thereof.

Mohamed Bouazizi

Mohamed Bouazizi was a 26-year-old unlicensed fruit vendor in Sidi Bouzid, Tunisia. According to an article published in *Foreign Policy*, Bouazizi was from a modest family, which he was forced to support from the age of ten (De Soto 2011). He was a street vendor who did not have a permanent kiosk at the market, making his economic security more perilous than secure. By many accounts Bouazizi was a talented vendor (De Soto 2011; Abouzeid 2011), but was not able to transform his skill into the type of earnings that could materially change his and his family's lives. Events are said to have unfolded as follows:[24] on December 17, 2010, Bouazizi went to the street market where he habitually sold his fruit. At that time he was harassed by municipal police officers regarding an allegedly unpaid fine. His offer to pay was refused and his cart and goods were confiscated, including an electronic set of scales. During this confrontation a female police officer is said to have slapped and insulted Bouazizi. After his livelihood was taken away Bouazizi tried to appeal to the municipal government, who refused to hear him. An hour later, at 11:30am, Bouazizi set himself on fire in front of the main government building in Sidi Bouzid. As is the case with many self-immolations, Bouazizi survived for a time, finally succumbing to his injuries on January 4, 2011. By the time of his death, politics in Tunisia had fundamentally changed. Despite attempts to deal with the increasing mobilization in the wake of the immolation, including visiting Bouazizi in the hospital, within ten days of his death President Ben Ali had fled to Saudi Arabia.

The protests incited by the self-immolation spread quickly from his small city to the rest of the country and encompassed many different sectors of society.[25] Using both violent and non-violent means, these protests seem to have been loosely connected, relatively spontaneous, uprisings and not the product of an entrenched organized movement. In the wake of the immolation and subsequent protests in Tunisia, other states in the Middle East experienced similar uprisings, known as the "Arab Spring."

Was this an act of protest? There are differing opinions about why Bouazizi chose to self-immolate. The two most commonly cited ones claim that his suicide was the result of either a profound sense of humiliation, or alternatively, economic desperation. The former would suggest that Bouazizi had no

Suicide protest from a global perspective   137

political or economic motivation for his decision to immolate, while the latter might do so. Based on my own reading of the events it is likely that a combination of these two motivations, and others, underlay Bouazizi's actions. Either way, Bouazizi's act resonated with others; maybe among those who had been humiliated by government officials themselves, or those young people facing similar economic situations. But in some ways the motivations behind Bouazizi's actions no longer matter. Whether he planned to or not, he became the emblem for a revolution. His protest action also incited a number of other people to self-immolate throughout the Middle East. Why did Bouazizi's act resonate where other single acts of suicide protest have not?

Malachi Ritscher

In 2006 I was a grad student working on my dissertation in Madison, Wisconsin. Despite my heightened interest in acts of suicide protest it took me a week to become aware that an anti-war activist named Malachi Ritscher had self-immolated in Chicago. It seems almost impossible that such an extreme act of protest could occur in the United States and be almost unmarked in the media. While Ritscher's actions were reported at the time, the lack of response to his protest act is in startling contrast to the case of Mohamed Bouazizi.

Malachi Ritscher was a Chicago-based musician. He was an avid participant in the Chicago jazz scene (Margasak 2006) as well as a self-proclaimed human rights activist and anti-war protestor.[26] Ritscher, who was 52, self-immolated on the Kennedy Expressway in downtown Chicago during rush hour on November 3, 2006; according to accounts, the police were called in because of reports of a statue on fire. When they arrived "they found a video camera, a canister of gasoline, a sign reading 'Thou Shalt Not Kill,' and a human body so badly charred that it was impossible to determine its sex" (Abebe 2006). Despite the publication of his own obituary online, Ritscher's death was not widely reported and in contrast to the Bouazizi incident the event engendered what can best be described as ambivalent reactions.

In the face of numerous questions and controversies regarding the motivations behind this suicide, I believe it is best to turn to Ritscher's own words. On the morning of his death Ritscher's self-written obituary was uploaded to the website savagesound.com. In this document, entitled "Mission Statement," Ritscher provides an explicitly political reasoning for his actions:

> Many people will think that I should not be able to choose the time and manner of my own death. My position is that I only get one death, I want it to be a good one. Wouldn't it be better to stand for something or make a statement, rather than a fiery collision with some drunk driver? Are not smokers choosing death by lung cancer? Where is the dignity there? Are not the people who disregard the environment killing themselves and future generations? Here is the statement I want to make: if I am required to pay for your barbaric war, I choose not to live in your

world. I refuse to finance the mass murder of innocent civilians, who did nothing to threaten our country. I will not participate in your charade – my conscience will not allow me to be a part of your crusade. There might be some who say "it's a coward's way out" – that opinion is so idiotic that it requires no response. From my point of view, I am opening a new door.[27]

This statement directly engages with the politics of the day. Is it possible, or even probable, that Ritscher was lonely or depressed? Yes, but as Abebe points out in his article, Ritscher's mental and emotional state is almost beside the point. He placed himself within the political space. The aftermath of this act is similar to the moment it occurred. It is discussed and wondered at, but did not substantively change politics, or even anti-war sentiment. In fact, it is indicative that the most in-depth analysis of this action occured not in regular media, political science or sociology journals, but in music publications such as *Pitchfork*. It seems that the Chicago music community was the one most affected by the loss of Ritscher.

Bouazizi and Ritscher in comparison

Were either of these acts "successful?" While this book is primarily concerned with the issue of success and failure, I don't think that this is a fruitful discussion when talking about individual events. Even if we know the actor's goals, as we did in the case of Ritscher, those goals are likely to be unattainable. More problematic would be the case of Bouazizi, who never articulated a political goal at all. Instead of using the narrow understanding of success that I do in my main analysis, I think it would be more appropriate to gauge the level of interest that was attracted, and the responses to the protests themselves.

Why did the reactions to these protest actions differ so vastly? How is it that a possibly non-political act of self-immolation could cause widespread political mobilization, while an explicitly political suicide had little to no impact? Trying to apply my theoretical approach to the previous two cases exposes some of the possible limits of my approach. Moreover, the lack of information about one of the cases makes any of the conclusions I reach tentative at best. Nevertheless, I would like to engage with possible causes for the different reactions to these two suicide protest events.

Tactical depth and the level of political competition are not relevant in these cases, since the acts were not deployed by a movement. Looking at the remaining two critical factors of intensity and emotional narratives it is clear that they do apply to cases of individual suicide protest, but not in the way we might expect.

I begin with a discussion of intensity and its importance for cases of individual suicide protest. Like acts of suicide protest that are embedded within a larger movement, the death of the actor can connote the level of commitment of an individual protestor. However, death can also backfire, as individuals

Suicide protest from a global perspective   139

don't have the time or ability to explain their actions. The possible negative reactions to the death of the protestor brings us to what I believe is the most useful aspect of the tactical approach when discussing individual acts of protest; that is, the emotional narrative of the act. The counterintuitive nature of these two cases is that Ritscher actually narrated his choice – his obituary extensively discusses why he chose to engage in suicide protest – whereas Mohamed Bouazizi did not speak, not even in the days he remained alive. Yet it is Bouazizi's action that resonated with the public, while Ritscher's did not. I suspect that there are a few things going on. First, while both of these actions were necessarily individual, Bouazizi was a member of a large family unit who spoke for him as soon as the self-immolation occurred. In many ways it was Bouazizi's family that outlined and deployed the narrative of frustration, anger, humiliation and familiarity for the rest of the nation. Bouazizi's mother is quoted as saying of the police harassment: "[I]t got to him deep inside, it hurt his pride" (Ryan 2011). Ritscher, in contrast, was much more isolated; he was estranged from his family (Abebe 2006) which consisted of an ex-wife, son and grandchildren. No one even knew his identity until days later. Based on the previous discussion, is it the occurrence of a narrative that matters, or the presence or absence of social networks that can and will speak for the protestor?

Another possible factor that helps explain the contrasting responses is the setting and staging of the protests themselves. Bouazizi set himself on fire in the middle of a major town square. People were present and tried to save him. One of the aspects of suicide protest that I have highlighted in the book is its visceral nature. Self-immolation can be a horrifying act to witness and not easily forgotten. While Ritscher self-immolated during rush hour on a busy highway, he was not within sight of people, making it possible for them to mistakenly ignore what was happening. The lack of reaction to Ritscher's suicide protest suggests that the setting and staging of these actions could be a critical factor in how the public receives them.

Finally, another explanation for the contrasting reactions might be contextually driven. Could it be possible that the United States is not a country that can easily accept or comprehend suicide protest, whereas Tunisia is more amenable to this type of political expression? I find this sort analysis disingenuous. There have been a number of self-immolations within the USA, starting with Norman Morrison outside the Pentagon in protest against the Vietnam War. Moreover, many individuals and groups in the USA have used fasting to death as a protest tactic. In other words, I don't believe that cultural or even political contexts factor in the responses to individual acts of suicide protest. What does seem to matter is the deployment and narration of these events. Who speaks for these actors once they die?

My presentation of these four cases illustrates the limits of my approach and points to some new directions for research on suicide protest. First and foremost, I utilize a narrow conception of success and failure in this book. While I believe this approach was necessary, I must also acknowledge that

140 *Suicide protest from a global perspective*

movement and protest success can be measured by a number of standards. Suicide protest is a type of political action that can raise strong emotions among different populations, and may have long-term cultural and social effects that my analysis cannot contend with. Also, the discussion of individual protests suggests that this category of suicide action is not well served by the tactical approach. Despite this disjunction, individual acts of suicide protest have become common enough to necessitate serious scholarly inquiry. Based on this chapter, I believe that the tactical approach can be applied to different geographical contexts, but is less relevant to non-movement-based acts of suicide.

Notes

1 Excluding the Indian Emergency, which took place from 1975–1977.
2 Freedom House has labeled Sri Lanka as "partly free" since 1999 (freedomhouse. org). In Chapter 6 I described Sri Lanka as having a deeply divided society and political system during the time covered in my analysis. Recently there has been troubling evidence that the Sri Lankan government has been centralizing its power within the post-war landscape.
3 In Chapter 1 I discuss the differences between suicide protest as outlined in the majority of the book, and this category of protest – which I name "social suicide protest." Initially I separated these two categories for a very simple reason; it can be very difficult to discern the motivations and intentions of individual suicide protestors. The lack of organization often also means a lack of stated goals. Since I define movement success as the accomplishment of stated goals, these individual protests wouldn't fit into my model, which leads me to excise that category of suicide protest from the main empirical examination. However, if political goals can be understood in individual suicide protests, it does make sense to see whether or not the tactical approach can apply and to what extent the lack of movement may help or hurt the effectiveness of individual acts of suicide protest.
4 In his book *Domination and the Arts of Resistance*, James Scott describes what protest and resistance may look like in highly repressive regimes. He introduces twin theories of the public and hidden transcript; the public transcript represents that space in which the dominated perform for those in power, while the hidden transcript is that space in which the dominated express their critique of the powerful. The public transcript is the performance; the hidden transcript takes place off-stage, between members of the same powerless group. This notion would suggest that there are higher levels of protest occurring within repressive regimes, but that we are not meant to recognize them. In such contexts would acts such as protests and demonstrations have the same type of political and cultural significance in repressive regimes in the long run? I would argue that in repressive regimes suicide protest stands between the public and hidden transcript as it communicates very different things to the oppressors and the oppressed.
5 Though prison fasts are generally referred to as hunger strikes in the literature and by activists, I am maintaining the nomenclature I have used throughout the book wherein political, or in this case prison, fasts are those actions that are meant to be indefinite, while hunger strikes have a previously discussed finite time span.
6 One of the most famous depictions of the totalizing nature of prison is, of course, Bentham's Panopticon (2011), a theoretical prison that he designed in the eighteenth century. What for Bentham was simply an efficient method for incarcerating and observing criminals, Foucault later describes as a mechanism through which

Suicide protest from a global perspective 141

modernity "automatizes and disindividualizes power" (Foucault 1995, p. 202), and helps to transform people into subjects. Foucault goes further in his discussion on prisons in general, asserting that the modern prison was meant to not only deprive people of liberty, but also to transform them into "docile bodies" (Ibid., p. 233). The point being that modern prisons can and do exert more influence than simple punishment, but are designed to physically and psychologically control the incarcerated to a previously impossible degree. That level of control relies on the notion that the bodies in prison will in fact begin to incarcerate themselves, rendering the notion of mundane protest a moot point. In the face of such totalizing control, it makes sense that inmates might turn to the option of transforming their own bodily functions into a location of protest.

7 Ujjuwal Kumar Singh describes three responses that the British used to deal with prison fasts in the early twentieth century: (1) force-feeding; (2) releasing prisoners temporarily as they weakened; and (3) "Letting the prisoner take his own course" (1998, p. 124). These responses were designed to apply to different types of prisoners. For example, suffragettes were more likely to be released as the British government did not want to deal with the consequences of allowing upper class women to die for their cause in prison. This was not the case for Irish Republicans or Indian prisoners.

8 "Hunger Strike at Guantanamo," Editorial Board. *New York Times*, April 5, 2013; Moqbel, Samir Naji al Hasan. "Gitmo is Killing Me," *New York Times*, April 14, 2013.

9 Force-feeding prisoners often occurs through the nasal cavity or esophageal tubes, and is mostly described as very painful. Alice Paul, the American suffragette, famously described her experience with force-feeding when she was arrested for protesting at the Lord Mayor's Banquet in London in 1909. She states: "During this operation the largest Wardress sat aside my knees, holding my shoulders down to keep me from bending forward ... Sometimes they tied me to a chair with sheets. Once I managed to get my hands loose and snatched the tube, tearing it with my teeth. I also broke a jug, but I didn't give in" (Paul 1909).

10 For example, Irom Chanu Sharmila of Manipur, India, has been on an indefinite fast for the last 13 years. Chanu began her fast in 2000 to protest against the Armed Forces Special Powers Act in Manipur. Since suicide is officially illegal in India, she is continually placed under arrest, forcibly fed through her nasal cavity, then released, only to resume the fast and be rearrested.

11 British policy towards Northern Ireland was much less democratic than its dealings with other members of the Union (England, Scotland and Wales). For example, the Emergency Provisions Act of 1973, which changed the way trials worked for IRA activists.

12 Gandhi was also greatly influenced by Jesus and Christian saints in the development of his theory of *satyagraha* (*Collected Works of Mahatma Gandhi*, 1960–94).

13 See Allen Feldman's *Formations of Violence* (1991) for an in-depth ethnographic of the Blanket and Dirty protests. Feldman's book is based on extensive interviews with participants in the protest events.

14 According to David Beresford (1997 p. 27) these demands were: (1) the right to wear their own clothes; (2) the right to refrain from prison work; (3) the right to free association with other prisoners; (4) the right to organize their own leisure activities; and (5) the right to have "remission lost" restored after the blanket protests.

15 In a session of Prime Minister's Questions on May 5, 1981, Thatcher responded to a number of questions regarding Sands' death. She is quoted as saying that "the Government's job always is to protect the law-abiding, and to defeat terrorism. To grant political status would be to give a licence to kill. That is why this Government will never grant political status, no matter what the extent of any

142 *Suicide protest from a global perspective*

hunger strike," indicating the inability of the tactic to shame the state (House of Commons Prime Minister's Questions, May 5, 1981. Accessed from the Margaret Thatcher Foundation website: http://www.margaretthatcher.org/speeches/display-document.asp?docid=104641)

16 The repression of the 1989 protests was extremely brutal, with countless dead and more detained. The lack of large-scale protest since that time can, in part, be attributed to those repressive mechanisms as well as to a tacit agreement between the government and the population that places economic advancement over political freedoms.

17 The notion that Buddhism is an inherently non-violent religion has interesting implications for the use of suicide protest. The self-immolations by Buddhist monks in Vietnam were some of the first recorded in the twentieth century and may have added weight to the non-violent character that many suicide protestors claim. However, as I discussed, this clearly discounts the extreme violence these protestors are doing to themselves. Moreover, assigning any religious system with inherent characteristics such as violence or non-violence seems very problematic. For example, see Stanley Tambiah's very interesting account in his book *Buddhism Betrayed?* (1994) of how Buddhist monks in Sri Lanka have both justified and legitimized the use of violence. Tambiah provides a persuasive historical analysis of the creation and consolidation of Buddhist nationalism; his work is concerned with both the influence that religion has had on the nature of political discourse and political action, as well as the effect that politics has had on Buddhism, suggesting that any religion, once intermixed with politics, can and will justify behavior that contradicts sacred texts or tenets. This may also be a possible explanation for why Buddhist monks and nuns in Tibet are using self-immolation, when Buddhism has a negative view of suicide.

18 Over time both of these groups have begun to advocate for more autonomy within Chinese borders as opposed to outright independence. This shift is one reason why the Dalai Lama no longer supports the goal of the Independence Movement of Tibet.

19 Moreover, Tibet is not the only issue that other states would like to take up with the PRC. Others include, human rights generally, labor conditions and trade agreements.

20 Gladney 2004.

21 Individual members of the spiritual movement, Faulon Gong, have self-immolated in China, among others.

22 I don't mean to indicate that the PRC is not keenly interested in the protests and the narrative surrounding it, but that these acts are more likely to resonate within the Tibetan and international community than with the state.

23 See Kevin J. O'Brien's edited volume entitled *Popular Protest in China* (2008). The articles in this book address movements that don't seek to overturn the state or insert democratic norms into China, but rather to bring about political change within the existing system.

24 There has been some dispute regarding the accuracy of these events. While I believe that it is important to excavate the truth of what happened that day, the very fact that this narrative has been propagated is interesting in light of my analysis. The story of Bouazizi's "humiliation" has seemingly become an integral part of his narrative.

25 Shadid, Anthony. "Joy as Tunisian President Flees Offers Lesson to Arab Leaders," *New York Times*, January 14, 2011.

26 Based on his self-written obituary, which can currently be found at: www.savage-sound.com/galleray99.htm

27 Ibid.

8 Conclusion

At the start of this book, I presented a single overriding question: can suicide protest be successful? I have spent the last seven chapters demonstrating how and why I believe that suicide protest is more than simply a dramatic action, but can also, when deployed in particular ways, result in positive political outcomes for movements. In this conclusion I review the argument and evidence, and answer some possible questions raised in the book. I then present a comprehensive comparison of the three main cases and examine some of the broader consequences of suicide protest and my argument. Finally, I briefly wrestle with some of the normative implications inherent within suicide protest and our approach to it.

What have we learned so far?

The book began in Chapter 1 with a discussion of the conditions that can help to create long- or short-term success for movements that choose to use suicide protest. I contend that the effectiveness of suicide protest lies not in whether groups choose to use the tactic, but in how they deploy and then frame the tactic once it has been used. My argument cites a number of organizational and structural variables that either help or hinder groups once they use suicide protest. A comprehensive analysis of three critical cases of suicide protest in India revealed what I believe to be four significant factors that help to determine movement success. Those factors are: the overall tactical depth of the movement, the intensity of the protest act itself, the attempts of the movement to create an emotional narrative surrounding its use of suicide protest, and finally the perceived or actual level of political competition in the state. As groups utilize or take advantage of these factors, the likelihood that suicide protest will result in policy shifts in support of movements increases.

Chapter 2 examines possible cultural antecedents to suicide protest within India. In particular, I explore Gandhi's use of fasting and what I believe to be the consequences of his philosophy and practice of that tactic. I argue that Gandhi engendered a new political idiom in India wherein self-sacrifice, especially that of the body, became an acceptable form of political expression. I investigate the implications of that new idiom by analyzing three cases of

144   *Conclusion*

suicide protest in post-Independence India in Chapter 3 through Chapter 5. Finally, the sixth and seventh chapters of the book move away from both suicide protest and the Indian context to investigate the impacts of empirically and theoretically distinct forms of this phenomenon, including suicide bombing and suicide protest in other regions of the world.

In applying this argument, which I call the tactical approach, to three cases of suicide protest in India, this book illustrates how and why suicide protest can be a very effective tool for social movements. I also consider when the tactic might hinder movements from attaining their goals. Of the three Indian cases, one, the fasting death of Potti Sriramulu, resulted in long-term policy change, whereas the Narmada Bacho Andolan's use of and approach to suicide protest only resulted in short-term success. Finally, the anti-reservationist students represent a case of failure to translate suicide protest into policy changes.

My explanation for movement success really rests in the interconnectedness of the significant factors I describe. No *single* variable is the most important, but it is how these variables work together that can aid in creating the conditions for success or failure. In Chapter 1 I describe the way that these factors interact as a complex dance. Another way to think of it would be as a string quartet in which all four instruments must work collectively to produce the desired outcome or emotions. One instrument may take precedence at some point in the performance, only to then give way to another one, but all of the instruments are integral to the outcome. If just one were missing, the piece would not work. The factors I describe interact in the same way; one may seem to take precedence at times, but the others are always necessary components. I emphasize the intermingled and reactive nature of this approach because the use of protest, especially one that can become so symbolically and emotionally laden, is complicated and messy. Many scholars within social science strive for parsimony above all things. While I agree that it is important to take a frugal approach in our attempts to explain political phenomena, emphasizing simple models in spite of empirical complications threatens to relegate our work into ever-continuing abstraction. My approach is an attempt to marry the hoped-for elegance of social science with the messiness of real-life political mobilization.

And protest can be very messy. For example, I opened Chapter 4 by describing a National Poor People's Alliance rally that I attended in Delhi in 2004. There is one part of the story that I did not relate, which I think encapsulates the arbitrary and even capricious nature of protest. As I explained, after the rally in Jantar Mantar ended, the protestors walked to the Parliament Police Station. I was there and talking to some people who had come from outside Delhi to attend the event. We all began to walk, and after about ten minutes realized that we had taken a wrong turn and were now lost. The protestors who had taken a bus from out of state may have missed a significant portion of the protest simply because of a lack of direction and knowledge of the city. In the end my story turned out fine; we retraced our steps and were then

Conclusion   145

motioned by the police to the station (which admittedly caused a bit of tension among the group), which we then entered, slightly embarrassed but ready to attend the rest of the rally.

This simple and somewhat embarrassing story illustrates a number of important aspects of protest. On its own the loss of a small group of protestors really couldn't change the outcome of an event; but what if we multiplied our small number of people by ten? What about people who never made it to Jantar Mantar at all? What if there was a small typo on flyers announcing the protest, or, especially relevant in multilingual India, what if there weren't enough translators available to communicate the message to disparate groups? Protests can live and die by these small details. Witnesses to demonstrations and rallies can be filled with awe by the drama and power of those events, but these things can also be derailed by something as simple as a wrong turn. I don't mean to imply that mobilization is a delicate act, but it is something that relies on a number of moving parts, which may or may not work well together. In my description of these suicide protests, I try to reveal the clockwork behind the façade of these events. If it is the case that protests rely on a complex set of components, then it makes sense that the effectiveness of protest, or lack of it, will also rest on a number of different factors. The four variables I highlight are not the only things that can help or hinder social movements, but I believe that they are the most significant when we look at the possible impact of mobilization and protest tactics.

The previous section leads to another common question regarding my take on movement success; who is to say that it is suicide protest and not something else that creates political change? Is it really suicide protest that is important, or something else? This is a valid point, but not one that completely weakens my overall analysis and argument. First, not only do I acknowledge the presence of other types of protest, I also argue that the presence of alternative protest tactics contributes to the effectiveness of suicide protest. Second, there are many reasons why a group might choose to use suicide protest,[1] but generally once a group makes the decision to deploy suicide protest those events take a primary position within the movement's campaigns. The drama of suicide ensures that this type of protest will become a central component within movement strategy, which in turn suggests that suicide protest has the ability to shift the outcome of mobilization.

My argument, which combines structural, organizational and performative factors helps to demonstrate how suicide protest can transform the potentiality of power into actual political outcomes and policy shifts.

Case comparisons

Recognizing the importance of these factors is much more easily accomplished if we can compare the cases across variables. Table 8.1 shows how each case compares with the others. I include all cases under consideration in the book, though I will only discuss the main Indian cases.

146 *Conclusion*

Table 8.1 A comparison of suicide protest inputs and outcomes

	Tactical depth	Intensity	Emotional narratives	Political competition	Outcome
Movement for Andhra	HIGH	HIGH	HIGH	HIGH	LONG-TERM SUCCESS
The NBA	HIGH	LOW	HIGH	HIGH	SHORT-TERM SUCCESS
Anti-Reservation Movement students	LOW	HIGH	LOW	BLOCKED	FAILURE
The LTTE	LOW	HIGH	HIGH	LOW	SHORT-TERM SUCCESS
The IRA	MEDIUM	HIGH	HIGH	REPRESSIVE	SYMBOLLIC SUCCESS
Tibet	HIGH	HIGH	HIGH	REPRESSIVE	SYMBOLLIC SUCCESS
Mohammed Bouazizi	N/A	HIGH	HIGH	N/A	ENGENDERED PROTEST
Malachi Ritscher	N/A	HIGH	LOW	N/A	NO REACTION

What does the comparison of cases tell us about suicide protest and how it is utilized? If we look at the three main cases under consideration a few interesting and even counterintuitive conclusions become apparent. For example, it is clear that intensity, or the death of the actor, does not always result in movement success. This finding challenges two commonly held assumptions regarding suicide protest. First, many would guess that suicide protest, from its very name, should end with high intensity events. As I discussed in Chapter 4, because of factors such as lack of volition or government intervention many types of suicide protest do not result in the death of the protestor. Second, and more relevant for this project, one might assume that for suicide protest to be an effective tactic, an actual suicide needs to take place. However, in looking at the three cases we can see that the NBA was able to deploy low intensity suicide protest resulting in short-term success, while the anti-reservationist students' high level of intensity was unable to create any policy change. In Chapter 5 I posit that too much intensity, too many deaths, may actually backfire on movements. Reasons for this could include a sense of fatigue with the tactic itself or a dampening effect that occurs when the high number of deaths becomes background noise to possible constituents and state officials. We have seen cases where the effect of too many deaths has been mitigated. Reasons include the application of specific emotional narratives, how long the conflict is, or the level of government response, as in the case of the LTTE. But the anti-reservationist students do illustrate a potential weakness of suicide when it is used as a strategic tactic; after a while people

Conclusion 147

can get used to anything. Acts that were once dramatic and attention-grabbing can become as mundane as anything else. To harness the potential power of suicide protest movements have to carefully consider how to maintain the unique and "special" characteristic of the tactic.

Table 8.1 also reveals another interesting aspect of how suicide protest may or may not create positive political outcomes, which is that suicide protest does not work well on its own. I argue that the presence of multiple tactics is a crucial element to successful suicide mobilization. I further contend that non-violent forms of protest make suicide protest more effective in general as they signal to opponents the presence of willing negotiating partners. The presence of viable partners within a movement is a crucial element in the transformation of protest into policy change. Movements that choose suicide as an overriding aspect of their approach to mobilization must also demonstrate that they are aware of the political system and can work within it. Moreover, the presence of alternative tactics helps to keep the movement in the public eye, as well as helping with recruitment and the transmission of the emotional narratives that they construct surrounding suicide protest – as we saw with the NBA.

Table 8.1 also demonstrates the importance that an emotional narrative can have on political outcomes. Throughout this book I have referred to the inherent drama of suicide protest. Witnessing the violence, pain and self-sacrifice of these events can leave indelible impacts on individuals. However, just because an event is dramatic does not mean that it will have the ability to shift political policy outcomes. It is not a coincidence that the two cases where the tactic completely failed were also the ones where emotional narratives were either captured (the anti-reservationist students) or not attempted (Malachi Ritscher). Like all types of political expression, suicide protest cannot simply speak for itself or explain the meaning behind it, the actors who practice it, or the problems it is trying to redress; the movement itself must communicate all of these things to the public. But unlike other types of protest, suicide usually means that the actors are no longer available to speak for themselves. The movement *must* speak for them. When I talk about this project with others they generally know certain people like Gandhi, Cesar Chavez, Bobby Sands or the students in Tiananmen Square, precisely because those individuals and their acts continue to be discussed, written about and mythologized. It is that sense of "knowing" the pride and sympathy that can give suicide protest a legacy beyond the death of the actor, movement or political goal.

Moreover, that emotional narrative must highlight the self-sacrificing nature of these acts. It does not seem surprising that the most successful movements discussed were the two that were able to harness and advance Gandhi's political philosophy. All three Indian movements claimed non-violent Gandhian status, but only Potti Sriramulu and the NBA were convincing. This clearly relates not only to their narrative, but also to their use of non-violent tactics. While the Gandhian narrative is more powerful within India,[2] I believe that

148   *Conclusion*

most states have some notion of non-violent ethos; movements that utilize suicide protest must try to frame their tactics in relation to that ethos.

Finally, the structure of politics comes into play as we examine the level of political competition. For a variety of reasons it seems that both non-violent and violent forms of political mobilization "work" better within democratic contexts. This can be attributed to the influence of electoral politics and public opinion, or even the ways movements will try to influence the political system (Goldstone 2004; Pape 2005; Giugni 2008). But democracy, or even the existence of political competition, is not a guarantee of success for movements. For example, the anti-reservationists acted within a very active political system, one that had many openings, but they were effectively blocked from taking advantage of those openings. Thus, the perception of competition and opportunity play just as important a role for movements as the actual structural context of the political system.

What are the implications?

This book raises a number of implications for both suicide protest and other forms of extreme and more mundane political mobilization. First and foremost, my analysis confirms that suicide protest and, by extension, other forms of extreme protest, can create political change. This conclusion may seem somewhat simplistic considering the rest of the book, but I feel the need to emphasize this point. Suicide protest is not an irrational act or an overabundance of passion, but an attempt by groups to act and influence the political process. In other words, we need to give as much weight to *protest* as we do to *suicide* when we observe and analyze these events. Moreover, if we extend this idea beyond suicide protest to other types of extreme protest, violent or non-violent, then we can see that people take these actions not because they necessarily want to, but because they believe it will help them in some way.

Suicide protest can be effective, but this leads to the next important implication of my analysis. Over the course of writing this book it has become clear to me that like suicide protest, other forms of political violence or extreme mobilization can "work," but not on their own. Purely violent groups are much less likely to translate their campaigns into real political outcomes. The idea that violence is more effective when accompanied by non-violence has far-reaching repercussions, especially for a state like India which tolerates high levels of political violence. Can we untangle when groups act violently or non-violently? How and why are some groups labeled as purely violent, even if they use non-violent tactics as well? Can states stem violence by emphasizing and validating the non-violent strands of a movement?

Finally, this book examines this issue from the perspective of the movements; but clearly the state is just as important in determining the success and failure of these tactics. To echo my first point, states and policy-makers must take suicide protest seriously. Dismissing acts of suicide protest will

Conclusion 149

simply exacerbate the underlying conflict. States must begin to anticipate and respond to the use of this tactic as more groups decide to use it.

Is this really *suicide* protest?

One of the major claims I make throughout this book is that suicide protest is powerful, in part because it occupies a liminal space between violence and non-violence, demonstrating the power that collective violence can have but stripping away many of the negative connotations of that violence. In this section I want to examine another type of duality: that of suicide and self-sacrifice. As I was starting this project, I struggled for a long period about how I should refer to these tactics. For quite some time I used the term "self-directed violence," which didn't seem to capture it very well. I was initially very reluctant to use suicide protest for a number of reasons, the most important of which are the negative connotations many associate with the word "suicide," a thought that was also articulated by my informants in the field. Groups that use suicide protest do not think of these actions as suicide, but as self-sacrifice. However, self-sacrificing protest was also a problematic term as it could connote a positive value judgment of these acts. The distinction between these terms is significant, because it semantically demonstrates the contested normative space that these types of acts inhabit. The lack of a value-neutral label for these actions ensures that any term we choose to describe these events could lead to troubling normative consequences. In the following section I briefly examine some of the different values placed on the terms "suicide" and "self-sacrifice." In doing so I hope to trouble our use of these labels to describe this type of political phenomenon.

Suicide

The term suicide protest is an uneasy fit with the empirical reality of these tactics. These protestors are not necessarily suicidal but claim to be making a positive decision to benefit the movement they support, and by extension their vision of the public good. Yes, they have a willingness to die, but not as an act of self-annihilation, rather as an act of self-actualization. So why did I choose to use the term suicide protest in the face of these issues? I liken suicide protest to Durkheim's (1979) category of altruistic suicide in which he claims that this type of suicide is practiced by individuals who are subsumed by a larger institution or identity, the best example of which would be the relationship between soldiers and the military. He was trying to disaggregate our idea of suicide, and using the modifier "altruistic" permits us to invest this particular type of suicide with some form of nobility. Durkheim's notion of altruistic suicide was integral to my own decision to use suicide protest to describe these events. Despite Durkheim and others' attempts to unpack and complicate our understanding of suicide, generally speaking those actions continue to

150   *Conclusion*

be negatively regarded in Indian and other societies. Actions that would fall under the rubric of altruistic suicide are simply called self-sacrifice.

Beyond the contradictions I have discussed above, other harmful connotations of the word suicide can impact our consideration of fasts to the death and self-immolation. Suicide tends to be a very solitary act, so to what extent does the term suicide protest hide the organizational aspects of these acts? Moreover, collective acts of suicide are viewed much more negatively, implying that there is a lack of volition on the part of many of the participants, who are regarded as being under the sway of a powerful organization. Could we think of suicide protest this way?

Finally, I want to discuss how societies approach the issue of suicide and the possible implications of that on suicide protest. Not only is the act illegal in India and other places, but many states have also spent a considerable amount of time, energy and money trying to reduce the number of suicides. Increases in suicide rates are thought to be a troubling indicator of greater social problems. Likewise, literature and films are rife with examples of the anger, sadness and bewilderment that accompany acts of suicide. While the dramatic presentations of suicide are complex, they tend to focus on particular emotional states such as sorrow or despair, or attribute the act to some form of weakness or punishment. For example, in *The Sorrows of Young Werther* by Goethe, a young man decides to end his life because of a doomed romantic love. The book demonstrated the possible romantic reasons behind, and implications of, suicide, sparking a wave of "Werther Fever" in Europe; a number of young men chose to follow Werther's example. Indian artists have also explored the many motivations and impacts of suicide. Two examples that come to mind explore the position of young women driven to suicide in West Bengal. Film directors Satyajit Ray in his film *Devi* (Goddess) and Rituparno Ghosh in *Antar Mahal* (Inner Chamber) both ended their films with suicides in order to highlight the tragic circumstances that they were presenting, the suicides of their characters providing a focal point for the raw emotions of the films. There have been countless depictions of suicides as tragic, sad, upsetting and desperate in Eastern and Western media, literature, art, myth and legend, most of which differs from the types of emotions and motivations that suicide protestors would like to embody. I bring up the portrayal of suicide within culture and politics not to dispute the negative consequences of these acts but to question the implications of these depictions on our intrinsic response to events like fasting to the death and self-immolation. Do negative conceptualizations of suicide implicate how we may react to suicide protest? Should we find another way to describe these protest events, even if they share a basic similarity with personal suicide?

Self-sacrifice

In contrast to both the term and the act of suicide, we tend to celebrate and reward self-sacrifice. But would the term self-sacrifice really be a better way

Conclusion 151

to describe these tactics? Gandhi and others employed the term self-sacrifice to explain what they were doing, which seems to makes sense, and places such acts in a positive light. But using that terminology masks the degradations that Gandhi and others forced on themselves. We are left with a situation where similar acts of self-directed violence are given vastly different meanings. Why and how can the understanding of these acts differ? The differences between our narrations of self-sacrifice and suicide are simply magnified once we turn to popular representations of self-sacrifice. The trope of the self-sacrificing individual is common in Indian and many other cultures. Our vision of these individuals is one of nobility and a willingness to die for the good of others. As Mr. Spock says after sacrificing his life in *Star Trek II: Wrath of Khan*: "The needs of the many outweigh the needs of the few." But I believe that conceptual dissonance is the crux of the distinction between the words "suicide" and "self-sacrifice." Self-sacrifice is much more relational and collective; there is an acknowledgement that these individuals are not killing themselves for self-reflexive but rather for other-regarding reasons. They are sacrificing themselves for the good of others; to save a spaceship, to save a romance between others, to save a nation. We allow ourselves to celebrate this type of self-inflicted harm because there seems to be an active volition behind it and maybe we would like to imagine that we would respond in the same way. Since groups that use these tactics would call their actions self-sacrificing, why don't we follow suit?

Though the narrative surrounding self-sacrifice may enmesh itself more closely with the desires and standpoint of activists, self-sacrifice is not a perfect fit for the phenomena under discussion in this book. First, all protest, in some shape or form, relies on the sacrifice of individuals, whether it be sacrificing pay to go on strike or sacrificing time to attend a rally; calling acts of fasting and self-immolation self-sacrificing protest does not connote the largest visceral difference between such acts and, say, a mere demonstration. Thus, self-sacrifice can be thought of not only in terms of life and death, but also in terms of protection from harm, economic sacrifice and so on. One famous portrayal of a self-sacrificing individual can be seen in Ritwik Ghatak's film *Meghe Dhaka Tara* (Cloud Capped Star). In it, the heroine Neeta shuts herself away from her family when she is diagnosed with tuberculosis. This type of sacrifice, where one does not actively seek death, is just as celebrated. Another example of self-sacrifice would be to deliberately put oneself in harm's way in order to protect others. These actions may result in death, but that is not the primary purpose of the action. In other words, you can sacrifice yourself without dying. There are parallels for the multiplicity of self-sacrifice within political contention. Activists will often engage in risky actions as part of their protests, which can result in anything from arrest to death. For example, the *Asociación Madres de Plaza de Mayo* (The Mothers of the Plaza de Mayo) risked their lives every day when they protested in Argentina. Should we include them within the category of protests considered in this book? I (and most likely they) would argue no, we should not.

152 *Conclusion*

The issue at heart with using the term self-sacrifice to describe these actions is that self-sacrifice is too big, too varied and too vague a term to really denote the kinds of acts under discussion. Finally, the positive emotional and social associations with the word self-sacrifice may also impact our thoughts on fasting and self-immolation. So, what should we call these tactics? I picked my side of the argument in writing this book. But I think it is necessary to engage in a discussion of the possible normative values and implications behind the labels we choose to use.

The discussion that I deliberately avoided in this book is the complicated issue of the morality (or lack therof) of these actions. Is suicide protest a good thing? If so, for whom? Can the decision to deploy suicide protest have negative reverberations in politics and society? What are the implications of the habitual use of suicide protest on political culture and approaches to mobilization? The answer to these question will depend on long-term, systematic enquiry, not only on the use of suicide protest but also on the social, cultural and psychological contexts of these actions. This book demonstrates how suicide protest can be effective. Other work is being done on the causes and consequences of suicide protest, but there is certainly space and a need for further examination of these actions. Suicide protest is a visceral form of political mobilization. It has the power to inspire some and disgust others. Underlying that confusion of motivations and responses is a form of political expression that continues to be used throughout the world, and one that requires serious and thoughtful scrutiny.

Notes

1 In a forthcoming article I argue for a complex understanding of strategy based on the motivations for both suicide protest and suicide bombing. I contend that groups will use these tactics precisely because they can evoke particular emotions, which in turn makes them effective.
2 Gandhi's rhetoric and tactics are not only powerful in India. It is clear that Gandhi has had a profound effect on many other movements and leaders, globally.

Bibliography

Interviews

Interview with media source (unnamed to preserve anonymity). June 29, 2005, Colombo, Sri Lanka

Interview with the family of a Black Tiger (unnamed to preserve anonymity), July 8, 2005, Sri Lanka

Interview with LTTE representative (unnamed to preserve anonymity), July 7, 2005, Kilinochchi, Sri Lanka

Interview with member of the EPDP (unnamed to preserve anonymity), July 12, 2005, Colombo, Sri Lanka

Interview with Ramaswamy Iyer, December 16, 2005, New Delhi, India

Interview with Ramaswamy Iyer, June 2005, New Delhi, India

Interview with NBA leader (unnamed to preserve anonymity), December 18, 2005, New Delhi, India

Government documents and unpublished letters

"Being Fed Through Nostrils is Described by Alice Paul, Young American Suffragette," December 1909, London, England. Part of *Miller NAWSA Suffrage Scrapbooks*, 1897–1911; Scrapbook 8, p. 134. Library of Congress, Rare Book and Special Collections Division. http://hdl.loc.gov/loc.rbc/rbcmil.scrp6014301

Government of India, Linguistic Provinces Commission, *Dar Commission Report*, 1948

Indian National Congress, *Report of the Linguistic Provinces Committee*, 1948

Indira Sawhney vs. Union of India. Indian Supreme Court Cases. 1992

Lok Sabha Debates. Part II. December 8, 1952. Government of India Press

Rajya Sabha Debates. July 16, 1952. Government of India Press

Rajya Sabha Debates. July 21, 1952. Government of India Press

Rajya Sabha Debates. August 7, 1990. Government of India Press

Rajya Sabha Debates. September 4, 1990. Government of India Press, p. 251

Rajya Sabha Debates. October 1, 1990. Government of India Press, p. 6

Report of the First Backward Classes Commission, 1955. Government of India

Report of the India States Reorganization Committee. Ministry of Home Affairs, Government of India, 1953

Report of the Linguistic Provinces Commission, 1948. Government of India

Linguistic Provinces Committee. Delhi: Indian National Congress

154 *Bibliography*

Unpublished letter from Lord Willingdon to Sir Samuel Hoare, 1932. Archived at the India Office Library, London, UK

Unpublished personal correspondence from J. Nehru to C. Rajagopalachari, December 3, 1952

Writ Petition (©) No. 319 of 1994: Judgment. Supreme Court of India

Newspaper and magazine articles

Frontline. September 15–28, 1990, p. 31–4. "Student Ire in A.P.," D. Keseva Rao; and "Battle in Bihar," Ramesh Upadhyaya

Frontline. January 19–February 1, 1991, p. 99. "A March Damned," Mahesh Vijapurkar

Frontline. August 27, 1993. "The Sardar Sarovar Project, Beyond the Deadline," Praveen Swami

Frontline, September 10, 1993, pp. 106–9. "The Sardar Sarovar Project, Manibeli Revisited," R. Padmanabhan

The Hindu, August 4, 1952, p. 4

The Hindu, August 17, 1952, p. 6. "Andhra State Demand: Harijan Youth on Fast"

The Hindu, October 18, 1952, p. 6

The Hindu, October 21, 1952, p. 6. "Demand for Andhra State Formation," no author given

The Hindu, December 18, 1952, p. 6. "'Follower of Gandhiji' Tribute to Potti Sriramulu, Performance of Last rites"

India Today, "Pirabhakaran 'We reviewed out stand'," August 15 1987, pp. 54–55, Anita Pratap

India Today, August 15, 1987. Bobb, Dilip and Anita Pratap, with S.H. Venkatramani and Mervyn De Silva. "Sri Lanka: Accord Discord," p. 52–56

India Today. September 15, 1990, p. 98. "Mandal Commission Dividing to Rule," Inderjit Badhwar

India Today. September 30, 1990, p. 36. "A Spreading Stir," Saba Naqvi Bhaumik

India Today. October 15, 1990, p. 27. "Rajeev Goswami Act of Desperation," Nonita Kalra

India Today. October 31, 1990, pp. 22–31. "Mandal Commission fall-out. Pyres of Protest," Harinder Baweja with N. K. Singh and Kanwar Sandhu; "The Ragtag Warriors," Pankaj Pachauri with Farzand Ahmed and Dilip Awasthi

The Indian Express, December 17, 1952

The Indian Express, January 1, 1991

Tehelka, December 17, 2005, p. 22. "Ma Rewa Tera Paani Amrit," Shivani Chaudhry

Time, January 21, 2011. "Bouazizi: The Man who Set Himself and Tunisia on Fire," Rania Abouzeid

"Fast and Win" in Time Magazine, December 29, 1952. Accessed from http://content.time.com/time/magazine/article/0,9171,822565,00.html

Times of India, November 18, 1963, p. 1. "Narmada Valley Development: Gujarat & M.P. Reach Accord on Plans"

Times of India (Bombay), August 20, 1978, p. 1. "Man Ends Life Over Award"

Times of India, December 28, 1990, pp. 1, 3. "We can't desert our Narmada," Lester Coutinho

Times of India (Bombay), August 7, 1993, pp. 1 and 13, by Meena Menon "Medha Calls off 'Jal Samparan'"

Times of India, April 16, 2012

New York Times, January 14, 2011. "Joy as Tunisian President Flees. Offers Lesson to Arab Leaders," Anthony Shadid

New York Times, April 5, 2013. "Hunger Strike at Guantanamo," Editorial

New York Times, April 14, 2013. "Gitmo is Killing Me," Samir Naji al Hasan Moqbel

The Statesman, Editorial, September 3, 1947, p. 4

The Statesman, Editorial, December 5, 1947, p. 6

Books and secondary materials

Abebe, Nitsuh. (2006), "Malachi Ritscher, 1954–2006" on pitchfork.com http://pitchfork.com/features/articles/6483-malachi-ritscher-1954-2006/

Abufarha, Nasser. (2006), *The Making of a Human Bomb*. Unpublished dissertation. University of Wisconsin-Madison

Ackerman, Peter, and Christopher Kruegler. (1994), *Strategic Nonviolent Conflict*. Westport, Connecticut: Praeger

Ahmed, Sara. (2004), *The Cultural Politics of Emotions*. New York: Routledge

Ambedkar, B. R. (1946), *What Congress and Gandhi have Done to the Untouchables*. Bombay: Thacker & Co.

Amenta, Edwin, and Michael P. Young. (1999), "Making an Impact: Conceptual and Methodological Implications of the Collective Goods Critierion" in *How Social Movements Matter*, edited by Marco Giugni, Douglas McAdam and Charles Tilly. London: Cambridge University Press

Aminzade, Ron, and Doug McAdam. (2002), "Emotions and Contentious Politcs." *Mobilization* 7(2):107–9

Anderson, Patrick. (2009), "There Will Be No Bobby Sands in Guantanamo Bay" in *PMLA* 124(5):1729–36

Anderson Patrick. (2010), *So Much Wasted: Hunger Performance and the Morbidity of Resistance*. Durham: Duke University Press

Andrews, Kennth T. (1997), "The Impacts of Social Movements on The Political Process: The Civil Rights Movement and Black Electoral Politics in Mississippi." *American Sociological Review* 62: 800–19

Andrews, Kenneth T. (2001), "Social Movements and Policy Implementation: The Mississippi Civil Rights Movement and the War on Poverty, 1965 to 1971." *American Sociological Review* 66:71–95

Babb, Lawrence A. (1975), *The Divine Hierarchy*. New York: Columbia University Press

Baviskar, Amita. (1995), *In the Belly of the River*. New Delhi: Oxford University Press

Baviskar, Amita. (1997), "Displacement and the Bhilala Tribals of the Narmada Valley" in *The Dam & the Nation*, edited by J. Dreze, M. Samson and S. Singh. New Delhi: Oxford University Press

Bell, Rudolph. (1985), *Holy Anorexia*. Chicago: University of Chicago Press

Bentham, Jeremy. (2011), *The Panopticon Writings*. New York: Verso

Beresford, David. (1989), *Ten Men Dead: The Story of the 1981 Hunger Strike*. New York: Atlantic Monthly Press

Beteille, Andre. (1997), "Caste and Political Group Formation in Tamilnad" in *Politics in India*, edited by S. Kaviraj. New Delhi: Oxford University Press

156 *Bibliography*

Bew, Paul, Peter Gibbon, and Henry Patterson. (1979), *The State in Northern Ireland: Political Forces and Social Class*. New York: St. Martin's Press

Biggs, Michael. (2005), "Dying Without Killing: Self-Immolations 1963–2002" in *Making Sense of Suicide Missions*, edited by D. Gambetta. New York: Oxford University Press

Bishop, Patrick, and Eammon Mallie. (1987), *The Provisional IRA*. London: William Heinemann Ltd.

Bloom, Mia. (2005), *Dying to Kill*. New York: Columbia University Press

Blumer, Herbert. 1969, *Symbolic Interactionalism, Perspective and Method*. Englewood: Prentice-Hall Inc.

Bondurant, Joan V. (1988), *The Conquest of Violence*. Princeton: Princeton University Press

Brass, Paul. (1996), "Introduction: Discourses of Ethnicity, Communalism, and Violence" in *Riots and Pogroms*, edited by P. Brass. New York: New York University Press.

Brass, Paul. (1997), *Theft of an Idol*. Princeton: Princeton University Press

Brown, Judith. (1977), *Gandhi and Civil Disobedience*. New York: Cambridge University Press

Brown, Judith. (1989), *Gandhi Prisoner of Hope*. New York: Oxford University Press

Brym, Robert, and Bader Araj. (2006), "Suicide Bombing as Strategy Interaction: The Case of the Second Intifada." *Social Forces* 84(4):1969–86

Burstein, Paul. (1999), "Social Movements and Public Policy" in *How Social Movements Matter*, edited by Marco Giugni, Douglas McAdam, and Charles Tilly. London: Cambridge University Press

Campbell-Johnson, Alan. (1953), *Mission With Mountbatten*. New York: Dutton

Dabholkar, Dattaprasad. (1990), *Oh Mother Narmada*. Pune: Wiley Eastern Limited

Dalton, Dennis. (1967), "The Gandhian View of Caste and Caste After Gandhi" in *India and Ceylon: Unity and Diversity*, edited by P. Mason. London: Oxford University Press

Dalton, Dennis. (1993), *Nonviolent Power in Action*. New York: Columbia University Press

Deegan, Chris. (1995), "The Narmada in Myth and History" in *Towards Sustainable Development?* edited by W. F. Fisher. London: M. E. Sharpe

DeNardo, James. (1985), *Power in Numbers*. Princeton: Princeton University Press

de Silva, K. M. (1983), *A History of Sri Lanka*. New Delhi: Oxford University Press

De Soto, Hernando. (2011), "The Real Mohamed Bouazizi." *Foreign Policy*. Online. http://www.foreignpolicy.com/articles/2011/12/16/the_real_mohamed_bouazizi

Durkheim, Emile. (1979), *Suicide*. New York: Macmillian Publishing Company

Edelman, Murray. (1967), *The Symbolic Uses of Politics*. Chicago: University of Illinois Press

Edelman, Murray. (1988), *Constructing the Political Spectacle*. Chicago: University of Chicago Press

Elster, Jon. (1999a), *Alchemies of the Mind*. New York: Cambridge University Press

Elster, Jon. (1999b), *Strong Feelings*. Cambridge: The MIT Press

Elster, Jon. (2000), *Ulysses Unbound*. New York: Cambridge University Press

Elster, Jon. (2005) "Motivations and Beliefs in Suicide Missions" in *Making Sense of Suicide Missions*, edited by D. Gambetta. New York: Oxford University Press

Erikson, Erik H. (1969), *Gandhi's Truth*. New York: W. W. Norton

Bibliography 157

Esherick, J. W., and J. N. Wasserstrom. (1990), "Acting Out Democracy." *Journal of Asian Studies* 49(4)

Feldman, Allen. (1991), *Formations of Violence*. Chicago: University of Chicago Press

Fisher, William F. (1995), "Development and Resistance in the Narmada Valley" in *Towards Sustainable Development*, edited by W. F. Fisher. London: M. E. Sharpe

Fligsten, Neil, and Douglas McAdam. (2011), "Toward a General Theory of Strategic Action Fields." *Sociological Theory* 29:1

Foucault, Michel. (1972), *Archaeology of Knowledge*. New York: Pantheon Books

Foucault, Michel. (1995), *Discipline and Punish: The Birth of the Prison*. New York: Vintage Books

Franda, M. F. (1962), "The Organizational Development of India's Congress Party." *Pacific Affairs*. 35(3), Fall

Frank, Robert H. (1988), *Passions within Reason*. New York: W. W. Norton & Company

Freedomhouse.org, 2013. *Sri Lanka Country Report.*

Gambetta, Diego (ed.) (2005), *Making Sense of Suicide Missions*. New York: Oxford University Press

Gamson, William A. (1968), *Power and Discontent*. Homewood, IL: The Dorsey Press

Gamson, William A. (1975), *The Strategy of Social Protest*. New York: Wadsworth Publishing

Gamson, William A. (1995), "Constructing Social Protest" in *Social Movements and Culture*, edited by H. Johnston, and B. Klandermas. Minneapolis: University of Minnesota Press

Gamson, William A., and David S. Meyer. (1996), "Framing Political Opportunity" in *Comparative Perspectives on Social Movements*, edited by J. D. M. Doug McAdam, and Mayer N. Zald. Cambridge: Cambridge University Press

Gandhi, Mohandas K. (1960–1994), *The Collected Works of Mahatma Gandhi*, edited by I. G. Publications. Vol. 1–90. New Delhi: Indian Government Publications

Gandhi, Mohandas K. (1965) *Fasting in Satyagraha*. Ahmedabad: Navijan Publishing House

Gandhi, Mohandas K. (1982), *Autobiography: The Story of My Experiments with the Truth*. New York: Dover

Gandhi, Mohandas K. (1997), *Hind Swaraj and Other Writings*, edited by Anthony J. Parel. Cambridge: Cambridge University Press

Ghosh, P. A. (1999), *Ethnic Conflict in Sri Lanka and the Role of Indian Peace Keeping Force*. New Delhi: A. P. H. Publishing Corp.

Ghosh, Partha S. (2003), *Ethnicity Versus Nationalism*. New Delhi: Sage Publications

Giugni, Marco. (2004), *Social Protest and Policy Change*. New York: Rowman & Littlefield Publishers

Giugni, Marco. (2008), "Political, Biographical and Cultural Consequences of Social Movements." *Sociology Compass* 2(5):1582–1600

Giugni, Marco, and Douglas MacAdam (eds.) (1999), *How Social Movements Matter*. Minneapolis: University of Minnesota Press

Gladney, Dru C. (2004), *Dislocating China: Reflections on Muslims, Minorities, and Other Subaltern Subjects*. Cambridge: Harvard University Press

Goel, Radhey Shayam. (2000), "Environmental Impact Assessment of Water Resources Projects" in *Series on Management of Water, Power, and Environmental Resources*, edited by R. S. Goel. New Delhi: Oxford and IBH

158 *Bibliography*

Goel, Radhey Shayam, and Prasad, Kamta. (2000), "Environmental Management in Hydropower and River Valley Projects" in *Series on Management of Water, Power, and Environmental Resources*, edited by R. S. Goel. New Delhi: Oxford and IBH

Goethe, Johann Wolfgang. (1989), *The Sorrows of Young Werther*. New York: Penguin

Goffman, Erving. (1974), *Frame Analysis*. New York: Harper Colophon Books

Goldie, Peter (ed.) (2002), *Understanding Emotions*. Burlington: Ashgate Publishing Company

Goldstone, Jack. (2004), "More Social Movements or Fewer? Beyond political opportunity structures to relational fields." *Theory and Society* 33

Goodwin, Jeff. (2001), *No Other Way Out*. Cambridge: Cambridge University Press

Goodwin, Jeff, James M. Jasper, and Francesca Polletta (eds.) (2001), *Passionate Politics*. Chicago: University of Chicago

Goodwin, Jeff, James M. Jasper, and Francesca Polletta. (2001), "Introduction: Why Emotions Matter" in *Passionate Politics*, edited by J. Goodwin, J. M. Jasper and F. Polletta. Chicago: University of Chicago Press

Gopoian, J. David. (1993), "Compassion & Voting Behavior in Presidential Elections." *Polity* 25(4):583

Gurr, Ted R. (1970), *Why Men Rebel*. Princeton: Princeton University Press

Hafez, Mohammed. (2006), *Manufacturing Human Bombs*. Washington DC: United States Institute of Peace

Hare, Paul A., and Herbert H. Blumberg. (1988), *Dramaturgical Analysis of Social Interaction*. New York: Prager Publishers

Hawley, John Stratton. (1994), "Introduction" in *Sati the Blessing and the Curse*, edited by J.S. Hawley. New York: Oxford University Press

Hobbes, Thomas. (1994), *Leviathan*. Indianapolis: Hackett Publishing Company

Hopgood, Stephen. (2005), "Tamil Tigers: 1987–2002" in *Making Sense of Suicide Missions*, edited by D. Gambetta. New York: Oxford University Press

Horowitz, Donald. (2001), *The Deadly Ethnic Riot*. Berkley: University of California Press

Horsburg, H. J. N. (1968), *Non-Violence and Aggression*. London: Oxford University Press

Hume, Robert Ernest. (1983), *The Thirteen Principal Upanishads*. Delhi: Oxford University Press

Irvin, C. (1999), *Militant Nationalism: Between Movement and Party in Northern Ireland and the Basque Country*. Duluth: University of Minnesota Press

Irving, Iyer, and Ramaswamy R. (2003), *Water Perspectives, Issues, Conerns*. New Delhi: Sage

Jasper, James M. (1997), *The Art of Moral Protest*. Chicago: University of Chicago Press

Juergensmeyer, Mark. (2000), *Terror in the Mind of God*. New Delhi: Oxford University Press

Kalyvas, Stathis, and Ignacio Sanchez-Cuenca. (2005), "Killing Without Dying: The Absence of Suicide-Missions" in *Making Sense of Suicide Missions*, edited by D. Gambetta. New York: Oxford University Press

Kearney, Robert N. (1985), "Ethnic Conflict and the Tamil Separatist Movement in Sri Lanka." *Asian Survey* 25(9) (September):898–917

Keck, Margaret, and Kathryn Sikkink. (1998), *Activists Beyond Borders*. Ithaca: Cornell University Press

Kertzer, David. (1998), *Ritual, Politics, and Power*. New Haven: Yale University Press

Khagram, Sanjeev. (2004), *Dams and Development*. Delhi: Oxford University Press

Kim, Hyojoung. (2002), "Shame, Anger and Love in Collective Action: Emotional Consequences of Suicide Protest in South Korea, 1991." *Mobilization* 7(2):159–76

King, Robert D. (1997), *Nehru and the Language Politics of India*. Delhi: Oxford University Press

Koopmans, Ruud, and Paul Statham. (1999), "Challenging the Liberal Nation-State? Postnationalism, Multiculturalism, and the Collective Claims Making of Migrants and Ethnic Minorities in Britain and Germany." *American Journal of Sociology* 103(3): 652–96

Kuchimanchi, Ravi, Aravinda Pillalamari, Kirankumar Vissa, Om Damani, Nigamanth Sridhar, and Mohan Bhagat. (2005), *245 Villages*. New Delhi: AID INDIA

Kuhn, Thomas. (1996), *The Structure of Scientific Revolutions*. Chicago: University of Chicago Press

Kumar, Dharma. (1992), "The Affirmative Action Debate in India." *Asian Survey* 32(3):290–302

Lahiri, Simanti. (2014), "Choosing to Die: Suicide Bombing and Suicide Protest in South Asia." *Terrorism and Political Violence*.Forthcoming

Laqueur, Walter (ed.) (2004), *Voices of Terror*. New York: Reed Press

Le Bon, Gustave. (1965), *The Psychology of the Crowd*. New York: Viking

Lewis, Marc D., and Isabela Granic. (2000), "Introduction: A New Approach to the Study of Emotional Development" in *Emotion, Development, and Self-Organization*, edited by M. D. Lewis and I. Granic. Cambridge: Cambridge University Press

Liberation Tigers of Tamil Eelam. (2004), "Black Tiger Commemoration Day Pamphlet"

MacAdam, Doug. (1996), "Conceptual Origins, Current Problems, Future Directions" in *Comparative Perspectives on Social Movements: Political Opportunites Mobilizing Structures and Cultural Framings*, edited by D. McAdam, J. D. McCarthy and M. N. Zald. Cambridge: Cambridge University Press

MacAdam, Doug. (1999), "The Biographical Impact of Activism" in *How Social Movements Matter*, edited by Marco Giugni, Douglas McAdam, and Charles Tilly. London: Cambridge University Press

MacAdam, Doug, Sidney Tarrow, and Charles Tilly (eds.) (2001), *Dynamics of Contention*. Cambridge: Cambridge University Press

McCarthy, John D., and Mayer N. Zald. (1977), "Resource Mobilization and Social Movements: A Partial Theory." *The American Journal of Sociology* 82(6):1212–41

McCully, Patrick. (1998), *Silenced Rivers*. New Delhi: Orient Longman

McGee, Mary. (1991), "Desired Fruits: Motive and Intention in the Votive Rites of Hindu Women" in *Roles and Rituals for Hindu Women*, edited by J. Leslie. Madison: Fairleigh Dickinson University Press

Machiavelli, Niccolo. (1998), *The Prince*, translated by H. C. Mansfield. Chicago: University of Chicago Press

McPhail, Clark. (1991), *The Myth of the Madding Crowd*. New York: Aldine De Grutyter

Margasak, Peter. (2006), "Malachi Ritscher's Apparent Suicide" in *The Bleader* http://www.chicagoreader.com/Bleader/archives/2006/11/07/malachi-ritschers-apparent-suicide

Matena, Karuna. (2012), "Another Realism: The Politics of Gandhian Nonviolence." *American Political Science Review* 106:2

160   *Bibliography*

Meyer, Michel. (2000), *Philosophy and the Passions*, translated by R. F. Barsky. University Park: The Pennsylvania State University Press

Morse, Bradford (Chairman), and Thomas Berger (Deputy Chairman). (1992), *Sardar Sarovar: Report of the Independent Review*, edited by H. Jarman, Scrivner, Brian. New Delhi: Many: NBA, Sanctuary Magazine, Center for Education and Documentation Consortium of Indian Publishers

Mukta, Parita (1990), "Worshipping Inequality: The Pro Narmada Dam Movement." *Economic and Political Weekly* 25(41):2300–1

Murty, Suryanarayana. (1984), *Life and Mission in Life: Potti Sriramulu*, translated by D. Anjaneyulu. Hyderabad: International Telegu Institute

Nagaraj, K. (2008), *Farmers Suicides in India: Magnitudes, Trends and Spatial Patterns*. Chennai: Bharthi Puthakalayam

Nandy, Ashis. (1994), "Sati as Profit versus Sati as Spectacle: The Public Debate on Roop Kanwar's Death" in *Sati the Blessing and the Curse*, edited by J. S. Hawley. New York: Oxford University Press

Narayana Rao, K. V. (1973), *The Emergence of Andhra Pradesh*. Bombay: Popular Prakashan

Nehru, Jawarlahal. December 3 (1952), *Unpublished personal papers of C. Rajagopalichari*, Nehru Memorial Library, New Delhi, edited by C. Rajagoplaichari

Nehru, Jawarlahal. (1987a), *Jawalahal Nehru: Letters to Chief Ministers*, edited by G. Parthasarath. Vol. 2. New Delhi: Oxford University Press

Nehru, Jawarlahal. (1987b), *Jawarlahal Nehru: Letters to Chief Ministers*, edited by G. Parthasarath. Vol. 3:52–4. New Delhi: Oxford University Press

Nissan, Elizabeth, and R. L. Stirrat. (1990), "The Generation of Communal Identities" in *Sri Lanka, History and the Roots of the Conflict*, edited by J. Spencer. London: Routledge

O'Brien, Kevin J. (ed.) (2008), *Popular Protest in China*. Cambridge: Harvard University Press

Ohnuki-Tierney, Emiko. (2002), *Kamikaze, Cherry Blossoms, and Nationalism*. Chicago: University of Chicago Press

Ohnuki-Tierney, Emiko. (2006), *Kamikaze Diaries*. Chicago: University of Chicago Press

Oldenburg, Veena Talwar. (1994), "The Roop Kanwar Case: Feminist Responses" in *Sati the Blessing and the Curse*, edited by J. S. Hawley. New York: Oxford University Press

Olson, Mancur. (1965), *The Logic of Collective Action*. Cambridge: Harvard University Press

Pape, Robert, A. (2003), The Strategic Logic of Suicide Terrorism. *American Political Science Review* 97(3):343–61

Pape, Robert, A. (2005), *Dying to Win: The Strategic Logic of Suicide Terrorism*. New York: Random House

Parekh, Bhikhu. (1989a), *Colonialism Tradition and Reform: An Analysis of Gandhi's Political Discourse*. New Delhi: Sage

Parekh, Bhikhu. (1989b), *Gandhi's Political Philosophy*. South Bend: Notre Dame University Press.

Patel, Anil. (1997), "Resettlement Politics and Tribal Interests" in *The Dam & the Nation*, edited by J. Dreze, M. Samson, and S. Singh. New Delhi: Oxford University Press

Patel, Sardar Vallabhbhai, Dr Pattabhai Sitaramayya, and Jawaharlal Nehru. (1949), *Report of the Linguistic Provinces Committee*. Delhi: Indian National Congress

Bibliography 161

Patkar, Medha, and Smitu Kothari. (1995), "The Struggle for Participation and Justice: A Historical Narrative" in *Towards Sustainable Development?* edited by W. F. Fisher. London: M. E. Sharpe

Perry, Elizabeth J. (2009), "Permanent Rebellion? Continuities and Discontinuities in Chinese Protest" in *Popular Protest in China*, edited by Kevin J. O'Brien. Cambridge: Harvard University Press

Petersen, Roger D. (2002), *Understanding Ethnic Violence*. Cambridge: Cambridge University Press

Piven, Frances Fox, and Richard A. Cloward. (1979), *Poor People's Movements*. New York: Vintage Books

Post, Jerrold M. (1990), "Terrorist Psycho-Logic: Terrorist Behavior as a Product of Psychological Forces" in *Origins of Terrorism*, edited by W. Reich. New York: Cambridge University Press

Rao, G. V. Subba. (1982), *The History of the Andhra Movement*, edited by G. V. S. Rao. 2 Vols., Vol. 1. Hyderabad: Committee of the History of Andhra Movement

Rao, P. V. (1978), *History of Modern Andhra*. New Delhi: Sterling Publishers

Ritscher, Malachi. (2006), "Mission Statement" accessed on: www.savagesound.com/gallery99.htm

Roberts, Robert C. (2003), *Emotions*. Cambridge: Cambridge University Press

Rudolph, Susanne Hoeber, and Lloyd I. Rudolph. (1983), *Gandhi: The Traditional Roots of Charisma*. Chicago: University of Chicago Press

Ryan, Yasmine. (2011), "Tragic Life of a Street Vendor" on Al Jazeera.com. Available at: http://www.aljazeera.com/indepth/features/2011/01/201111684242518839.html

Sands, Bobby. (1997), *Writings from Prison: Bobby Sands Writing*. Cork: Mercier Press

Sangavi, Sanjay. (2002), *The River and Life*. Calcutta: Earthcare Books

Scarry, Elaine. (1985), *The Body in Pain: The Making and Unmaking of the World*. Oxford: Oxford University Press

Scott, James. (1992), *Domination and the Arts of Resistance*. New Haven: Yale University Press

Seth, Pravin. (1994), *Narmada Project*. New Delhi: Har-Anand Publications

Shah, Asvin A. (1995), "A Technical Overview of the Flawed Sardar Sarovar Project and a Proposal for a Sustainable Alternative" in *Towards Sustainable Development?* edited by W. F. Fisher. London: M. E. Sharpe

Sharp, Gene. (1973), *The Politics of Nonviolent Action: The Dynamics of Nonviolent Action, p. III*. Boston: Porter Sargent Publishers

Singh, Satyajit. (1997), *Taming the Waters*. Delhi: Oxford University Press

Singh, Ujjwal Kumar. (1998), *Political Prisoners in India*. New Delhi: Oxford University Press

Sisson, Richard, and Munira Majumdar. (1991), "India in 1990: Political Polarization." *Asian Survey* 31(2):103–12

Sprinzak, Ehud. (2000), "Rational Fanatics." *Foreign Policy* 120:66–73

Sreeramulu, B. (1988), *Socio-Political Ideas and Activities of Potti Sriramulu*. Delhi: Himalaya Publishing House

Sriramulu, Potti Shri. (1952), "Appeal to the people of Madras City and Others" in *Amarajeevi Potti Sreeramulu: Jayanthi Souvinir*, edited by Y. S. Sastry and Mallik. Madras: Amarajeevi Potti Sreeramulu Memorial Society

Subramanian, Nirupama. (2005), *Sri Lanka, Voices from the War Zone*. New Delhi: Vijtha Yapa Publications

162 *Bibliography*

Swamy, M. R. Narayan. (2002), *Tigers of Lanka*. New Delhi: Konark Publishing

Tambiah, Stanley J. (1992), *Buddhism Betrayed?* Chicago: Chicago University Press

Tambiah, Stanley J. (1996), *Leveling Crowds*. Los Angeles: University of California Press

Tarrow, Sidney. (1989), *Democracy and Disorder*. Oxford: Clarendon Press

Tarrow, Sidney. (1996), "Social Movements in Contentious Politics: A Review Article." *American Political Science Review* 90(4):874–83

Tarrow, Sidney. (1998) and (2011), *Power in Movement*. Cambridge: Cambridge University Press

Tata Institute for Social Sciences. (1997), "Experiences with Resettlement and Rehabilitation in Maharashtra" in *The Dam & the Nation*, edited by J. Dreze, M. Samson, and S. Singh. New Delhi: Oxford University Press

Taylor, Gabriele. (1985), *Pride, Shame, and Guilt*. Oxford: Clarendon Press

Thukral, Enakshi Ganguly (ed.) (1992a), *Big Dams, Displaced People*. New Delhi: Sage

Thukral, Enakshi Ganguly. (1992b), "Introduction" in *Big Dams Displaced People*, edited by E. G. Thukral. New Delhi: Sage

Thurman, Robert. (1997), *Essential Tibetan Buddhism*. New York: Book Sales Incorporated

Tilly, Charles. (1978), *From Mobilization to Revolution*. Reading: Addison-Wesley Publishing Company

Tilly, Charles. (2003), *Regimes and Repertoires*. Chicago: University of Chicago Press

Tilly, Charles. (2008), *Contentious Performances*. Cambridge: Cambridge University Press

Turner, Victor. (1974), *Dramas, Fields and Metaphors*. Ithaca: Cornell University Press

Turner, Victor. (1982), *From Ritual to Theatre*. New York: PAJ Publications

Turner, Victor. (1995), *The Ritual Process*. New York: Aldine De Gruyter

Udall, Lori. (1995), "The International Narmada Campaign: A Case of Sustained Advocacy" in *Toward Sustainable Development?* edited by W. F. Fisher. London: M. E. Sharpe

Varshney, Ashutosh. (2002), *Ethnic Conflict and Civic Life*. New Haven: Yale University Press

Weiner, Myron. (1954), "Prospects for India's Congress party." *Far Eastern Survey* 23(12):182–8

Whittaker, David. (2012), *The Terrorism Reader*. Fourth edition. London: Routledge

World Medical Association. (2006), "Declaration of Malta on Hunger Strikes," revised version. Available on: http://www.wma.net/en/30publications/10policies/h31/

Index

adivasi 61, 63, 67, 82 n. 4, 83 n. 5
ahimsa *see* non-violence
altruistic suicide 19 n. 10, 149–50
Ambedkar Dr. B.R., 7, 29–30, 32–3, 38 n. 15, 39 n. 18, 86
Amte, Baba 72
Andhra 1, 5, 15–7 *see also* Andhra Movement
Andhra Mahasabha 56
Andhra Movement 40–2campaigns 42–9use of suicide protest 50–2comparison to other cases 145–8
Andhra Pradesh 50
Anti Mandal Commission Forum 90
Anti Reservation Movement (ARM) 89–97comparison to other cases 145–8
Armagh Prison 127–8
Asociacion Madres de Plaza de Mayo 151

Bandaranaike, S.W.R.D 106
bandh 72
Baviskar, Amita 63, 68, 71
Ben Ali, Z.A. 136
Bengal 33
Bhagwat Singh 38 n. 12
Bhai, Devram 77
Bhai, Kaja 77
Bhai, Mathur 77
big dams 65
BJP 81, 88, 96
The Blanket Protests 128
Bouazizi, Mohamed 6, 18, 122, 136–9, 142 n. 24, 146
boycott 72, 74, 131
British Raj *see* The Raj
Buddhism 105, 129–30, 142 n. 17

Calcutta 33–5, 39 n. 22
Calcutta Fast 29, 33
Car bombs 119 n. 25, 127
Chicago 6, 18, 122, 136–8
China *see* The Peoples Republic of China
civil disobedience 41, 48, 72, 127 *see also* satyagraha
Cloward, Richard A. 10, 96
Communal Award: depressed classes 29–32, 34, 38
communal violence 34–5
Communist Party Of India (CPI) 56, 81, 88
The Communist Party Of India-Marxist (CPIM) 81, 88
Congress Party *see* Indian National Congress
cultural practice 16, 20, 23, 25, 86, 104–5

Dalai Lama 129, 142
Dalits 18, 86 *see also* Harijan; Untouchables
Dalton, Dennis 26, 33–5, 38–9
Dar Commission 43
Dar Commission Report 44
Das, Jatindranath 38 n. 12, 124
Delhi University 88, 90
demonstrations 4–5, 19, 140, 145; by the Narmada Bachao Andolan, 72; during the Anti Reservation Movement, 90; in Tibet, 131
Devine, Mickey 131
dharna 26, 72, 127
direct action 70–2, 76, 83 n. 20, 90, 91
The Dirty Protests 128
disruption 23, 44, 71, 85, 113
Doherty, Kiernan 131

164 *Index*

drowning 1, 3, 5, 37; and the NBA 62, 64, 69, 72, 74, 77 *see also* jal samadhi; jal samparan
Durkheim, Emile 19 n. 10, 149

Eldelman, Murray 21–3
emotional narratives: definition 12–13, 17, 19; within the movement for Andhra 42, 52; within the NBA 79, 80; in the Anti-Reservation movement 85, 93–7; within the LTTE 103–4, 109, 114, 117; within the IRA 132–3; within the movement for Tibet 132–3; within individual acts of suicide protest 138–42
environmental movements 17, 19 n. 14, 63
environmentalism 62–3, 69
episteme 21, 37 n. 1 *see also* political idiom; paradigm

fast to the death 5, 7, 16; pattern of use in India 2–3; use by Gandhi 20, 30; use by Potti Sriamulu 40, 42, 47–51, 53; use by Narmada Bachao Andolan 72, 77; use by the Liberation Tigers of Tamil Eelam 111, 113
Faulon Gong 142 n. 21
Fear: and Gandhi 27; and suicide bombing 13, 93, 114, 116
Five Member Group (FMG) 74, 78
Foucault, Michel 37, 140–1
Free Tibet Movement 129, 132–4
full reservoir level (FRL) 65–6, 83 n. 13

Gamson, William 7, 10, 12, 113
Gandhi, M.K.: definitions of suicide protest 6–7; influence on modern political contention in India 16, 20–1, 49–50, 52–4, 72, 78, 147; and the LTTE 111; attitude towards hunger strike 28; attitudes toward prison fasts 28, 124–5; practice of spiritual fasting 28–9; the communal award 30, 32; and self-sacrifice 20–1, 30, 36–7, 151; theories of fasting 29; and Ambedkar 29–33; funeral 54
Gandhi, Rajiv 109
Ghatak, Ritwik 151
Ghosh, Rituparno 151
Giugni, Marco 8–10, 18–19, 124, 148
Goswami Chowk 94
Goswami, Rajiv 1, 88–9, 92, 94

Goethe, J.W 150
Great Calcutta Killings 33
Gurr, T.R. 116

Harijan 30, 32, 035, 38–9, 41, 58–9
  see also Dalits; Untouchables
hartal 53, 60 n. 42
Hinduism 24–6, 30
Hughes, Frances 131
hunger strike 18, 28, 31–2, 42, 47, 48–50, 53, 58–9, 76–7, 92, 122, 131, 140 n. 5, 141 n. 15
Hurson, Martin 131
Hyderabad 89, 91, 160–1

Independence Movement of Tibet 142 n. 18
The Indian Emergency 2, 140 n. 1
Indian National Congress 26, 29, 43–5, 49, 55–6, 59, 88, 96
The Indian Nationalist Movement 20, 24, 26, 28, 41; influence on modern politics 16, 20, 24, 26, 53, 56, 60; use of fasting 28–9, 33, 35–6, 38, 61, 124; Potti Sriramulu 41, 43; use of satyagraha 72, 83
intensity: definition 12; within the movement for Andhra 49–52; within the NBA 76–9; within the ARM 92–3; within the LTTE 113–14; within the movement for Tibet 131–2; within the IRA 131–2; in individual acts of suicide protest 138–9; negative effects 93, 146–7
Irish National Liberation Army 132–3
Irish Republican Army (IRA) 6, 107, 122, 126–8, 130–4, 141, 146

jal samadhi 62, 70, 72, 76, 80, 83
  see also jal samparan; drowning
jal samparan 72, 74, 77–8, 80, 84
  see also jal samadhi; drowning
Jan Sangh 56
Janata Dal 61, 68, 81, 88
Japan 75
Jayewardene, J.R. 109
JVP Report 44

Kalelkar Commission 87
Kamikaze Pilots 101
Kanwar, Roop 25
Khosla, A.N. 83 n. 10
Khosla Commission 65–6
Kumaratunga, Chandrika 100, 111, 117

Laxmiben 77
Liberation Tigers of Tamil Eelam
  (LTTE) 5, 12, 17, 130–2; historical
  use of suicide bombing 102–4;
  history of the conflict 106–12; suicide
  bombing 112–18; comparison to other
  cases 145–8
linguistic provinces 44, 50
  see also vernacular states
Linguistic Provinces Commission
  see Dar Commission
Lok Sabha 46
Long Kesh Prison 122–3, 127
  see also The Maze
Lord Williningdon 31
Lucknow Prison 38 n. 12, 124
Lynch, Kevin 131

McCreesh, Raymond 131
McDonnell, Joe 131
McElwee, Tom 131
Madras 40–2, 44–5, 48, 50–1, 53
Mandal Commission 18, 85, 87–91,
  93–4, 98
Manibeli 78, 84 n. 34
Martyr 54–5, 79, 81, 115
Martyrdom 13
The Maze 18, 122, 124, 126–8, 130, 132
  see also Long Kesh Prison
Meghnath 77
memory 13
Ministry of Water Resources 74
Morrison, Norman 139
The Morse and Berger Report 72
movement success 8–10
The Muslim League 26, 56

Naranyana, P.V. 44–5
Narmada Bachao Andolan (NBA) 61–3;
  history of the movement 67–9; use of
  suicide protest comparison to other
  cases 145–8
Narmada Development Plan (NDP) 62,
  64–5, 69
Narmada River 62, 64–7, 71
National Alliance of People's
  Movement 61
Nationalism 44, 101, 105, 110, 116,
  142 n. 17
Nehru, J: attitude towards linguistic
  states 44–5; responses to Gandhi's
  fasts 31, 33; responses to Potti
  Sriramulu 41, 46–7, 49–51, 54, 56–7,

60; role in the Sardar Sarovar Project
  64, 75
Nimar 63
Nimar Bachao Andolan 68
Non-Cooperation Movement 39 n. 23
non-violence 6–8, 12, 18–19, 28, 32, 36
Northern Ireland 18, 122–3, 126–7,
  130, 132–4

O'Hara, Patsy 131
Other Backward Classes (OBCs)
  87–8, 96
Outcomes

pain 26, 36–8, 81, 124, 141, 147
  see also suffering
panopticon 140 n. 6
Pape, Robert 15, 102–3, 124
paradigm 21, 37 n. 1 *see also* political
  idiom; episteme
Parekh, Bhikhu 26–7, 47
Partition: 33–4, 44; of Bengal 58 n. 2; of
  Ireland 127
Patel, Chimanbhai 81
Patel, S.V. 33, 59 n. 14
Patkar, Medha 61–2; use of fasting
  to the death 63, 72, 74, 77, 82; jal
  samadhi 80; leadership of the NBA
  71, 75–6, 79, 81, 84 n. 41; testimony in
  front of USA Congress 76
The Peoples Republic of China (PRC)
  6, 18, 121, 123, 126; protest in 128–9,
  131, 133–4
performance 1, 23–4, 37 n. 6, 140 n. 4, 144
Piven, Frances Fox 10, 96
political competition: definition 14–15;
  within the movement for Andhra
  55–7; within the NBA 81–2; within the
  ARM 96–7; within the LTTE 116–17;
  within the IRA 133–5; within the
  movement for Tibet 133–5
political idiom 21–3, 31, 33, 37, 125, 143
  see also episteme; paradigm
Political Process Approach 10, 14, 55
political spectacle 21
political theater 21
Prabhakaran, V. 107–8, 110, 112,
  115, 119
Praja Socialist Party 56
Prakasam, T. 54, 59 n. 37
Pride 13, 52, 79, 93–4, 114–15, 132, 147
prison fast 122–3, 125, 127–8, 130, 140–1
project affected persons (PAPS) 63, 72–4

166   Index

Quinn, Paddy 132

Radhakrishnan, S. 45
The Raj 29–30, 33, 40, 58 n. 4, 64, 86
Rajagopalachari, C. 45, 51, 59
Rajiv Goswami 1, 88–9, 92, 94
Rajya Sabha 45, 59 n. 23, 91, 95, 98 n. 7,
  99 n. 99
Rao, T.A. 48
Rao. Dr. 47
Ray, Satyajit 150
Reddi, R. 47
reorganization of states in India 43, 57
repression 30, 61, 88, 103, 108, 126,
  134, 141
reservations 86–8, 94
resettlement 62, 66–7, 71–3, 129
riots: in Calcutta 33–4; after Sriramulu's
  death 51; during the Anti-Mandal
  campaign 89, 91, 98; in Sri Lanka
  106–7, 109; in Northern Ireland 127
Ritscher, Malachi 6, 18, 122, 136–7, 147
ritual 13, 20, 24, 80, 94, 103, 114

sacrifice see self-sacrifice
sacrifice squad 78
Salt March 29, 38 n. 13, 41, 58 n. 4
Sands, Bobby 128, 131–2, 134, 147
Sardar Sarovar Project (SSP) 17, 62–3,
  66, 68, 71, 73
sati 24–5, 38 n. 7 and 8
satyagraha: Gandhian philosophy
  24, 26–9, 35–6; use by movement
  for Andhra 41, 43, 45, 47–50; use
  by the NBA 71–3, 78 see also civil
  disobedience
satyagrahi 27, 29, 47, 49
Schedule Castes 86
Scott, James 23, 140 n. 4
self-immolation: pattern of the practice
  in India 2–3; threats 6–7; possible
  cultural antecedents 24–6; Gandhi's
  opinions 36–7; use by ARM 88–9, 92–
  6; use by Mohamed Bouazizi 135–40;
  use by Malachi Ritscher 137–40
self-sacrifice: and Gandhi 20–1, 37; of
  the body 26, in Indian politics 36–7;
  and the LTTE 113, 115; and the ARM
  94–5; and the NBA 61, 78, 81; and
  the movement for Andhra 54; as a
  political idiom 20–1, 125, 143; as a
  positive narrative in politics 149–52
Separate Electorates 7, 31

Setting 24–5, 60, 79–80, 126, 136, 139
  see also staging
shame 13; within dharna 26; within the
  movement for Andhra 47, 52, 54;
  within the NBA 79–80; within the
  ARM 93–5; within the LTTE 114,
  116; in Ireland 127, 132
Sharmila, Irom Chanu 141 n. 10
Shatiben 77
Shukla, V.C. 74, 78
Sidi Bouzid 136
Singh, Viswanath Pratap 61, 81, 87,
  89–90, 92, 94
Sitaram, Swami 41–2, 45–51, 53
Sitaramayya, P. 59 n. 14
Social drama 22–3
Spock 151
Sri Lanka: conflict with the LTTE 104–
  8; negotiations with the LTTE 111–13;
  reactions to suicide bombing 116
Sriramulu, Potti: early life 41–2; death
  and aftermath 41, 53–4; method of
  fasting 52–3; comparison to other
  cases 145–8
staging 13, 52, 80, 92, 126, 136, 139
  see also setting
submergence 66–7, 72–4, 78, 84 n. 34
success see movement success
suffering 28, 36–7, 40 see also pain
Suhrawardy, H.S. 34
suicide see altruistic suicide
suicide bombing: difference from
  suicide protest 7–8, 13; theoretical
  explanations 101–4; use by the LTTE
  113–16
swaraj 27–8, 30, 33, 36
symbolism
sympathy 13, 52, 79, 93–4, 114–15,
  132, 147

tactical depth: definition 11–12; within
  movement for Andhra 42–9; within
  the NBA 70–6; within the ARM 90–2;
  within the LTTE 109–13; within the
  movement for Tibet 130–1; within the
  IRA 130–1
tactics: effects on social movements 4–6;
  genesis of 20, 23–6
Tarrow, Sydney 4, 8, 14, 18, 23, 37, 55
Telegu
Telegu Linguistic State see Andhra
Telengana 2
Thatcher, Margaret 128, 130, 141 n. 15

Thich Quan Duc 129
Tianamen Square 128, 147
Tibet 6, 122, 128–34, 142, 146
Tilly Charles, 4, 12, 23–4, 26, 37, 49
Transgression 22
Tunisia 6, 18, 122, 136, 139
Turner, Victor 22–4

Untouchables 29–30, 32, 38–9, 41, 58–9, 86 *see also* Dalits; Harijan

vernacular states 44, 57 *see also* linguistic provinces
Vietnam 129, 139, 142 n. 17

West Bengal 82 n. 3, 150
World Bank 62–4, 66, 69, 72–6
World Commission of Dams 75

Yeravada Fast 29, 32, 38
Yeravada Prison 30